Also by Kirsten Grind

The Lost Bank

HAPPY AT ANY COST

The Revolutionary Vision
and Fatal Quest of
Zappos CEO Tony Hsieh

KIRSTEN GRIND

AND

KATHERINE SAYRE

Simon & Schuster
New York   London   Toronto   Sydney   New Delhi

Simon & Schuster
1230 Avenue of the Americas
New York, NY 10020

First Simon & Schuster hardcover edition March 2022

SIMON & SCHUSTER and colophon are registered trademarks of Simon & Schuster, Inc.

For information about special discounts for bulk purchases, please contact Simon & Schuster Special Sales at 1-866-506-1949 or business@simonandschuster.com.

The Simon & Schuster Speakers Bureau can bring authors to your live event. For more information or to book an event, contact the Simon & Schuster Speakers Bureau at 1-866-248-3049 or visit our website at www.simonspeakers.com.

Interior design by Erika R. Genova

Manufactured in the United States of America

1   3   5   7   9   10   8   6   4   2

Library of Congress Cataloging-in-Publication Data has been applied for.

ISBN 978-1-9821-8698-2
ISBN 978-1-9821-8700-2 (ebook)

For Steve Grind.
Even though I dedicated my first book to him,
he deserves it even more this time.
—Kirsten

For my mom
—Katherine

CONTENTS

You will never be happy if you continue to search for what happiness consists of. You will never live if you are looking for the meaning of life.

—Albert Camus

NOTE TO READERS

Tony Hsieh's sudden death in late November 2020 at only forty-six years of age sent shock waves through the business community and around the world.

One of America's most beloved entrepreneurs, Tony was adored and respected for his unconventional ideas on workplace culture and happiness, which he detailed in his best-selling book, *Delivering Happiness: A Path to Profits, Passion, and Purpose.* A near billionaire, he had almost single-handedly developed downtown Las Vegas over the previous decade. He had built one of the most joyful companies on earth as chief executive officer of the shoe-selling site Zappos, now owned by Amazon. Thousands of people around the world, many of whom didn't even know him, loved him because of his singular ability to lift people up and see the best in them.

His story might have ended there, with the beautiful obituaries published in newspapers and magazines that detailed his life and accomplishments, including where we work as reporters, the *Wall Street Journal*.

But Tony died under mysterious circumstances at a young age in a shed fire in Connecticut. Almost immediately after his death, we began hearing stories about his last year as he embarked on a new vision in a new town, Park City, Utah. He had surrounded himself with people who were taking advantage of him. We were told that alcohol and drugs had played a role in his death, but we weren't sure how. We learned that he might have suffered from mental health issues, possibly worsened by the isolation of the Covid-19 pandemic. Meanwhile, few details about the fire that had killed him were released in the weeks after his death, including why Tony was in New London, Connecticut, at all. A much bigger story needed to be unraveled.

As a result, we were faced with a challenge. On the one hand, we had a mystery: How did Tony Hsieh die? But we also had a biography, the storied career of a person who saw the world differently and encouraged others to believe in themselves, to write. And so we ended up with two intertwined stories: one about Tony Hsieh's life and one about his death. Because this is a deeply personal story, and to differentiate from other members of the Hsieh family, we have opted to refer to Tony by his first name throughout, while we use the last names of other people who are mentioned in this book. The exception is Jewel, who is commonly referred to by her first name.

Tony Hsieh moved to Park City—which he had often visited for the Sundance Film Festival—in early 2020 after leaving rehab with big plans. He wanted to boost arts in the community, support local businesses, and bring people together. It was in some ways modeled after his famous Las Vegas Downtown Project, in which he had invested $350 million in the development of a struggling part of the city. But like so many of us, he was privately struggling. He began heavily abusing drugs, exacerbating lifelong mental health issues that he had always hidden from others. He spent tens of millions of dollars in just a few months, with people around him vying for pieces of his fortune. It all caught up with him one night in a riverside house in New London, Connecticut, when a shed he was in caught fire.

We have based this account on more than two hundred interviews with his close friends, employees, business associates, and others such as lawyers, doctors, consultants, and professors who interacted with him in the last year of his life and throughout his career. Some people are quoted on the record; others spoke to us anonymously.

This book is also based on thousands of documents, photos, and videos. We obtained hundreds of police, local government, business, and court records—from New London, the San Francisco Bay Area, Las Vegas, and Utah. Some we received through filing Freedom of Information Act requests or from public disclosures, others from people involved in the story.

Related to Tony's last year in Park City, we viewed dozens of pictures taken of Tony's multimillion-dollar mansion in Park City known as the Ranch, watched videos taken by those who had interacted with him, and reviewed dozens of employees' schedules during the summer and fall of 2020. We viewed internal communications, such as emails and text messages, between members of Tony's inner circle. We have detailed our sourcing in full at the back of the book, including our efforts to obtain some documents that have not been released by Park City officials and responses from some of the parties involved.

We have also benefited from Tony's own book, *Delivering Happiness*, which he published in 2010, as well as a more recent book about Zappos in Tony's and his employees' own words, *The Power of WOW: How to Electrify Your Work and Your Life by Putting Service First*.

We ask you not to assume that a person or a business that appears prominently in the narrative, or is mentioned, participated in this book, although every person and entity cited was given the opportunity to do so. Dialogue is in quotes only when it is described in a record, or when it was relayed by someone directly involved, or by someone who witnessed a particular scene. Please keep in mind that even in seemingly private moments, Tony was nearly always surrounded by multiple friends or employees.

A note about Cirque Lodge, the rehabilitation facility in Utah, in particular: it was enormously generous in granting us access to its owner, therapists, and other staff. We were allowed to tour its facilities and experience its program (including a helicopter ride!). However, the employees did not breach doctor-patient confidentiality by giving us information about Tony Hsieh's stay there or his medical condition in general, nor did they discuss any other patients who had visited the facility.

Some of the scenes in this book, particularly at the end, will be hard to digest. We're especially aware of how difficult it might be for Tony's loved ones. This is a story of a business pioneer who pushed countless boundaries throughout his career but also suffered from addiction and mental health issues, particularly in his last year. From the very nature of his death, parts of the story will be disturbing. But at the heart of Tony's life story is his drive to connect with people—to solve problems for others and generally make the world a kinder place in which to live—a legacy that has continued even after his death and that we hope this book will contribute to.

Know that we have chosen the descriptions of his mental, emotional, and physical states with the utmost care and that we have not included many devastating accounts and details from friends, employees, and visitors that would have only served to repeat descriptions of his condition or make the story appear salacious. What we did choose to use, we did so with the intention of showing his unfortunate decline at a time when many people around him were taking advantage of his condition. Our primary hope, however, is that through these carefully selected scenes and details, Tony's story will serve as a warning to many others not to ignore looming mental health and addiction issues.

Indeed, many of the people we spoke to for this book were understandably concerned about how Tony's last year would ultimately reflect on his legacy as a vaunted entrepreneur and beloved CEO. We would argue that not only will that legacy remain but one of his more unexpected gifts to the world will be to serve as an example of someone who could have been saved, by himself or others, if mental health issues weren't so stigmatized. Tony's struggles are also emblematic of the impossible expectations, often unspoken, that we place on society's most respected figures—those whom we look to for answers and perfection. It is our hope that his story will shine a light on these issues, possibly helping others in the process.

If you or someone you know is struggling, we have included an appendix with information on mental health and substance abuse resources. Our goal in telling Tony's story is to break the cycle of silence and isolation around these issues with the hope of destigmatizing reaching out for help when you're struggling. People are there to help, even when it might not seem like it, and the National Suicide Prevention Lifeline, 1-800-273-8255, and Crisis Text Line, 741741, provide immediate, around-the-clock assistance.

A fuller list of mental health resources can be found at the end of the book.

PROLOGUE

"A FREAK ACCIDENT"

New London, Connecticut, November 18–19, 2020

F ire Chief Thomas Curcio drove across the dark neighborhoods of New London, Connecticut, in the early morning of November 18, 2020, the crackling sound of his car scanner the only noise breaking the silence in his SUV.

He had been awakened by a call to his cell phone around 3:30 a.m. by dispatch with reports of a fire and a person trapped inside a house or possibly a nearby structure.

That wasn't unusual. New London is only six square miles, with a population of about 27,000, but it is a densely populated urban area—"like someone took a slice out of New York City," his fire marshal, Vernon Skau, likes to tell people. The small department is busy enough on most days, handling about 7,500 calls a year. A large glass cabinet at the fire station showcases pictures and artifacts from some of New London's most memorable fires, large and small: a blown fuse at a fast-food restaurant that had charred the inside; a Samsung cell phone that had exploded.

Once the largest of a string of affluent coastal towns in southeastern Connecticut, New London has been in decline since the 1980s, when the Crystal Mall opened on the outskirts of town, sucking business away from local shops on State and Bank Streets in the downtown area. A recent attempt to infuse arts into the city stalled during the Covid-19 pandemic.

Chief Curcio was born and raised in New London and has worked at its fire department since he was twenty-two. As a kid, he pretended to respond to fires using his Matchbox toy cars. He had been given the top job at the department two years earlier, at an official ceremony covered by the local newspaper.

Fifty-eight now, with salt-and-pepper hair and a pleasing New England accent, Curcio knows many of New London's residents by name and its streets by heart. The address of the fire, 500 Pequot Avenue, was only half a mile away from his house in a high-end neighborhood of New London. It was the middle of the night and freezing—about 20 degrees Fahrenheit.

He was not the first to arrive. It was a serious incident, and New London's three fire trucks, including a ladder truck, had been dispatched to the scene. Several police cars and an ambulance had also pulled up in front of a fairly large gray house, not unlike others on the residential street overlooking the water. Curcio knew its previous owner, a local doctor, but not who lived there currently.

If it was a house fire, it didn't look serious upon arrival. A thin plume of smoke rose from the backyard. The front of the house, with a sloping roof and a round attic window, appeared undamaged. Most of the lights were on, turning the property into a glowing beacon in the middle of a very dark street. Curcio stepped out of his SUV in his firefighting gear and a face mask, a department precaution during the pandemic.

As he hurried across the street, he could see the ambulance crew loading a man on a stretcher into the back of the ambulance. The person appeared to be alive but unconscious, with an oxygen mask strapped around his head.

Curcio didn't stop to examine him further. His job as chief was to direct the firefighters at the scene while also performing an initial evaluation of what had occurred. He went to the backyard, where several of his colleagues were gathered around a small shed attached to the house.

The shed faced a rectangular pool, which was covered for the winter months, and beyond a short wall at the end of the property, Curcio knew, was the Thames River, although he couldn't see it in the darkness. In New London, the Thames River spills into Long Island Sound.

The shed was where the man who had been pulled out had been found. He had been lying on a blanket inside, unconscious. The wooden door had been locked, and firefighters had had to pry it open with "forcible hand entry tools" to pull him out, a later fire department report said. "He's barricaded," one rescue worker shouted into her radio to a dispatcher. The man hadn't been badly burned, and the fire had been put out right away.

Parts of the inside still smoldered, and it was a jumble of beach chairs and long foam floaties used in pools. A propane space heater was partially charred, as was the edge of the blanket the man had been lying on. A candle had tipped over, spilling wax over a plastic ziplock bag stuffed with Post-it notes. Small metal canisters littered the ground that fire investigators later identified as cartridges of nitrous oxide, the kind you might attach to a whipped cream dispenser, known as whippets. Cigarettes were strewn around, and a pool of Tiki torch fluid had spilled onto the floor. All of those objects Curcio's department would later describe as possible causes of the fire.

Curcio moved on to the basement of the house, which was attached to the shed and could be accessed by sliding doors from the backyard. The basement could theoretically have been harmed during a fire. It was there that he saw something unusual.

All of the walls of the finished room were covered in bright yellow sticky notes, a mosaic of paper squares that traveled all the way to the ceiling. Words and messages were scrawled on them, but Curcio couldn't make out what they said. "The man must be a scientist or an engineer," he thought to himself, "someone who lays out their thoughts on many pieces of paper, like a map." In addition to his day job, Curcio worked part-time at Lawrence + Memorial Hospital nearby, performing stress tests on patients in the cardiology department. He would sometimes see sticky notes or other scraps of paper tacked up on meeting room walls.

Soon Curcio's phone lit up with a text message. The New London police chief, also on the scene, had sent the name of the victim to everyone else working there: Tony Hsieh. The chief speculated in his text that he might be the CEO of the online shoe retailer Zappos. Later the fire chief researched Tony more.

He found that Tony Hsieh (pronounced "Shay") was only forty-six and had become something of a business legend through his nearly two decades at the helm of Zappos, the online shoe company now owned by Amazon. Tony was known worldwide for his radical ideas about company culture and had led a redevelopment of downtown Las Vegas, plowing hundreds of millions of dollars into the downtown area of the city and funding dozens of new companies. Early in his career, before Zappos, he had sold a startup to Microsoft during the internet boom of the 1990s, cementing his reputation as a genius entrepreneur. Later Chief Curcio would ask his wife to buy him a copy of Tony's best-selling book, *Delivering Happiness*, for Christmas. The book, published in 2010, detailed Tony's life and the company culture at Zappos, inspiring business leaders, government officials, and readers around the world.

Tony's ties to New London were unclear; the articles Curcio found all showed that Tony lived in Las Vegas but had recently been buying properties in Park City, Utah.

In a later police report, one officer at the scene of the fire had also googled Tony and written the barest of details, likely from his Wikipedia page: Anthony "Tony" Hsieh was an "American Entrepreneur and venture capitalist who has a net worth of $850 million dollars. He was born in Illinois on 12-12-73 and grew up in California. He earned his Computer Science degree at Harvard University. He retired as the CEO of Zappos in August 2020, after 21 years."

The night of the fire, the firefighters and police noticed three large Mercedes passenger vans, the kind that transport celebrities to events, parked in front of the house on Pequot Avenue. In New London, where the streets are filled with more economical vehicles, they stood out. Inside one of the vans, a group of men and women sat silently, looking shaken.

Curcio and his team soon learned that many of them were employees of the wealthy businessman. The fire department had split up the interviewing with the police, a standard procedure in an investigation with many witnesses. An officer spoke to one of them, Brett Gorman, who described himself as an employee of Tony's. Gorman said he was engaged to another employee, a young woman named Elizabeth Pezzello.

When the officer asked for more information about Tony, Gorman explained that Tony had several investments in and out of the country. The officer asked him to elaborate, but he just shrugged.

"Does the business have a name?" the officer prodded.

"No," Gorman replied.

"Well, how does the business make money?"

Gorman laughed. "I don't mean 'business' in that way, as in making money," he said. "Tony is very rich, and he is retired except for a project we have going on in Utah."

He, Pezzello, and three other employees, he told the officer, were part of Tony's "core team."

The Mercedes vans had been waiting to take them all on a trip to Hawaii.

How does an accomplished chief executive officer, one of America's most beloved entrepreneurs, end up in a burning shed thousands of miles away from his home city of Las Vegas in the middle of a devastating pandemic?

As reporters at the *Wall Street Journal*, we wanted to find the answer. In stories for the *Journal* in 2020 and 2021, we explored Tony's struggles with alcohol and, later, drugs. We deeply examined the entourage who surrounded him in Park City, Utah, during 2020, a group of friends and employees—including his own brother—many of whom enabled Tony's worsening drug addiction while feeding off his wealth.

But we quickly realized that Tony's path to the burning shed in New London, Connecticut, was much more complicated and heartbreaking than we had first realized. His journey had actually started years earlier, with a fundamental goal that many people can surely relate to: he wanted to be happy. His desire to achieve happiness, and especially to spread it to those around him, was so great that he staked his entire career, and his livelihood, on that goal. It was his life's mission, and it was ultimately his downfall.

At Zappos, he infused the company with a culture known for its outrageous parties, constant happy hours, and a list of values that encouraged workers to be "a little weird," an unusual workplace renaissance he detailed in his book, *Delivering Happiness*. Determined to bring joy to people who bought shoes from Zappos and those who worked for him, he believed strongly in the value of customer service and in building a workplace culture that would allow all employees to be themselves.

With the line between friends and employees already blurred, Tony took his happiness goal one step further by empowering his workers to take on more responsibility in a much-watched management experiment called *holacracy*. This decentralized organizational theory meant that he refused to adhere to a traditional company structure or the confines of a chief executive officer role; he thought everyone should be empowered to achieve his or her own goals.

In downtown Las Vegas, Tony Hsieh dedicated $350 million of his own fortune to turning the forgotten corner of the city into an urban theme park filled with brightly colored art, bars, and event venues. He wooed entrepreneurs from across the country, investing in their businesses in exchange for their moving to Vegas. He asked his friends and acquaintances, "What do you need to live up to your full potential?" and then gave them the money or time they required. He rarely directed those questions inward, in part to avoid addressing his own problems. He failed to take care of himself.

Tony was endlessly generous. He never asked for anything in return.

Across the tech industry, charismatic, eccentric innovators have often been exalted—lifted up and put onto unrealistic pedestals for the rest of us to admire or vilify. Tony Hsieh was no different, and he was viewed as a sort of business culture messiah, a leader who could solve all the riddles plaguing the workplace. Thousands of business owners, government officials, and academics made the pilgrimage to Zappos each year to learn from his genius.

But the relentless pursuit of happiness has a darker side. Beneath his public, happiness-focused veneer, Tony struggled privately: he had undiagnosed mental health issues and facial recognition problems that he kept hidden from even some of his closest friends. Across Silicon Valley, a work-until-you-break ethos is common as superstar CEOs and founders race to build products they believe will help humanity, whether they are operating social media platforms, renting out co-working space, or selling shoes. There is no time to stop. There is no room to stumble.

Only recently has it become more accepted for high-performing people such as CEOs, celebrities, and athletes—the tennis star Naomi Osaka and the Olympic gymnast Simone Biles, for example—to admit that they need a break. There is, however, still a great stigma.

Tony, despite his close friendship with the singer and songwriter Jewel, a mental health expert in her own right, refused to seek help, always believing, as many in the tech industry do, that he could some-how hack his own problems through diet or exercise or cold baths. The Covid-19 pandemic and the resulting quarantine away from his closest friends took a terrible toll on him. Tony never married or had children.

Always a heavy drinker—a way of life, particularly at Zappos*— Tony increased his drinking in the latter years of his life as he con-

---

* Zappos has a drug- and alcohol-use policy that prohibits illegal drug use in the workplace and requires that any alcohol consumption at company offices or at work-related events be done responsibly.

tinued to ignore his own internal suffering in the pursuit of others' happiness. Even in his darkest moments, he wanted to make sure that those around him felt they were loved and taken care of.

Ultimately, he turned to drugs—ketamine and nitrous oxide—to help free his mind and to try to find some relief.

His life reached a devastating conclusion in Park City, Utah, where he tried to build a utopian community in 2020. He wanted his loved ones, and the people of the world, to live together free of Covid-19 and achieve the lasting peace he sought. By that time, though, his mental health problems had worsened, and he suffered a series of breakdowns that could no longer be ignored.

By that point in his life, though, a new entourage surrounded him, including his brother. At their best, many of these people, paid handsomely from Tony's fortune and beholden to a man they worshipped, simply stood by as he unraveled before them. At their worst, others enabled all his most terrible instincts and drug use. By the time he locked himself into a shed in New London, Connecticut, in November 2020 at a house owned by a woman considered to be his "soul mate," Tony was lost, a wisp of the man so many people had loved.

The man peddling happiness couldn't make himself happy. By the time his friends and family tried to save him, it was too late.

This is the story of one great and flawed entrepreneur and the long, fateful journey he took to try to make the world a better place. It is also the story of a man who struggled silently with his inner turmoil for decades, even as he was surrounded by dozens of people who loved him and, in the end, some others who didn't.

More than anything, it is the story of the great desire in all of us to find happiness, and bring happiness to others, at any cost.

Two days after the shed fire in late November 2020, a neighbor, Patricia Richardson, was at her house in New London, which shared a side yard with the site of the shed fire, 500 Pequot Avenue.

The former publisher of the local newspaper, *The Day*, Richardson didn't know her neighbors well, since they were almost never home. When she did see them, they seemed nice, and polite.

A group of them had moved in that September of 2020, but the house appeared to be owned by just one of them, Rachael Brown, whom Richardson had greeted on several occasions. Brown was a middle-aged woman, friendly enough, with light brown hair that looked like it had been dyed blonde.

One day in the fall of 2020, Richardson had looked down into her side yard to find a small lavender metal canister that fit into the palm of her hand. She had no idea what it was and, after examining it a little, had thrown it away. By that time, she had heard about Tony Hsieh and knew he was somehow affiliated with the property. She'd looked him up but had never seen him.

The house at 500 Pequot Avenue stood empty for weeks at a time, and when Brown was home, she was usually with a small group of people. They were generally quiet, but one time in the fall of 2020 the neighbors were treated to an unusual spectacle. Spotlights were set up on the side of the house, and a wrestling ring was assembled. A group of people came out dressed in costume, including the actor David Arquette. Arquette is a former professional wrestler and a friend of Tony's, but the neighbors didn't know that.

On the night of the fire in late November 2020, Richardson woke up to the sound of several people screaming outside. "Tony!" she heard the people yell. "Tony!"

She rushed to open her sliding glass door and looked over her balcony, from which she could see Brown's backyard. A woman was on the neighbor's balcony, pacing and yelling "1014!" over and over. Richardson later learned that it was the code to the nearby pool shed. Below, she saw two men clawing desperately at the door of the shed, which appeared to be locked. An alarm blared.

Richardson couldn't figure out what was going on until she heard one of the neighbors yell something about a fire. She immediately ran back inside and called the police. Later she watched from her yard as thick smoke poured from the shed. It smelled acrid, like an electrical fire.

Across the fence the next morning, she saw one of the neighbors, a man named Anthony Hebert who visited there sometimes with Brown. There was a memorial on their side of the fence, a tacky, brightly colored thing that appeared to be marking a small grave. The memorial included a stack of white rocks, a bird feeder, two Tiki torches, and plastic flowers arranged over an arch.

Hebert greeted her and explained, "Rachael's dog died. It was really old and blind and sick, and she's really upset.

"And now her friend . . ." he trailed off. Richardson told him she had called the police the night before and said she hoped their friend would be okay. The details of who had been pulled from the shed had not yet made national news. Soon reporters from all over the country would be stationed on the residential street, and Richardson would be followed by camera drones as she walked down the beach.

"It was a freak accident," Hebert acknowledged, "but he's young. He's going to be okay.

"It was really just a freak accident."

PART I

CHAPTER ONE

"A VERY OPTIMISTIC, INNOCENT TIME"

Park City, Utah, February 2020–March 2020
San Francisco, California, 1995–1998

My role is about unleashing what people already have inside them.
That is maybe suppressed in most work environments.

—Tony Hsieh

Tony Hsieh was free.

He pushed through a set of double glass doors, pulling a suitcase with several changes of clothes, cell phone in hand. His eyes were clearer than they had been in weeks, and his face looked fuller. His black hair, which he had recently shaved off completely, had grown back into little spikes. He already needed a haircut.

Tony paid little attention to the majesty of his surroundings as he hurried to a Mercedes van waiting in the sprawling parking lot. Directly in front of him towered the Provo Peaks, a set of mountains in Utah's Wasatch Range, only miles away. To his left was what the locals called the "Wasatch front" side of Mount Timpanogos, one of the largest mountains in the range. On the "Wasatch back" side of the mountain, out of Tony's view, was the Cascade Cirque. Even at a distance, the Cirque, a glacier-carved amphitheater, is recognizable by the dark, jagged slashes across its white surface, as if a tiger had run its claw horizontally across the snow.

It was the end of February, and a light snow was falling. Earlier in the month, there had been several blizzards in the area, and snow from those storms was still piled high in some corners of the parking lot.

The drug and alcohol rehabilitation facility in the town of Orem, Utah, that Tony had just left was named for the glacier—Cirque Lodge—and Tony would have seen plenty of the surrounding area during his stay. The facility, known as "the studio," because of its affiliation with the Osmonds singing band in the 1970s, has a panoramic view of the mountain range through large windows in its dining room and common areas, and winding hallways that resemble dorm rooms. Cirque Lodge charges most patients $38,700 a month to stay in the studio, typical for a celebrity facility.

Cirque Lodge was founded in 1999 by Richard Losee, a devout Mormon whose background was in the beauty and jewelry industries. After watching a relative deal with drug addiction without the right mix of treatment options, Losee made a life-altering decision to change the plans for a wellness center he had been planning to build in the mountains. Instead, he turned it into a rehabilitation clinic. He has since turned down several offers from private equity firms to purchase it. Losee, who keeps an office at the studio location, is known by clients for his quiet kindness and flexibility. Despite its reputation as a facility for the rich and famous, Cirque Lodge routinely cuts its prices for clients who can't afford it, and many staff members have worked there nearly since it was founded. Others have been addicts themselves or watched loved ones suffer.

Because of his stature, Tony would normally have been staying at Cirque's smaller, more private facility, a mountain chalet known as "the lodge," about a twenty-minute drive away, hidden at the top of an unmarked driveway in the mountains near Sundance, Utah. The treatment plan is about the same, but the rooms are private and guests are allowed more access to phones and computers. The monthly cost is also higher, about $64,000 a month.

Big-name former clients such as Lindsay Lohan and Kirsten Dunst typically preferred to stay at the more intimate lodge facility because of its privacy and because it looks more like a cabin retreat. Never more than sixteen clients are in residence at any one time. But Tony stayed at the studio location, which resembled dorm rooms, instead so that he could quickly adapt to his preferred habitat—with a lot of people around him.

He did not want to stay at either location—or any facility at all, for that matter. But his friends had insisted. By the end of 2019, Tony had begun acting erratically. He had always been a heavy drinker—his cologne was the smell of his favorite drink, the Italian liqueur Fernet-Branca, his friends liked to joke—but he had begun experimenting with more drugs as well. He had started taking ketamine, a drug used medically as an anesthetic that can cause hallucinations, but also thought to help with inspiration and creativity. The practice had been encouraged by a shaman, a religious leader believed to fall into a trancelike state to communicate with the spirit world. Tony told his friends that the shaman was taking him on trips into the desert. Usually Tony reserved his drug use for his annual trip to the Burning Man art and music festival in the Nevada desert, one of his favorite events.

His strange behavior started becoming noticeable at Zappos, where he had been CEO for two decades, veering from his standard silliness to downright puzzling. Working on his acres of new development plans, Tony was talking a lot, all the time, about outlandish ideas and plans as he walked around downtown Las Vegas. Usually reserved, he was even chatting to strangers, who didn't know him and would stare curiously at him on the street.

His friends really began to worry in January 2020, after he decided to throw one of his close friends, Ryan Doherty, a surprise party. Doherty, a clean-cut Boston native, is a longtime, well-known bar owner in Las Vegas. One of his most popular bars in the downtown area, Commonwealth, has a secret speakeasy tucked inside the back. Called the Laundry Room, the small brick-walled room has plush brown couches, small tables, a chandelier hanging from the ceiling near the wooden wraparound bar, and framed black-and-white portraits lining the walls.

Tony had spent his life throwing parties for his friends, often with themes. And this time he wanted to give the entire parking lot where he lived in an Airstream trailer with a dozen other Airstreams and a scattering of tiny, wooden homes the same old-timey feel of a speakeasy in honor of Doherty. He wanted to somehow recreate the feeling Doherty gave others when they walked into his popular bar. So his plans weren't unusual. But the entire night seemed off-kilter.

The party started in downtown Las Vegas. Someone picked up Doherty, blindfolded him, and handed him a cold package wrapped in paper, instructing him to hold it. He was then placed in a car that sped around the city, so he wouldn't know where he was going. Doherty needed to brace himself in the car during the crazy drive, so he stuffed the package awkwardly down his shirt. He knew the Airstream park where Tony lived, but when the car pulled up and his blindfold lifted, he found a maze of sheets and makeshift walls, an experience that someone later explained had been aimed at "sensory deprivation." In the twenty-four hours spent constructing the party, Tony had dispatched friends to Doherty's speakeasy to borrow some of the furniture, arranging it in front of the Airstream trailers.

The cold package Doherty carried was a bundle of raw fresh fish. He was expected to hand the fish to a waiting chef, who would cook it for the group's dinner. Its significance was unclear. Attendees, most of them wearing white, speculated that it must be Doherty's birthday for Tony to plan such an elaborate celebration. It wasn't.

His friends were confused, with the night not coming together fully and Tony acting strangely, and they tried to make sense of what was unfolding. Perhaps Tony was trying to create his own version of the Jejune Institute, an underground alternative universe in which players complete tasks based on a made-up story line that an artist invented in San Francisco. "A fake protest, drawing 250 people, was enacted for a 'minichapter,' created to delight hard-core gamers," the *New York Times* wrote about the experience in 2012. Tony had recently discussed a vision of an immersive, real-life "game" experience in downtown Las Vegas like the one organized in San Francisco years earlier, and maybe, they thought, they were living through a trial run.

The party became one of the incidents that ultimately convinced

Tony's friends that he might need help. Soon after, several of them began to broach the subject of Tony going to rehab. Talking him into something, however, always required careful framing, especially about more delicate issues. Some of his friends came on too strong, telling him that he was an addict or that he had a problem. Doherty, who knew Tony well, took another tack, persuading him in an hours-long conversation that if he went to rehab by his own choice, he could control the narrative. He wouldn't want Zappos to discover that something was wrong and then force him to go, Doherty argued.

Doherty had prepared for the conversation, having researched the best rehab facilities in the country. He ultimately landed on Cirque Lodge, chosen in part because Tony loved the area. Almost every year he and his group traveled to the annual Sundance Film Festival, and they typically stayed in a rental in Park City, Utah. Tony was actually in the process of buying a property there in the winter of 2020 for vacation use, a wood-frame house across from the ski resort on Empire Avenue. It provided a cover for him to be out of town.

Of utmost importance was keeping it quiet. Tony was a business celebrity, and Las Vegas was insular; word could spread quickly. No one wanted executives at Amazon, which had bought Zappos in 2009, to find out. Zappos operated largely autonomously from Amazon, but the parent company was likely to get involved if the company discovered that Tony had a drug problem. If anyone in Las Vegas asked, they were told that Tony and Doherty were visiting the new vacation property, getting it ready for visitors. The Sundance Film Festival would also have just ended, and parties sometimes continued in the days after.

The program at Cirque Lodge seemed perfect for Tony. It is "experiential," relying on various activities throughout the day to help treat patients. Its facility in the town of Orem, Utah, about an hour from Park City, has a state-of-the art ropes course housed in a 17,000-square-foot room that also features an indoor rock-climbing area and storage closets packed with outdoor gear. A recording studio featuring musical instruments and equipment that would make any professional band jealous is on hand for music therapy. In the summer, Cirque Lodge employees lead clients on hikes through the rising rock walls of nearby Provo Canyon, often taking the 1.5-mile trail to Bridal Veil Falls, a two-tiered waterfall gushing from the rocks. They go rafting and tubing down the Provo River. In the winter, they snowshoe. Most clients participate in equine therapy with a skilled, long-standing staff member, Dave Beck, an intense man with piercing blue eyes who is himself a recovering alcoholic. At indoor and outdoor staging areas, Beck teaches patients how to issue commands to the horses, trying to get them to trot in a circle around the client or change the direction in which they are walking. It is a challenge, even for people used to animals; so Beck hopes to break through patients' egos so they will ask for help when they are struggling. That is a skill he is hoping they will take back to the real world.

Though the program at Cirque Lodge employs the twelve-step program of Alcoholics Anonymous, among other traditional therapies, Beck and Losee early on introduced experiential therapies as a way to get clients distracted and perhaps interested in another activity besides their addiction. This awakening to something new is what Beck refers to as an "internal spiritual experience," one of the main steps in the AA manual. "This is a very simple program," said Beck, as he picked up his own manual, which was falling apart and duct taped in some places. "It's very difficult to execute."

Tony agreed to go to Cirque Lodge after Doherty spoke to him and left Las Vegas in a private jet. When Doherty had broached the topic with Tony, much of their conversation had involved Tony negotiating his length of stay at Cirque Lodge, refusing to go for the full thirty days that is common in most addiction programs today. It is very rare for a client to stay at Cirque Lodge less than a month. Usually it takes a week or ten days just to become adjusted to the daily schedule and acknowledge the need for help. Some centers now promote stays as long as three months. "The longer someone stays, the more likely their chances are of staying sober," Losee said later.

Tony agreed to two weeks total. On day thirteen, he left. Though there is a small front desk, there is no security, only a reception desk. Clients can leave at any time.

As he walked out, Tony climbed into the waiting Mercedes Sprinter van in the parking lot, and it drove through a pair of wrought-iron gates and away from the treatment facility.

It wasn't the first time Tony had left somewhere important early.

In 1995, he sat at a desk in a row of other desks in a large room full of rows of desks at the database management giant Oracle Corporation. He had just graduated from Harvard University with a degree in computer science. Oracle had hired him for a software engineering position, even though Tony didn't really know what the job entailed.

He was twenty-two, the son of Taiwanese immigrants, with a penchant for playing pranks, programming computers, and eating at Taco Bell. He wore his black hair shaggy, and it crept down the back of his neck. He looked no older than fifteen.

Oracle's business is not exciting; it helps companies around the world manage information. But it is one of the founding companies of Silicon Valley, and its chief executive officer, Larry Ellison, remains well regarded as one of the area's original tech founders. When Tony arrived almost two decades after its 1970s founding, Oracle, located in the small South Bay community of Redwood City, was one of the Valley's greatest success stories. Its custom-built headquarters spanned several multistory green glass towers that half circled a small lake. Employees called it "Larry's Lagoon." Oracle had gone public in 1986 and was bringing in more than $2 billion in revenue each year.

The $40,000 salary that Oracle offered Tony straight out of college seemed like a staggering amount at the time. He had been raised in nearby Marin, California, just north of San Francisco, so he would be returning home, sort of, and definitely to warmer weather than in Cambridge, Massachusetts, where he had spent the last four years of undergrad.

Tony was one of hundreds of software engineers at Oracle, and he quickly became bored. His parents, Richard and Judy, a chemical engineer and a psychologist, had imposed intense structure and discipline on his life and that of his two younger brothers, Andy and Dave, while they were growing up. As a result, Tony hated monotony and routine. He had gone to Harvard for his parents' sake, but what he really wanted to do was start his own business. He wanted to make money, not because he needed it—his family had always lived comfortably—but because he wanted to build something that would deliver freedom from having to worry about the cost of anything. He didn't have expensive tastes; he preferred jeans and a T-shirt over any other outfit and was happy sharing a rental with his roommate, Sanjay Madan, who also had graduated from Harvard and taken a job at Oracle. Madan was an ultrasmart computer programmer of Indian descent who, improbably, spoke less than Tony did.

Tony learned that at Oracle, no one was tracking his time in the office. He came in late and left early, taking an hour-long nap break during the day at his apartment nearby. He waited it out a few months and then quit.

Madan also left his job at Oracle. Together the two planned to design company websites, a venture Tony's parents did not support. Richard Hsieh told him frankly, "It didn't really sound like that could ever become a big enough business to be meaningful."

Back then, the internet was in its infancy, a novelty called the World Wide Web—which helps explain why Richard Hsieh was doubtful about his son's new career path. In 1995, only about 3 percent of the US population had ever signed on to the Web. Yahoo! had launched the previous year, and Craigslist, eBay, and Amazon all got their start as Tony was thinking about a web business. Oracle became one of the first software companies to design a strategy for the internet.

It was a defining moment for Silicon Valley, a feeling in the air that people there were on the verge of something big, a small quivering that was about to turn into an earthquake. "It was all brand new to everyone," recalled Alan Shusterman, one of the founding team members in the business Tony would start at the time, LinkExchange, and the director of product management. "It was like 'Oh, my God, I could have my website visited by people all over the world! I can sell golf balls or anything I want online!' It was a very optimistic, innocent time."

In August 1995, the web browser Netscape went public, with shares priced at $28 each. Demand for the stock was so high that the opening of trading was delayed by almost two hours. It closed at $58 a share that day. The frenzy set off what would later be described as a gold rush, a flood of money set to spill into the coffers of startups across the region. "Until then, Silicon Valley was just a place where microchips were made, not the fountainhead of global commerce," the business magazine *Fortune* wrote a decade later.

Tony and Madan had an idea for how to revolutionize internet advertising. The industry was burgeoning at the time, and few companies allocated any of their advertising budget to websites. Most of the money still went to traditional media such as television, radio, and print. When they did advertise online, companies purchased banner ads, usually directly from the website where they wanted to advertise. The banner ads were cartoonish and clunky; the first one had launched in 1994 on HotWired with faded white text on a black background: "Have you ever clicked your mouse right HERE? → YOU WILL."

Tony and Madan came up with an idea for a collective advertising system, one that would lower the barrier to entry for smaller websites especially. It worked like this: any business could join the network for free and insert a code on its own website; banner ads from a variety of other businesses would then start showing up. The website would earn half a credit for every ad it displayed. The credits would rack up, and then the website could use them to purchase its own advertising banners on other sites in the network. Tony and Madan called the business LinkExchange. (LinkExchange kept about half of the advertising from its member businesses and sold it for a profit to larger companies. Members could also purchase advertising.)

LinkExchange grew much faster than Tony and Madan had anticipated. After only a few months, they had tens of thousands of customers. After six months, they had fielded their first purchase offer from a private investor, for $1 million. They turned it down. LinkExchange was growing so rapidly that it seemed like a bad idea to sell so quickly.

By 1997, LinkExchange had about fifty employees and had moved out of the cramped San Mateo apartment that Tony and Madan shared where it had been housed for almost a year. Now employees worked from two floors of a nondescript brick building in an area of San Francisco that was less than desirable at the time, the South of Market neighborhood known as SoMa. A sign in the lobby of the building warned tenants that it was not earthquake safe. Rather than pay for desks, which were expensive, Tony and Madan bought dozens of doors that came with holes for doorknobs from a local hardware store. Computers sat on the wooden doors, which rested on concrete blocks and sawhorses, their power cords snaking through the doorknob holes and into wall outlets.

Underneath the desks, Tony and most of the other employees kept sleeping bags. They often worked late into the night, crashing on the floor afterward only to start over in the morning. Internet advertising had taken off, and LinkExchange had fierce competitors, including its biggest one, DoubleClick, which would be acquired about a decade later by Google.

When an important World Wide Web conference, Internet World '97, was held in Los Angeles, LinkExchange couldn't afford to pay for flights, admission, and the cost of an entire booth. But the conference was an important chance for startups to be noticed and promote themselves—Microsoft was introducing its next web browser, Internet Explorer 4.0, and AOL was showing off its latest software, Casablanca. Tony wanted to be there, so he rented a Winnebago, nicknamed it "Web-a-bago," and drove a small group of employees the six hours to Los Angeles. He parked the RV, littered with junk food, guitars, and pagers, at a prime spot at the conference. He draped a banner with the LinkExchange logo across the front, a much lower-quality version of a booth than the nearby flashy digs of AltaVista, a new web search engine.

The LinkExchange executives sent an email blast to their customers, telling them that they would get a free T-shirt if they showed up at the "booth" by noon on the day of the conference. Soon dozens of people were lined up and then walked through the conference venue wearing bright blue shirts with LinkExchange's logo, far outpacing the impact of the more upscale booths.

Tony had brought in two more recent Harvard graduates: his former college classmate Alfred Lin and the identical twin brother of an Iranian-American friend, Ali Partovi, to help with the business. Lin, whose parents had also immigrated from Taiwan, had met Tony at Harvard when Tony had devised a scheme to sell slices of pizza to his classmates, buying and installing a pizza oven in a campus hangout area. The way Tony remembered it and later described it in *Delivering Happiness*, Lin had one-upped him by buying whole pizzas and reselling slices to other students at a higher price. Though Lin wasn't trying to make money off his roommates, he found that when he charged $1.25 or $1.50 per slice, his customers gave him $2 anyway. No one wanted to give up the precious quarters needed for laundry, vending machines, and arcade games. He and Tony would joke about Lin's apparent pizza arbitrage.

However it happened, the move impressed Tony, forever endearing Lin to him. The pizza story became their origin story. They shared a similar upbringing, both having been raised by strict parents who had high expectations for their sons. In their early years in business, they also shared a feeling of not always fitting in at the party and hated being onstage to make presentations before both grew into business leaders with big successes.

Tony didn't know Partovi well, but his identical twin brother, Hadi, had been on the Harvard computer programming team with Tony. They had competed together at a renowned worldwide coding competition in 1994. Ali Partovi, Tony joked, was basically Hadi's stunt double.

Ali Partovi, who was also twenty-three at the time, helped Tony with aspects of management that didn't suit him. LinkExchange was so small that Tony was essentially a co-CEO with all his other business partners: no one really held the formal title. Tony preferred it that way. He didn't like bureaucracy and had chafed at the company structures set up by Oracle. At LinkExchange's monthly all-hands meetings, Partovi would often handle the speaking, while Tony might say something brief and then step to the side. A *San Francisco Focus* magazine article on startup culture at the time referred repeatedly to Tony and his partners as "the kids," and the reporter described how Tony, in his T-shirt and running shoes, "stares ahead, looking bored." Partovi, by comparison, was a "chatterbox," the article reported.

In one-on-one meetings with employees, Tony sometimes never spoke. He sat silently, absorbing what the other person was saying. Some employees were disarmed by this and sat awkwardly waiting, while others kept talking to fill the silence. "It was the ultimate Socratic method," observed Scott Laughlin, who headed up LinkExchange's sales department at the time. "He would look at you until you asked all the questions you should have asked yourself. He didn't like to hear himself talk."

Laughlin, who had moved over to LinkExchange after working at a popular Web magazine, recalled a meeting he had had with Tony and LinkExchange's engineering director. In the meeting, Laughlin and the engineering director explained to Tony that some customers were unhappy with an aspect of the website—they couldn't easily find the types of businesses where they wanted to place their own ads. But fixing the problem would require a massive overhaul of the website. Tony remained mostly quiet as the two detailed the problem, and the meeting ended without a solution.

The next morning, Laughlin woke up to a one-sentence email from Tony: "Is this better?" with a link to the LinkExchange website. Tony had spent the whole night since the meeting rewriting code so that the issue was fixed. He had done it himself, rather than assign it to someone else. "I was swayed by your argument," he told Laughlin.

There was a playfulness about Tony, a wry wit that shined through even when he wasn't talking much. Despite his awkwardness, he had the ability to connect with people in a way that others didn't, mostly because he truly seemed to care about everyone around him.

It was clear that he thought about the world in an unusual way, with an almost childlike enthusiasm. "If you're looking at a model of something, he would go off to the side and look at it at a twenty-degree angle because he saw the contours differently," said Shusterman. "He would say these things all the time that were just really remarkable insights."

Tony once decided to take a road trip across the country to talk to other companies about advertising—itself an extraordinary move for a young startup founder. After he returned, he sent off a detailed email to the LinkExchange team with his predictions about how the advertising industry would change over the next decade, including how companies would want more control over their advertising by managing their own in-house platforms, a seemingly unlikely trend at the time. All of Tony's predictions ultimately came true, Shusterman recalled later.

At a time when workplace culture looked more like *The Office* or *Dilbert*, Tony instituted silliness. He hazed new employees, customers, and even prospective business partners. Shusterman was deputized as the "pledgemaster," in charge of planning whatever zaniness might occur. Ahead of one companywide meeting, Shusterman asked Tony what was on the agenda from the executive team.

"Oh, we have nothing," Tony replied. The meeting was being held strictly to make the new employees dress up in business suits and do push-ups and jumping jacks in front of everyone else. Though it might sound harsh to some and could have been under a different CEO, Tony encouraged LinkExchange employees to have fun and laugh at themselves, as opposed to a suit-and-tie culture of seriousness and business metrics.

Tony came up with an unusual low-cost marketing strategy, dispatching his team to email thousands of customers, asking them to display the LinkExchange logo in an unusual way and then mail in a picture of it. Within weeks, the company was overwhelmed with postcards. One customer was shown walking through a mall holding a large, homemade LinkExchange sign; another mowed the logo onto his suburban lawn. One man had shaved it into his hair, another had painted it across his pet snake. The photos covered an entire wall of LinkExchange's San Francisco office and frequently delighted visitors and job candidates. Ultimately Tony helped create a loyal, devoted customer base not unlike the fans of Steve Jobs's Apple products.

Tony and Partovi—who was much more anxious than Tony, even in his early twenties—one day discussed LinkExchange's customer service department. Typically companies don't like to focus on customer service because it doesn't make money and in fact usually drains money because of the cost of employing people to answer phones and emails of existing customers. Partovi was brainstorming ways that LinkExchange could automate aspects of customer service to keep costs from ballooning as the business continued to grow.

Tony thought about it and then challenged Partovi: "What if instead of controlling customer service costs, we just paid the employees more?" Tony theorized that if the division was handled well, it would translate to good marketing for LinkExchange. He also seemed to genuinely care about the people working in the department. The strategy worked.

Sometimes Tony's ideas didn't translate to the real world, though, and it was up to Partovi and Lin to rein in his most outlandish schemes. "He had an extremely positive, creative energy," Partovi said later. "There had to be a counterbalance to temper that."

Soon Jerry Yang, a cofounder of Yahoo!, came calling, interested not in investing in but in possibly buying LinkExchange. At the time, Yang was a legend, the Mark Zuckerberg, before the tech backlash, of his day. Yang had cofounded Yahoo! with a colleague, David Filo, in 1994 while a PhD candidate in electrical engineering at Stanford, and the company's success had been rapid, attracting many big-name investors. Named for *Gulliver's Travels*—a "yahoo" is an uncouth and uncivilized being, a description that attracted Yang and Filo—Yahoo! tried to list websites for users in a directory format. It later became one of the first internet search engines.

Yang wanted to buy LinkExchange for $20 million, a massive amount in the 1990s that would give Tony and his executive team the gift of financial independence at a very young age. Yang invited Tony and Partovi to Yahoo!'s small office in Sunnyvale to discuss a potential deal. For days leading up to the meeting, Partovi felt stressed. He wanted to talk about it constantly, weighing the pros and cons of selling versus growing more. Tony, in contrast, seemed unconcerned and not at all focused on the coming meeting. He continued addressing day-to-day issues at LinkExchange that seemed trivial in the context of the potential windfall at stake.

When they met Yang, Tony smiled and shook his hand. "Hey, I

heard you just got married—congratulations," he said warmly. Yang had indeed just married a Costa Rican woman he had met in Japan.

Immediately the tension in the room dissipated, and Partovi marveled at his twenty-four-year-old friend. "His ability to think about the other person and connect at a human level was amazing," Partovi said later.

The group debated selling to Yahoo! but ultimately decided against it. Again, LinkExchange's rapid growth convinced them to hang on, although a second deal months later for five times as much nearly came together before Yahoo! got cold feet.

After Tony and Madan turned down Yahoo!'s first offer, they drew the attention of Michael Moritz, a forty-two-year-old Welsh former journalist turned venture capitalist, who was a Yahoo! investor and aware of the company's courting of LinkExchange. Moritz was among the best-known Silicon Valley investors, representing Sequoia Capital. His reputation would only grow due to his then-recent investment in Yahoo! and his early, prescient bet on Google. Meanwhile, Sequoia's stature also increased, and it became one of the most sought-after venture capital firms by startups. Moritz invested $3 million in LinkExchange and was forced by Tony to awkwardly perform the macarena in front of employees.

LinkExchange continued to grow, and around it, San Francisco was going through a renaissance. Raves had become part of the culture in the late 1980s and early 1990s, starting with meetups after dark hosted by bands with names such as Wicked that grew a cult following. Sometimes parties took place under the Golden Gate Bridge, along the wild, unpopulated shoreline of Baker Beach, and then moved to repurposed garages and underground clubs in the city's iconic Haight-Ashbury neighborhood. In the earliest meetups on Baker Beach, attendees constructed a giant statue of a person using driftwood that had washed up along the rocks. They then lit it on fire, creating a "burning man," the genesis of the art and music festival that would later gain popularity after it moved to the Nevada desert.

Before the days of group invitations on social media, ravers joined secret listservs, calling a phone number the day before to figure out the location. Much like the 1970s-era hippies before them, the ravers were a community, and they operated under the acronym PLUR—Peace, Love, Unity, Respect. Many of them wore bright-colored necklaces, shirts, or backpacks, but there was no real dress code.

Tony was skeptical of raves, even though he was slowly realizing how much he valued his close friends and having a group of them around all the time. He liked to throw parties, in large part because he wanted to make his friends happy and observe them as they enjoyed a well-planned get-together. At parties, he could also usually avoid one-on-one conversations.

One night, he tagged along with his friends to a rave. They drove outside of the city to a warehouse with nothing else around it, except for hundreds of cars parked outside. The warehouse was massive, "the size of ten football fields," Tony later wrote in *Delivering Happiness*. Green laser beams crisscrossed the crowd, and a machine churned fog into the cavernous space. Ultraviolet lights stationed around the warehouse caused the decorations on the wall to light up, giving the room an eerie glow.

Not a fan of techno music—the backbone of raves—Tony didn't understand the draw of the constant, repetitive thumping with no words. But then he entered the warehouse and, unlike in a typical nightclub, where people dance in small groups, often facing each other, here everyone moved at the same pace, bouncing up and down, looking toward the DJ. Tony was struck by an inexplicable feeling of awe and was greatly moved by the scene.

"As someone who is usually known as being the most logical and rational person in a group, I was surprised to feel myself swept with an overwhelming sense of spirituality—not in the religious sense, but a sense of deep connection with everyone who was there as well as the rest of the universe," he later wrote.

"It was as if the existence of individual consciousness had disappeared and been replaced by a single unifying group consciousness, the same way a flock of birds might seem like a single entity instead of a collection of individual birds. Everyone in the warehouse had a shared purpose. We were all contributors to the collective rave experience." He would spend the rest of his life chasing that feeling and trying to recreate what he called a "tribe" wherever he went.

At raves, he also discovered ecstasy, a staple of the culture, and enjoyed the intense feeling of happiness and energy that spread through him after he placed the small round pill on his tongue. He'd usually add to the mix with vodka—Grey Goose was his favorite brand—straight or with soda. His friends noticed that drinking made him more confident and less shy, a feeling he seemed to crave.

At LinkExchange, Tony supported Partovi and Shusterman when they organized a social club called DrinkExchange, open to anyone in San Francisco. The club held events at local bars, usually once a month, with operating rules similar to those of LinkExchange: attendees were asked to buy two drinks and give them away to two people they didn't know, and then they would theoretically receive drinks back the same way. Hundreds of people showed up.

One clunky online invitation read, "We're hoping to build THE definitive social event for Wuppies (Web Yuppies), and we need YOUR attendance to get us there. Make sure you come and buy somebody a drink! Invite as many Internet-savvy people as you'd like, but make sure to tell them about the important DrinkExchange model."

At LinkExchange, the culture was souring. Tony, Madan, and Partovi had operated as a three-pronged chief executive officer team for most of the company's existence. But LinkExchange had grown too large to sustain that unusual approach. Moritz stepped in to run it temporarily, but then the group hired an outsider, Mark Bozzini, the former CEO of Pete's Brewing Company. Bozzini, who had no real internet experience, brought in senior executives, and the group did not mesh well with the younger team.

Bozzini and his team planned to take LinkExchange public, but a financial crisis in Russia suddenly triggered a temporary shutdown of the public market in the United States. Instead, LinkExchange began looking for buyers. The LinkExchange team found itself in a bidding war between Netscape and Microsoft, sparked in part by Partovi's twin brother, Hadi. Hadi worked at Microsoft and told then president Steve

Ballmer, "I haven't talked to you about my brother's company before, but they're about to get acquired, and I've spent the last five years competing with Netscape."

Microsoft won the bid. The Seattle-based software behemoth, at the time the "evil giant" among tech companies, paid $265 million, more than ten times Yahoo!'s offer only a year earlier. In the local San Jose *Mercury News*, a story about the deal ran on the front page, packaged next to the day's events in the government's antitrust lawsuit against Microsoft.

Tony was only twenty-four, part of the first crop of startup superstars who helped create the myth of the fortune to be found in Silicon Valley.

"Against the backdrop of a booming economy, capital aplenty and the wide open frontiers of technology, a new generation of entrepreneurs are utterly prepared to amass their fortunes under their own steam," the *Wall Street Journal* wrote in 2000, describing Tony and other entrepreneurs' good fortune.

Startups that sold themselves or went public during those two years were affectionately called 98ers and 99ers, a reference to the wildly successful 48ers and 49ers during the Gold Rush. eBay, the online auction site, went public a few months before LinkExchange was sold in 1998, priced at the top of its range (and breaking the earlier IPO dry spell that had dissuaded LinkExchange from going public).

"The 98ers cleaned up in the same way that the 48ers did," said David A. Kirsch, an associate professor of management and entrepreneurship at the University of Maryland, in an interview. Kirsch had once maintained a giant database of Silicon Valley startup failures in the 1990s.

Tony earned $32 million from the LinkExchange sale. He would have earned 20 percent more if he had stuck to an agreement with Microsoft to stay with the company for a year.

But Tony no longer liked the culture, even though LinkExchange had of course hazed Ballmer and his deputies after the sale, making them don silly clothes and dance. He found Microsoft to be much more political, and more formal. Tony dreaded getting up in the morning to go to work. He quit a few weeks after the deal was signed.

CHAPTER TWO

TREASURE MOUNTAIN

Park City, February 2020–April 2020
San Francisco and Las Vegas, 1998–2008

To dare is to lose one's footing momentarily. To not dare is to lose oneself.

—Soren Kierkegaard, quoted in
Delivering Happiness by Tony Hsieh

In the 1950s, Park City nearly disappeared.

Today, the town is nestled among ski slopes and rustic mansions carved high into the craggy Wasatch mountain rocks. Cross-country skiers glide across snowy paths that become biking routes lined with wildflowers in summertime. Ski lifts ferry vacationers up the tree-lined mountainside, where Wild West miners once dug for silver in the hope of becoming rich. The town sits a thirty-minute drive east—and roughly three thousand feet above—its neighbor Salt Lake City.

Its roots, like those of other Western towns, go back to mining days after precious metals were discovered in the mid-nineteenth century. By 1898, the town was home to about 7,500 residents. Park City survived big fires and catastrophic mine collapses, but the late 1940s and 1950s brought an economic crisis after metal prices plummeted. Mines closed and thousands of people left, while Main Street businesses were boarded up. Park City appeared in a guidebook of Western ghost towns, even though 1,150 people still lived there.

When a mining company decided to convert its cableways used for carrying silver ore to ferry skiers and tourists instead, Park City was set on a new course in history. The Treasure Mountain ski resort opened in 1963; it later became Park City Mountain Resort.

Now about 8,400 people live in town. The snowy months are the lifeblood of local businesses that cater to wealthy second homers and vacationers. In January, the Sundance Film Festival takes over the town. More than 100,000 people attend over the eleven-day festival of movie screenings. Hollywood stars walk the press line at the Park City High School auditorium.

At the bottom of the ski slopes, tourists and locals stroll through Old Town, rows of quaint buildings that hint at the town's origins as a mining camp. Now family-owned restaurants, bars, and shops line Main Street. This American West charm resides uneasily with the Park City area's current booming industry: high-dollar real estate. Stacks of luxury modernist homes and towering resorts have been carved into the mountainsides. Meanwhile, pricey fur shops, yoga clothing chains, and art galleries have cropped up alongside the family-owned businesses. The arrivals have aggravated locals, who dislike the image of Park City as a playground of the wealthy.

"We look shiny when you see us in a Sundance story or some stupid *Entertainment Weekly* story," said one longtime resident, Teri Orr. "We're not based on shiny. We're based on being outdoors. We're based on being good neighbors. We're based in disproportionately caring about our small town, if you read letters to the editor in the paper. We're passionate."

Orr moved to Park City in 1979 with her two children to escape a bad marriage in Tahoe City, California. She had only $10,000 and no college degree when she arrived. "This was our second-chance place," she said. In Park City, "we all kind of screwed up, whether it was divorce or a business, and for some people, it was meant to be a Band-Aid." She worked for a ski shop, and she got a part-time gig writing a column for the long-running *Park Record* newspaper starting at $10 per month. Eventually she became editor.

In 1993, she left the newsroom and founded a nonprofit that would become the Park City Institute. The nonprofit brings performing arts and other cultural events to the town: touring ballets, summer concert series, and talks from high-profile figures such as Monica Lewinsky and Edward Snowden. The ambition, as she saw it, was to build an arts scene that would thrive beyond the expectations for a town of Park City's size.

The onslaught of the Covid-19 pandemic in 2020 hit Park City with a month left in the ski season. As news of the virus threat dominated worldwide headlines, the *Park Record* on March 14 reported the first known instance of community spread in Summit County, an adult man who "had not traveled recently and did not have contact with another person confirmed to have the virus."

"This really changes the picture," a local public health official told the newspaper. In the following days, many businesses were ordered to close, and limits were placed on public gatherings.

Park City business owners who stake their year on the ski season shuttered their shops with expenses looming. City Hall, too, foresaw an economic crisis due to the loss in tax revenues from the tourism economy. The future of a planned $100 million arts and culture district, a flagship project funded in part by tax dollars from tourism, was suddenly thrown into question. City leaders, including most recently Mayor Andy Beerman, had been working for three years to develop the district in partnership with the Sundance Institute, which would relocate its headquarters there. But Park City, like other cities around the world, fell nearly silent.

Orr stayed home alone in her two-story lavender house off Little Kate Road, her grown children and grandchildren thirty miles away and down the mountain in Salt Lake City. One day in April, she needed a break. She drove her Subaru Outback the two miles to Main Street to retrieve her mail at the post office and stop by Rocky Mountain Chocolate Factory to pick up dessert.

Outside Dolly's Bookstore, a figure quickly caught her attention.

A wiry, thin Asian man smoking a cigarette stood outside wearing no shoes despite the cold, his bare feet pacing the empty sidewalk. The man, she later learned, was likely the latest billionaire to move to town. And he had his own vision for the future of Park City. His name was Tony Hsieh.

After he left rehab in late February, Tony had his driver take him to the vacation home in Park City that he was in the process of buying, a wood-frame house on Empire Avenue. He planned to stay about a month and then return to Las Vegas.

The Sundance Film Festival had officially ended for the year a few weeks prior, though some of Tony's friends were still in town and the parties kept going. Over the years, Tony had become something of a regular at the festival, making friends not just with other executive producers who had helped fund films, as he occasionally did, but with the stars themselves. He had become particularly close with the forty-year-old actor Joseph Gordon-Levitt, known for *500 Days of Summer* and *Inception*, and with David Arquette of the *Scream* movie franchise fame.

Recently, Tony had helped fund an independent film, *Try Harder!*, by the Asian American director Debbie Lum, about students at San Francisco's largest high school trying to get into college. Tony is listed as one of ten executive producers, along with his longtime friend and assistant, Jennifer "Mimi" Pham, who for years had helped Tony run his day-to-day life.

In late February 2020, fresh out of leaving rehab early, Tony attended parties and bar meetups as if nothing had happened. Most people didn't know that anything had. He seemed more like his normal self, with his jeans and T-shirts not hanging quite so loosely off his frame. As he always did, he listened intently, made small jokes, and occasionally cracked his sly smile. A dimple punctuated his left cheek. He carried around a glass of Fernet, sipping it throughout the evening. The friends who knew about his rehab stay weren't worried about his drinking because he had always seemed to tolerate it well. They only wanted to keep him off ketamine, believing that that was the chief cause of his downward spiral. Some of his friends still didn't know that he had been to rehab, while the others were happy to avoid the topic. They wanted to make Tony comfortable. Though Tony hated being alone, he also avoided talking about himself, especially in social settings, curling inward mentally or walking away when he felt put on the spot.

Now he seemed even quieter, if that were possible, as though he were mulling some things over that he didn't want to discuss. He also seemed more closed off, the usual brightness in his eyes turned pensive. Noticeably absent was Ryan Doherty, who had convinced him to go to rehab. Tony had started telling people that Doherty had forced him to go, when he didn't need it. Doherty had also made clear to Tony that he did not want to be part of his Park City plans.

Tony had an immediate problem, one that demanded he focus on his role as CEO of Zappos: he had to get the company ready for a brewing global health crisis. Long before businesses began to send their employees home in March 2020, Tony recognized the severity of the coming pandemic. "Do you really think it's necessary to send everyone home?" one of his executives asked him as the staff worked night and day to ready Zappos to be run remotely.

"It's not a question of 'if,'" Tony replied. "It's 'when.'" Through the transition, as Zappos closed its headquarters and sent hundreds of employees home, Tony wasn't panicked by the unprecedented crisis, despite its long list of unknowns. He was as calm as he had been at LinkExchange, on the verge of selling his startup for millions of dollars.

Tony was effectively stuck in Park City in the early months of the pandemic. He could have driven himself the six hours back to Las Vegas, but he hated to drive, and his driver, Steve Moroney, the owner of Experience Transport Agency, was based in Las Vegas. Tony had known him so long that he and his friends called him "Steve-O." There also was the early fear of how the virus spread—could you get it walking outside or even in your car? No one knew for sure.

Tony had become famous for living in a small Airstream trailer, surrounded by friends in other Airstreams, in a parking lot in downtown Las Vegas with his small dog, Blizzy, and an alpaca named Marley. His communal way of living, though, was anathema to the pandemic lockdown. Even if he had managed to get back, few people wanted to live in the trailer park right now if they had the choice.

The pandemic isolated the world. For Tony, it quickly stole his foundation for being. He had spent two decades building communities in cities and with his friends in San Francisco and Las Vegas: at work, at parties he hosted, at raves he attended, and at Burning Man every year. Tony floated through crowds, preferred to have a lot of people around him, and had a repulsion to alone time. Even at night, he'd find himself waking up a friend and asking to go for a 2:00 a.m. walk. His friends always agreed because they loved and admired Tony, so they stepped outside into the darkness and waited for him to ask the first question.

His desire to create groups of people around him had started early in his life, in the years after the LinkExchange sale in the late 1990s.

Tony had walked away after the deal with Microsoft with $32 million, a newly minted twenty-four-year-old tech mogul little known beyond Silicon Valley. His seemingly limitless options stalled him, and he found that despite his wealth, he just wanted to spend time with friends.

One day in the rough Tenderloin neighborhood of San Francisco, he drove by 1000 Van Ness Avenue, a strikingly opulent 1920s building originally designed for a Cadillac dealership. Developers were converting the building into residential lofts and an AMC multiplex theater. Tony decided then that 1000 Van Ness would be his home base—for what, to be determined later. He and his friends would figure out what to do together with little space and few boundaries between them. He convinced Alfred Lin and other former Link-Exchange coworkers to move into the lofts, and the group eventually owned 20 percent of the apartments. He and Lin launched a venture capital fund, Venture Frogs, and opened an incubator for their startups in the building as well. The investment fund had a few hits—OpenTable, the restaurant reservation site, for example—and some misses.

In 1999, Tony got a voice mail from a stranger, cold-calling with an investment pitch for his website, shoesite.com, which sold footwear on the web. Nick Swinmurn, a native of England who had moved to Cupertino, California, with his parents when he was seven, was a marketing manager for an online car-buying service. He had come up with the idea for shoesite.com, which he hoped would be the Amazon.com of shoes, after being unable to find a specific pair of Airwalk boots in his size in a local mall. A search of the handful of online retailers had also failed.

Tony shared the same skepticism of online retail as most people did in the early days. Other websites were losing money. Tony would later recount that he had worried that people would not want to buy shoes without trying them on first. But Swinmurn offered up some statistics, which always impressed Tony: in 1998, 5 percent of the $40 billion footwear industry was transacted through printed catalogs, and the number was quickly growing. If people would order shoes through the mail without trying them on, why not online? Tony, intrigued by the hard numbers, agreed to a meeting.

Swinmurn, balding with a pointed goatee that grew longer over the years, showed up at the Van Ness Avenue lofts to meet with Tony and Lin, wearing board shorts and a T-shirt. Tony urged Swinmurn to find a person with retail footwear experience. Swinmurn called a Nordstrom store in a downtown San Francisco mall and found Fred Mossler, a shoe buyer.

Mossler, a tanned thirty-three-year-old with a bright white smile, bears a striking resemblance to Nicolas Cage, a fact Tony delighted in. The two would become like family over the ensuing years. At that moment, though, Mossler had risk factors to weigh: he had spent eight years moving up at the growing Seattle-based department store, had bought a house, and had had his first child. But once Venture Frogs agreed to make an investment in the new company, he quit Nordstrom. The partners changed the name of the retailer to Zappos, a play on the Spanish word for shoes, *zapatos*.

The Van Ness Avenue building, meanwhile, had become a nexus of partying alongside work. Tony organized elaborate nightlong events in his penthouse loft, number 810, which became known as Club BIO after a guest misread a sign in the elevator directing visitors to the apartment. He lived in a seventh-floor loft, but when the penthouse was listed for sale, he saw an opportunity—not for a real estate investment but for parties. "Owning the loft would ultimately enable more experiences," he later wrote in *Delivering Happiness*.

Meanwhile, Tony had been experimenting more with ecstasy and liked taking the drug, especially with friends.

At one rave in 1999, he spotted a man sitting at a booth toward the back of a giant warehouse. Emanuel Sferios, a community activist, had recently founded the organization DanceSafe to test ecstasy before people ingested it. Sferios wasn't a raver but had taken an interest in the drug after it had helped him recover from some of his own childhood trauma. By adding a particular substance known as a chemical reagent to MDMA, he could tell in thirty seconds whether it was truly the drug. He hoped to prevent rave attendees from dying from counterfeit pills, but his new organization could do only so much with its staff of unpaid volunteers. Sferios had just been rejected for a $25,000 grant.

Tony bounced up to his table—"clearly on MDMA," Sferios recalled later—and introduced himself. He said enthusiastically, "I love what you guys are doing, this is great." He explained that he had just sold his technology company to Microsoft. "If I could give you as much money as you wanted right now, how much would you ask for?"

Sferios, surprised by the unexpected, benevolent stranger, recounted to Tony the $25,000 grant he had just lost. Tony pulled out his checkbook and wrote out a check for the amount on the spot. "It catapulted us," Sferios said later. DanceSafe trained people around the country to test drugs at raves and has since become one of the preeminent nonprofits advocating for harm reduction in the electronic dance community. Tony was its first large donor.

In 2000, the investor euphoria that had helped propel LinkExchange and fueled huge valuations at other startups came crashing to an end. The Silicon Valley dot-com bubble burst, and investors shied away from the market just as Zappos was looking to grow. Tony, still an investor-adviser to the company, later wrote that he had felt he had something to prove, that LinkExchange "wasn't just dumb luck." So he stepped into the role of chief executive officer. "I decided that Zappos was going to be the universe that I wanted to help envision and build," he wrote in *Delivering Happiness*. "It would be the universe that I believed in."

On October 19, 2000, Tony emailed Zappos staff, laying out a nine-month plan for surviving the tough market. "Right now, because we are unprofitable with very limited cash, we are in a race against time," he said.

Over the coming months, Zappos imposed a round of layoffs. Tony worked closely with Mossler to develop faster shipping methods to grow sales, and he gave up Club BIO and moved five beds into the apartment for Zappos workers to live there rent-free before selling the loft in 2002 to help save the company. He poured millions of dollars of his own money into the fledgling company. That sort of move might have terrified some young entrepreneurs, but Tony had a large appetite for risk, and lived his life with little margin for error. In addition to his venture investments, he moved money into real estate and stocks. At one point, less than a decade after the LinkExchange sale, his cash balance, not including some assets he owned, was only $40,000. Tony didn't seem to care much about that number. He was always confident that he'd make things work out.

By 2003, Zappos was back on top and posted $70 million in gross sales that year. Tony implemented a new customer service incentive, designed to overcome customers' hesitation about buying shoes online and trying them on at home: Zappos would give them 60 days to return shoes free; by the end of the year, Zappos had increased that to 365 days. Tony later attributed that trial period as the reason Zappos had survived while other dot-coms had failed. It was two years before Amazon would launch its popular Prime service, offering free two-day shipping for an annual fee of $79.

Tony and his executive team then made a fateful decision: in 2004, they moved Zappos' headquarters to Las Vegas, in a low-tax state that, they hoped, employees would enjoy. In the Bay Area, it had become difficult to hire staff, especially customer service reps who saw the job as no more than a temporary gig. But Zappos' momentum as a company, along with the prospects of a lower cost of living and a bit of adventure, was enough to attract its existing staff. The built-up camaraderie was enough to convince seventy-two employees out of ninety to relocate.

In those early years in Las Vegas, the company was headquartered at an industrial park in the suburb of Henderson, Nevada. A new family in the desert was born out of necessity since almost all the employees who had moved didn't know anyone in Las Vegas. Zapponians—as they were called—invaded bars and restaurants together and explored the city.

It had been six years since Tony had sold LinkExchange, but he was still a young CEO, only thirty years old. Still, he had developed ideas about how companies should be run, and he had especially learned from his last year at LinkExchange, when the culture had begun to sour with the influx of new employees and executives and he hadn't wanted to go to work anymore. More than anything, he did not want that to happen at Zappos.

Zappos was growing rapidly in the early aughts, hiring between forty and eighty people every two weeks. That was a good problem to have, but before long, Tony couldn't interview every single person himself, nor could Fred Mossler or Alfred Lin. There had to be some way to lay the groundwork for the type of person Tony wanted to work at Zappos without their having to meet each one individually.

Tony began to study his friends and the employees that Zappos had already hired. He wrote down what he liked about them and what made them good or fun or interesting people. Over the course of a few months, he assembled a list that had dozens of different qualities on it, all the adjectives that described the people he cared about the most. He also asked his current employees what they thought about Zappos' culture. He came up with a list of thirty-seven core values, including some that seemed obvious, such as "Company growth," and others that were more specific, such as "Willing to laugh at ourselves."

Tony spent much of 2005 working with Zappos' human resources team revising the list, hoping that it would help guide which employees should be hired and which shouldn't. He emailed employees several more times to ask their opinions.

For a fairly new company, Tony's time spent on values was rare. In their early years, most startups are much more focused on their product and their growth. Decades later, it would become more common for companies of all sizes to adopt a values blueprint, following Tony's lead. He "was really good at scaling himself," one former executive observed.

Ultimately Tony ended up with ten values that became the foundation of Zappos:

1. Deliver WOW Through Service
2. Embrace and Drive Change
3. Create Fun and A Little Weirdness
4. Be Adventurous, Creative, and Open-Minded
5. Pursue Growth and Learning
6. Build Open and Honest Relationships With Communication
7. Build a Positive Team and Family Spirit
8. Do More With Less
9. Be Passionate and Determined
10. Be Humble

Value number 3 garnered the most attention, and quirky tales of Zappos' friendly customer service people and office antics prompted a growing number of media profiles of Tony and the company, glowing pieces about building community and passion in the workplace and keeping staffers invested in the culture. New hires were offered a $2,000 bonus to quit during their four weeks of training unless they wanted to stay, a new method developed by Tony that sparked more media attention.

When Tony was featured on his first magazine cover in the early aughts, one Zappos employee bought dozens of copies and handed them out to everyone else in the office. Throughout the day, each employee walked up to Tony and asked him to sign it, laughing and making fun of his newfound fame. Tony was in on the joke—he had had no desire to be interviewed, but he also understood that it was a necessary part of the job. He wasn't good at public speaking, but he was a relentless researcher and taught himself how to improve by studying comedians and carefully watching other experts.

The motto "Create Fun and A Little Weirdness" spread throughout Zappos' offices, and all employees had full license to make their workspace their own. The Henderson office was decorated year-round from floor to ceiling with personal knickknacks, posters, streamers, and stuffed animals, all crammed together.

TV camera crews following Tony around captured the weirdness: an Oktoberfest celebration with workers wearing German folk costumes, a toga party, toy cars racing among cubicles. It wasn't a silent office: noise machines went off, music played, and someone had one of those clapping toys.

In contrast, Tony guided journalists and Wall Street analysts on tours in a demure fashion, often wearing a Zappos-branded T-shirt and jeans. He twirled a small umbrella to signal that he was taking visitors around. Tony's own office was a space no larger than anyone else's in the middle of the mayhem, surrounded by giant jungle-style plants and stuffed animals, as in a zoo. His desk was cluttered with mementos given to him by friends and employees.

For outsiders, the Zappos tours could be overwhelming, like visiting Willy Wonka's Chocolate Factory, a crush of colors and noise and decorations. A giant wall featured ties that had been cut off the business suits of stiffly dressed visitors.

On tours, Tony hewed closely to his message of human connection, rarely revealing anything personal. "We really want people's true personalities to shine in the workplace," he said. Just like the DJs onstage at the all-night raves Tony loved, he orchestrated the fun from a place of power but somehow slipped into the background. He rarely mentioned shoes.

"It was a little bit surreal because everyone seemed so happy," said Wall Street analyst Colin Sebastian, who visited Tony on several occasions. "I've been to thousands of offices, and none of them were like this."

Some of the early employees who had moved from San Francisco suffered in the heat of the Las Vegas summers—"The coldest winter I ever spent was a summer in San Francisco" is a quip often heard among Bay Area residents—and soon a number of the Zappos men decided to shave their heads. Some of the women shaved their legs in solidarity. Later Zappos formalized the event, calling it "Bald and Blue," and asked Zapponians to either shave their heads or dye their hair blue in allegiance to the brand.

Visitors could see that Tony was a special, rare kind of CEO. He had come up with an unusual way to build a big company: by making sure that everyone wanted to come to work every day. "We call them 'magic leaders': they are able to build companies in ways that run against the grain of anything that has been done before," Sebastian, the Wall Street analyst, said later.

Under Tony's leadership, Zappos grew to more than $1 billion in gross merchandise sales ($635 million in net revenue after customer returns) by 2008, what *Inc.* magazine called "an e-commerce powerhouse." Internally, though, Tony and his board of directors disagreed about the company's next steps. Some early investors who sat on the board wanted a financial exit, such as being acquired, rather than riding along with Tony's big ideas. The board called those "Tony's social experiments."

"The board wanted me, or whoever was CEO, to spend less time on worrying about employee happiness and more time selling shoes," Tony said.

Meanwhile, Zappos was in a precarious financial position because of the unfolding 2008 financial crisis. Like many retailers, the company relied on revolving credit to pay for inventory, but if it missed certain monthly business targets, its current banks could walk away. In an environment in which access to credit was becoming incredibly hard, it was unlikely that another bank would step in to save Zappos, possibly leading to the company's bankruptcy. (Zappos had not actually missed any payments yet.)

Then in walked Amazon. The world's largest and most powerful online retailer had unsuccessfully approached Zappos about a deal in 2005 and two years later had launched its own competitor to Zappos, an online shoe retailer called Endless.com. For Tony and his management team, a sale this time around seemed to solve a lot of problems as pressure from the board mounted. Amazon founder Jeff Bezos was still interested. In April 2009, Tony met with Bezos in Seattle, an encounter he described in writing about why he had decided to sell in *Inc.* magazine. In a PowerPoint slideshow to the online magnate, Tony brought up how he strived to make workers and employees happy.

"Did you know that people are very bad at predicting what will make them happy?" Bezos asked, interrupting Tony's presentation.

"Those were the exact words on my next slide," Tony later wrote.

That year, Tony signed an all-stock deal to sell Zappos for $1.2 billion, marking Amazon's biggest acquisition in its fourteen-year history. Analysts speculated that Bezos, then Amazon's CEO, had bought Zappos because it was the only real competitive threat to his company.

Tony insisted that Zappos would continue to operate independently, its own weird family, despite Amazon's reputation as more aggressive and buttoned-down. A personal video Bezos sent internally to the Zappos team seemed to confirm that. In the video, Bezos, standing in the front yard of what looked to be his house in Seattle, introduced himself to Zappos employees. "Hello, my name is Jeff Bezos," he said, "and I started Amazon.com about fifteen years ago." Bezos, who would go on to become the richest person in the world, operating one of the largest tech companies, told Zappos employees how he had launched Amazon in his house with only a few employees and not enough electricity to power the startup's servers.

He then pointed to a sheet of paper on which he had written what he called "a short list" of the things he knew were important to any business: "Obsess over customers," "Invent," and "Think long term," points that Tony also clearly valued.

Bezos, who was effusive in the video, told the Zappos team, "I have never seen a company with a culture like Zappos, and I think that kind of unique culture is a very significant asset, and I'm super excited about that." He described all the time he had spent talking to Tony, Lin, and Mossler and sought to reassure employees that they wouldn't be going anywhere, saying that Zappos' workers were in good hands. "I've seen a lot of leaders of companies, and I haven't seen any better than those three," he said. He concluded, "That culture and the Zappos brand are huge assets that I value very much, and I want those things to continue."

As the CEO of Zappos, Tony asked for a salary of just $36,000, less than some call service reps were paid. The stock deal had been lucrative for him, boosting his net worth to nearly $1 billion. His risk-taking had paid off once again.

Under Amazon, Zappos expanded from a thousand brands of shoes to clothing and even cookware. Some small details changed, like the way budgeting happened, for example. But otherwise, Zappos was left alone, hundreds of miles away from Amazon's headquarters in Seattle.

Happy Zappos customers emailed constantly, asking Tony to take over the Internal Revenue Service or start a new business, such as an airline. "In 20 years, I wouldn't rule out a Zappos airline where we offer the best customer service," he said at a conference.

In March 2020, Tony started calling and texting friends, imploring them to come visit him in Park City, despite the nationwide quarantine due to the spread of Covid-19. He could be very convincing, and many of his friends had grown used to saying yes to any of his plans. Some didn't need much persuasion at all.

Tyler Williams drove the six hours from Las Vegas, often leaving his wife, who had been his high school sweetheart, back home. The drive is beautiful: the barren desert outside Las Vegas soon gives way to steep, rocky canyons, the Virgin River a trickle following the side of the highway for a stretch. After Interstate 15 briefly crosses through Arizona, the reds and beiges of the desert turn into vast stretches of green farmland, and finally, after more than five hours, the peaks of the Wasatch range open up in front of the highway.

Williams visited Tony several times over the ensuing weeks, driving back and forth from Las Vegas. He was the quintessential long-time Zappos employee, and he had invented his own title: "fungineer." A musician originally from Alaska with a chest-length beard the color of rust, Williams had been touring across the country a decade earlier with a little-known rock band before burning out and moving to Las Vegas. His wife had taken a tour of Zappos and encouraged him to apply. In 2011, the year he wanted a job, statistics showed that it was easier to get into Harvard than to get a job at the online shoe retailer.

So Williams made a short music video, hoping to set himself apart from the thousands of other applicants. He cloned himself on screen, seven copies of himself wearing a V-neck sweater and plaid shirt, his red hair teased into a mohawk. The song featured lyrics about Zappos' corporate values with a chorus repeating the company name over and over: "Za-a-a-apo-os."

Tony watched the video, and was impressed. Williams got the job, starting in Zappos' customer service department, and then worked his way up over the years until he eventually controlled one of the company's largest budgets outside of e-commerce, something called "Brand Aura." "Brand Aura" basically described experimental projects, sometimes at the behest of Tony and sometimes involving frivolous exploits, such as building unique porta-potties for events. Called "Porta Parties," the traveling toilets came with selfie stations and motorized squatty feet.

"Zappos is always making things fun, and now I'm excited about the toilet," one user said in a company promotional video.

For Williams, as for many Zappos employees, his work relationship with Tony blurred into close friendship, and he was well known as one of Tony's chief advisers, willing to do most anything for him and around him almost every hour of the day.

Tony asked him once, "What if we built a jacket that had charging ports in it with batteries?" Though there was no clear use for it, Williams made one anyway, a clunky prototype with wires hanging everywhere. It worked but was never used by anyone.

In Park City, Williams joined a small group of Tony's friends who had also come to visit, a hodgepodge of people who had touched his life at one point or another. Not all of them were part of Tony's close inner circle in Las Vegas. A large entourage surrounded Tony at all times, so it wasn't unusual to get to know a wide variety of people from all demographics anytime you spent time with him.

The first few weeks of the pandemic shutdown felt like a retreat. The mountains were covered in snow, but the ski resorts were closed, so the group mostly stayed in. Not too concerned about catching the virus, Tony found a masseuse who was willing to come to the rental house, where guests were treated to long massages. Tony joined meetings through Amazon's private online video service, continuing to run Zappos from afar.

In their downtime, the group read books together, and Tony always had a recommendation for a new nonfiction or self-help book he liked. A voracious reader his whole life, he constantly read and researched new ideas. Often he used books to express his thoughts about a new philosophy or way of life he was contemplating. In Park City, he recommended *The Slight Edge: Turning Simple Disciplines into Massive Success & Happiness* by Jeff Olson, a slim manual by a little-known marketing executive that proclaims it holds the "SECRET to a successful life." In life, the book argues, the people who succeed make small changes to their daily activities, focusing on time management and savings, rather than expect a big break to propel them to success.

Tony also kept a copy of *Stealing Fire: How Silicon Valley, the Navy SEALs, and Maverick Scientists Are Revolutionizing the Way We Live and Work* by Steven Kotler, a journalist, and Jamie Wheal, a leadership expert. The book outlines a process called *ecstasis*, a condition in which a group of people subconsciously act as one unit, with examples including Google engineers and Navy SEALs on a mission. This mode of acting makes one superhuman, with increased focus, quicker muscle reaction, and the ability to recognize patterns.

Tony had long been interested in ways to maximize his body's capabilities, a lifestyle that has become somewhat of an obsession in Silicon Valley. The process, called *biohacking* or *DIY biology*, involves activities that aim to increase a person's physical and cognitive abilities, many of them unproven by science. That can include everything from intermittent fasting and specialized diets to running experiments on yourself. In the latter, more controversial practice, some adherents of biohacking have inoculated themselves with healthy feces in attempts to improve their stomach function, while others have injected themselves with the blood of a younger person to try to improve their vitality. One biohacker described biohacking to the website Vox as "the art and science of changing the environment around you and inside you so that you have full control over your own biology."

Biohacking started gaining popularity in 2014 after a twenty-five-year-old engineer in Silicon Valley, Rob Rhinehart, introduced Soylent, a bland beige liquid that professed to include all the nutrients of a single meal. Even though some customers described it as tasting "rancid," it gained a cult following among people who wanted to skip the hassle of buying food and preparing meals. It soon raised over $70 million from well-known investors. Rhinehart claimed to have spent months drinking it, leading to big improvements in his health. The *New York Times* called it "the most joyless new technology to hit the world since we first laid eyes on MS-DOS."

In 2017, a thirty-two-year-old entrepreneur, Serge Faguet, published a series of controversial blog posts on the technology platform Hacker Noon, claiming that he had spent $200,000 on biohacking to try to improve his mood and energy level. The result was that he had become "calmer, thinner, extroverted, healthier & happier." He detailed his procedure: three hours before bed, he begins to block blue light with special glasses, and he tracks his sleep with an Oura smart ring, a product that registers a user's health information; he fasts intermittently throughout the week; he has an intense daily gym routine; he meditates regularly and practices not lying about anything; he takes more than two dozen drugs and supplements daily, including antidepressants, a growth hormone, an estrogen blocker, and lithium, a drug frequently used to treat bipolar disorder; and he uses a hearing aid, despite having normal hearing.

The posts were panned as "the embodiment of Silicon Valley's toxic machiavellian bro culture," according to the *Guardian*, but Faguet's thousands of mostly male readers applauded his efforts, particularly when he noted his increased sex drive.

Perhaps the most recognizable of Silicon Valley's biohackers is Jack Dorsey, until late 2021 the chief executive officer of both the social media giant Twitter and the financial payments service provider Square. Dorsey, who looks like the antithesis of an executive, with a long, scraggly beard and nose ring, has spoken openly about his unusual routines. He believes in intermittent fasting, which can take several different forms, including one known as "16/8"—fasting every day for fourteen to sixteen hours and restricting one's daily eating window to eight to ten hours. Dorsey's practice involves eating one meal a day, typically dinner. He starts his day with a drink he calls "salt juice," a mixture of Himalayan salt, water, and lemon juice that has questionable benefits. He takes ice baths several times a day, a process sometimes used by athletes to reduce inflammation. Though the practice can reportedly repair muscles, studies examining its benefits are mixed, research shows.

Tony had never been extreme about his own biohacking, but he had certainly run experiments on himself and gone on what some friends described as "exercise benders," climbing three peaks in southern California in just one day. Once he tried to limit himself to four hours of sleep a day. Another time he went on a twenty-six-day diet, progressing through the alphabet on each day. On the letter *A* day, he could eat apples, anchovies, and asparagus; by the time he reached the letter *Z*, he was nearly fasting.

His experimentation continued, including with drugs, where he added ketamine to the mix in late 2019, going farther than he had before. At the time, mind-altering drugs such as psychedelics were experiencing something of a renaissance. Decades after the government had banned the drugs in the 1960s, researchers were discovering that ecstasy, mushrooms, and ketamine could be used to treat post-traumatic stress disorder, depression, and anxiety.

The author Michael Pollan discovered their beneficial properties while writing his 2018 book about LSD and mushrooms, *How to Change Your Mind: What the New Science of Psychedelics Teaches Us About Consciousness, Dying, Addiction, Depression, and Transcendence.* "What was missing from my life?" asked Pollan, who is in his fifties. "Nothing I could think of—until, that is, word of the new research into psychedelics began to find its way to me, making me wonder if perhaps I had failed to recognize the potential of these molecules as a tool for both understanding the mind and, potentially, changing it."

Ketamine, used in medical procedures, is generally regarded as a dissociative anesthetic. Recreationally, it is snorted or injected. In small doses, however, it can operate like a psychedelic drug, and patients who take it often feel as though they have some kind of profound understanding of reality under its influence, according to the psychiatrist and neuroscientist Dr. David Feifel.

Dr. Feifel developed the world's first ketamine infusion program for psychiatric disorders more than a decade ago and uses it to treat patients with severe depression, anxiety, and post-traumatic stress disorder at his San Diego clinic. He has found that it can produce an almost immediate effect, one that can last for months, even though the drug stays in a patient's body less than twenty-four hours. "It blows the other treatments out of the water," he said. Taken in high doses, a process that users sometimes call "going to K-land" or a "K-hole," ketamine can cause disorientation and even temporary paralysis. Doing it illegally, he says, is "fraught with danger."

In 2018, twenty-eight-year-old Aaron Traywick, a well-known bio-hacker, drowned in a flotation tank filled with body-temperature salt water used for sensory deprivation and deep relaxation. A relative told the *New York Times* that he had likely taken ketamine, some of which was later found in his pants pocket, and lost consciousness. Traywick believed that people should be able to design and self-administer unap-proved treatments. Months before his death, he had stood in front of an audience at an annual biohacker conference, removed his suit pants, and injected himself in the thigh with a treatment he had devised that he claimed cured herpes. He had broadcast the controversial stunt on Facebook. "You would not be here today—if polio, malaria, if these diseases were still in place without self-experimentation," he had told the audience. "You are in your right to self-experiment. It is your right, and it is your body."

Ketamine was the drug that landed Tony in rehab in February 2020, and in the early days after he left, Williams and other friends in Park City tried to keep him away from it. He grudgingly went along with them. But he drank Fernet and occasionally took ecstasy. He wasn't fully sober, as someone who had just left a treatment program should be. He refused to talk in depth about his use of any drug; more often than not, he would hand a friend one of his favorite books to explain his thinking about most subjects.

Long before articles began examining the effects of isolation dur-ing the Covid-19 pandemic, Tony was experiencing it firsthand, and early. The handful of people around him couldn't make up for his nor-mal daily existence, in which he had regularly interacted with dozens of people, including coworkers, many of whom lived next to him in the Airstream park in Las Vegas.

By early April, he had devised a solution: he would buy a fleet of tour buses in Park City to shuttle people back and forth from Las Vegas. He dispatched Mimi Pham, his longtime personal assistant, to help handle the details. Soon he owned several large buses and had hired a company to supply drivers. His personal driver, Steve Moroney, came to town to help him.

Tony wasn't the first tech entrepreneur to discover Utah. Like the biohacking trend, Silicon Valley had already arrived first in the form of the Summit Series, an invitation-only series of events for entrepreneurs, artists, and wealthy elites that counted Tony among its audience. Summit Series founders had organized the purchase of an entire mountain a ninety-minute drive away from Park City, in Eden, Utah, for $40 million from owners in financial distress. Powder Mountain Resort would develop high-end ski resort homes marketed to Summit's elite members, curating a community from its rosters.

"The folks that are here aren't just here to have a second home in the mountains," Powder Mountain CEO Gary Derck told the *Wall Street Journal* in 2019. "They're also here to connect their family to other like-minded families and basically constantly better themselves and the world and their own particular initiatives."

Tony was starting to have other ideas for Park City as well. As he spent more time in the small town, cradled in the volcanic rock of the Wasatch Mountains, all he saw were possibilities.

CHAPTER THREE

COLLISIONS

No matter what your past has been, you have a spotless future.

—Tony Hsieh

In the darkness of the desert night, Tony Hsieh gazed across the pulsing mass of human bodies and lights known as Black Rock City. It was 2011, his first year at Burning Man, which had become a rite of passage for every techie in Silicon Valley. Tens of thousands of people, who adopt "Burner" names and dress in costumes, build a temporary village in the middle of the desert known as "the Playa," where they live in makeshift yurts, domes, and campers. DJs play throbbing music as dancers etch their feet through the sand. The minieconomy runs on gifting items—no money is allowed and there is no expectation of receiving anything in return.

The festival started in San Francisco in 1986, when its founders burned a wooden effigy on Baker Beach, and was later moved to the Black Rock Desert of northern Nevada. The tech community soon followed. In 1998, a startup called Google put a Burning Man stick figure onto its now-iconic search engine, a message that Google employees were headed for the desert. It was the first-ever "Google Doodle," which would become a regular feature. Soon executives from

Facebook, Twitter, and venture capital firms also descended on the festival, arriving on private jets, hiring chefs to serve tasting menus, and sleeping in luxury RVs. Some saw it as a betrayal of Burning Man's free community ethos. Still, the festival became intertwined with the tech community. As the billionaire Elon Musk told a reporter for Vox in 2014, Burning Man *is* Silicon Valley, "If you haven't been, you just don't get it."

Despite being a near billionaire, Tony stayed low profile as usual, joining the party with the humble masses on the Playa. He was instantly in love. Like an underground rave, Burning Man triggered what he referred to as a "hive switch," a term coined by a social psychologist: a body of people working together for the greater good rather than their own self-interest. "When you experience it, it is pure awe," he said later in an interview with *Playboy*, "like when you see something in nature that's bigger than yourself."

At Burning Man, people gathered with no schedules, talking and sharing meals and riding bikes around the trippy art sculptures that lit up the desert. Burning Man's stated values matched everything Tony had come to believe in: inclusion, civil responsibility, gifting, and communal effort. Perhaps because his own strict upbringing had lacked wonder and fun, Tony was attracted to activities that allowed him to view the world from a more innocent, childlike perspective. His friends likened him to Tom Hanks's character in the 1980s movie *Big*: a kid trapped in an adult's body. Nothing enabled Tony to feel small again more than Burning Man and its outsized, nearly overwhelming grassroots grandeur. The festival "ignited a light in him and altered the course of his life," the organization later wrote about Tony.

That first year, 2011, Tony wore his usual shorts and T-shirt. He watched the Burners float past him in scanty sequined attire and science fiction–inspired headdresses adorned with tentacles. He stood out as a plain-clothed newcomer late one August night as he came across Phil Plastina's art car. "Art car" is Burning Man vernacular for a vehicle transformed into a mobile sculpture, such as a fire-spewing rhinoceros or a dinosaur, that moves around the Playa like a parade float. In Tony's first year, the art cars would have been astounding and impressive, a collection of glowing and unusual vehicles moving improbably throughout the middle of nowhere. "Gluing a few tchotchkes on your car or covering it in glo-sticks does not an art car make," Burning Man has declared. "Your car must be approved by our Department of Mutant Vehicles and you must have a DMV sticker in order to drive it."

Plastina's art car, however, was in another realm altogether. A long-time Burner, Plastina had been driving from Santa Cruz to the Nevada festival for so long that he remembered when it had been dominated by beefy guys with guns and *"Mad Max* types."

By 2011, he had fallen on hard luck. The financial crisis had wiped out his construction business, almost causing him and his brother to lose their beachfront home in Santa Cruz. To save it, they had repossessed other houses for the banks, he recalled later. The job paid $10,000 a house but was heartbreaking. He had to force families and their children to leave, often in only a few hours. "We were cleaning out their books with photos in them, little dressers—everything. We were the devil," said Plastina, whose gruff accent reveals his Queens, New York, upbringing.

Plastina quit the job, and with the money he had saved—about $200,000—he spent the next two years building the largest, most outlandish art car that anyone at Burning Man had ever seen. He wanted to create something positive from all his heart-wrenching work.

With the help of some friends in California, he constructed a massive enclosed stage on top of a flatbed truck, which looked like a spaceship rising high above the ground. They welded giant pieces of metal together to create the stage, then took the type of reflective material used for greenhouses and stuck it around the outside of the stage, so that when dozens of neon lines are turned on, the reflection of the lights makes it seem as though you can reach your hand right through the panel. A jack in the shape of a Burning Man stick figure could raise and lower the entire metal stage at the press of a button— the art car's crowning jewel.

A second truck carried electronics, speakers, a sound system engineer, and DJs. Plastina had recently formed an electronic dance music group called the Dancetronauts, and together, dressed in elaborate white space suits, they gyrated inside the art car to the music.

Tony saw Plastina's art car for the first time during its debut event, and it was a knockout sensation. Thousands of people gathered around to watch, dancing and screaming under the desert stars, nothing else around for miles and miles. Tony was drawn to the crowd as if the art car's flashing neon lights were pulling him in. When Plastina climbed down carefully from the vehicle after the first set, Tony stood there, staring at him with intense interest, his eyes gleaming with admiration. He introduced himself, but the name meant nothing to Plastina.

"Hey, I want you in Vegas," Tony said.

Plastina laughed. "We're not for sale, man," he told Tony.

"Look, I'm Tony Hsieh, I run Zappos, the shoe company, and I'm developing Las Vegas, and we need to have this in Las Vegas," Tony continued in his characteristic style of wasting no time on pleasantries. Anyone else might have come across as a spoiled rich kid, but Tony was so earnest in his appreciation of beautiful things that made him happy and that might bring others joy that his selfless intent always seemed to shine through.

"How much is it going to cost? A million dollars? Two million?" he probed.

Plastina brushed him off and climbed back onto his spaceship. But Tony wouldn't give up.

After another round of dancing, one of the Dancetronauts went over to Plastina and whispered into his ear, "There are some people who want to talk to you." A line of people, producers, and event organizers who were attending Burning Man wanted him to bring the art car to their own events. The Dancestronauts would ultimately draw a niche following, playing at tech parties across Silicon Valley.

At the front of the line was Tony, waiting to speak with Plastina again. He was vibrating with excitement and blurted out, "I want you in Vegas at any cost."

Plastina quickly learned a key lesson about Tony: behind his quiet demeanor, he was powerfully convincing with both words and money. His childlike idealism and his sheer faith in everything working out made it hard for others to say no. He paid for the California-based Dancetronauts to perform in Las Vegas three times, priming Plastina for his bigger pitch: he offered to pay for Plastina to move to Las Vegas, including his housing and food, in exchange for performing only one night a month at the "First Friday" downtown arts festival. Plastina eventually agreed. He relocated to Las Vegas, upending his life to join the growing congregation of Tony Hsieh. Tony became an honorary Dancetronaut himself, donning a white space suit and sometimes performing on the art car along with the other dancers.

Tony's magnetism drew in Plastina, but there was something more than that about his excitement. It was like watching your own ambition reflected in Tony, so sure was he that you could live up to anything you strove to become. Plastina had never meant to stake his career on the Dancetronauts. It was basically an extracurricular activity that was fun on weekends sometimes and at Burning Man. Tony immediately recognized the group's, and Plastina's, potential. It was a trick he played: you thought you were following his vision, but really you were following your own.

"I never meant to do this, ever," Plastina said a decade later. "I gave up my company, I sold my home. I moved down here for Tony."

Tony was obsessed with what he called "collisions": the act of people—maybe strangers, maybe friends—randomly meeting to form bonds and partnerships but mostly to come up with great ideas or business projects, such as the one he forged with Plastina. He didn't actually believe in bad ideas; ideas that weren't fully formed simply hadn't benefited yet from the right collision. Often, he acted as a secret matchmaker, orchestrating collisions between people he had decided should meet by inviting them to a happy hour or a party so that they could run into each other "by accident." His friends usually enjoyed the happy "accidents," only grumbling sometimes about Tony's enthusiasm for a clearly terrible idea.

It was exactly the way Tony planned to build his own minicity, downtown Las Vegas, and how, a decade later, he planned to tackle another one: Park City, Utah.

Las Vegas evokes a mirage, a casino town that shines brightly out of nowhere in the black Nevada desert at nighttime. A series of entrepreneurs built the modern Las Vegas Strip, erecting bigger and bigger resorts filled with craps tables, noisy slot machines, booming nightclubs, and Cirque du Soleil shows. Before the pandemic began, about 42 million people from around the world flocked to the city every year, despite its oppressive heat.

The city's tourism boosters struck gold in 2003 when they launched a campaign that would become legend and made permissiveness its motto: "What Happens Here, Stays Here." And most of what happened in Vegas stayed on the Strip, compared to downtown.

Even before relocating Zappos to the Vegas area, Tony had grown to love the city. Starting around 1999, he had become fascinated by poker, first playing in card rooms in California and later taking weekend trips to Las Vegas. At crowded tables of mostly tourists, he discovered how to master the game through math and outdo his less astute rivals. But the thrill of winning money waned, and he became more interested in making friends with other players. "I realized that once I had learned the basics of poker, I wasn't really building anything by spending endless hours in casinos playing the game," he later wrote in *Delivering Happiness*. "I realized that I needed to be doing something more fulfilling. . . . It was time for me to change tables."

About six miles north of the Strip, downtown Las Vegas in 2011 was a collection of old, classic casinos, such as the Golden Nugget, that nodded to the town's Wild West roots with a grittier vibe, when Tony arrived. Along the major thoroughfare is the Fremont Street Experience, a pedestrian-only tourist attraction, with an overhead light show, zip-lining, live music, and cheap shops.

Beyond that area, crossing over into East Fremont Street, downtown had crumbled. Sex workers and homeless people had settled in. Residents knew to avoid the area. One of the only businesses on East Fremont Street was a weathered old hotel and casino called the Gold Spike. Across the street was a run-down motel, once the site of one of Las Vegas's deadliest bombings. "Most tourists never see downtown Las Vegas," the *New York Times* wrote in 2012.

The 2008 financial crisis had ravaged the entire city, and it had become "ground zero for the Great Recession," the *Las Vegas Review-Journal* reported, with some of the highest unemployment and foreclosure rates in the country.

In that broken-down, desolate side of Las Vegas, baking under the relentless desert sun, Tony saw only promise. He was first introduced in 2009 to the downtown area by one of the locals, a man named Michael Cornthwaite, who had recently opened one of the few new businesses in the struggling neighborhood, a classy bar called Downtown Cocktail Room that served craft cocktails amid low lighting and leather chairs. Cornthwaite had moved to Las Vegas more than a decade earlier from Chicago and asked the locals where to hang out. Their answer was a depressing chain of bars where people sat at a row of video-gambling screens and didn't talk to each other. Cornthwaite took that as a challenge. He wanted to open something better.

Tony walked the empty blocks of downtown Las Vegas, always asking "What if?" of his close friends and business partners: Cornthwaite; his wife, Jennifer; Fred Mossler, who was still helping run Zappos; and his soon-to-be-wife, Meghan. It was several years after Tony had moved Zappos to nearby Henderson, Nevada, and more than a decade after his brief foray into poker playing.

"What if this was an event space?" he would ask. "What if this bar had a speaking series that took place in the back?" "What if, what if, what if . . ." In 2012, Tony, who was living in a house in the suburbs, moved into the Ogden, a luxury tower in downtown Las Vegas. Late at night, he and his friends would stand around eating kabobs from the only nearby restaurant, brainstorming.

Tony scrawled ideas down on sticky notes, posting them around his apartment, desk, and computer monitor, perfect squares of possibilities. He had a wall filled with thoughts about how to change his adopted hometown. He sometimes invited friends or visitors to post their own notes. He wanted to reshape Las Vegas into his own Silicon Valley. He imagined the empty streets filled with talented entrepreneurs and their thriving startups, cool stores for visitors, and art everywhere to look at. One of the things that attracted him to downtown Las Vegas most was that unlike in many other cities, Tony saw the business owners working together, lifting each other up: a new kind of community. "The fact that people were really rolling up their sleeves and trying their best to create business and the community—he loved that," said Jennifer Cornthwaite later.

Tony fueled his ideas with the writings of intellectuals, and for downtown Vegas, he turned to the book *Triumph of the City: How Our Greatest Invention Makes Us Richer, Smarter, Greener, Healthier, and Happier.* It clearly explained the benefits of urban living, and Tony referenced it often when describing his plans for downtown Las Vegas. In it, the author, Edward Glaeser, an urbanist and Harvard University economics professor, argued that successful cities attract smart entrepreneurial people in part by being urban playgrounds. Echoing one of Tony's key tenets, Glaeser wrote that "human collaboration is the central truth behind civilization's success and the primary reason why cities exist."

Tony called Glaeser at his Harvard office after reading his book, so thrilled with it that he offered to have his father, Richard Hsieh, translate it into Mandarin. Glaeser, meanwhile, had had to Google "Tony Hsieh" and "Zappos" before they spoke. Tony asked Glaeser some detailed questions, such as what level of urban density is the most desirable, Glaeser recalled. (The answer to that question, Glaeser says, varies depending on the place and the person.)

Tony was most excited to connect with someone who agreed with him so fully. Sometimes his ideas seemed so strange to the average person that he needed validation. "I just seemed to give him some scientific support for his own viewpoint," said Glaeser.

At Tony's request, Glaeser made a three-day pilgrimage to Las Vegas in 2012, just before any real development took off. Tony took him on a tour and invited him to speak at Zappos. Glaeser found Tony to be intelligent and remarkably humble but focused less on the details of making his vision a reality. "How are your pedestrian pathways designed; the weather; making sure people are going to have a good walking experience—he was less engaged with things like that," he recalled.

Tony had already decided that moving Zappos to downtown Las Vegas would help create the sort of communal living and work situation that he hoped to achieve. Rather than working on a company campus that excluded outsiders, such as Apple's in Silicon Valley and Nike's outside Portland, Oregon, Zappos' 1,200 employees would live and spend money right where they worked. The company would rent the empty former City Hall building downtown, a 1970s-era brown behemoth with a horizontal panel of windows lining the very top and the back.

To convince city officials to approve the many complicated details of the plan, more than a dozen Zappos employees showed up at a Las Vegas City Council meeting in 2011 as a flash mob. Wearing light blue company shirts and waving blue and white pom-poms, they streamed into the front of the room facing the row of city officials. As the startled council looked on, they began to perform a minutes-long choreographed dance, bending and dipping and waving their hands.

Orchestrating the event hadn't been hard. At that point, Zappos operated almost like a high school, with various groups for employees' interests, including a dance club.

The city council ultimately approved Zappos' move into the building in 2012. At the time of the vote, then councilman Bob Coffin likened the project to the investments that the tycoon Howard Hughes had made in the city during a recession in 1967. "It is eerily similar to me that someone is coming into town who believes in this town, who wasn't here, stuck in the old ways, and sees something here that others didn't," he said.

Born in Texas, in 1905, Hughes had turned an inheritance from his father into an even bigger $2 billion fortune, through producing Hollywood films, speculating in real estate, and starting an airline, among other entrepreneurial ventures. A famous aviator himself, Hughes became a recluse later in life as symptoms of obsessive-compulsive disorder—in particular, a fear of germs—made him avoid human contact. He arrived in Las Vegas in 1966 before dawn on a train in his pajamas and checked into a penthouse suite of the Desert Inn on the Las Vegas Strip. From its confines, he began making big purchases in Vegas, motivated by a desire to be the largest single property owner in the city.

Hughes bought six casinos, enough to capture one-third of the annual revenue on the Strip—swiftly buying out Mafia owners and shifting the Strip away from organized crime and into an American vacation destination. He also bought nearly all of the remaining undeveloped land in Las Vegas, an old airport terminal, and a TV station. He left Las Vegas four years later, in 1970, having never ventured out of the Desert Inn.

Tony convinced dozens of entrepreneurs to leave Silicon Valley and other areas across the country as part of an ambitious goal to recruit ten thousand new residents to downtown Las Vegas in five years. The entrepreneurs could take advantage of $50 million of seed money Tony was putting aside, part of his $350 million plan for the area, which now had a formal name: Downtown Project. And it had a headline-grabbing goal: to build "the most community-focused large city in the world." Tony came up with a new reporting metric to measure a business's positive impact on its surroundings: return on community, or ROC. Ultimately, Downtown Project would create more than 1,500 jobs, including 130 at tech startups, and make more than 60 small-business investments. Over the ensuing decade, it would create more than $200 million in economic output.

Tony bought the Gold Spike casino and gave it a full renovation. He had the motel that was the former bombing site torn down. He ordered more than a dozen forty-foot shipping containers from Long

Beach, California, and workers stacked them in a rough circle across sixty acres, forming the basis of a completely new kind of development called Container Park. Inside the metal containers, bars and restaurants opened, as well as a playground with a giant treehouse right in the middle. Parents could watch their children play while sipping wine. The number of strollers outside the bars became one of the chief metrics the executives running Container Park used to measure its success.

"There was a lot of exuberance around that time, a lot of hopefulness, and a lot of big plans," Doug McPhail, a former director of Container Park, said later. Before he met Tony for lunch the first time, his colleagues warned him: he may just sit there, not speaking, or he may get up and leave without warning. In the end, Tony was perfectly normal, even chatty, when they met.

Tony also infused downtown Las Vegas with the whimsical, cartoonish art he had seen on the Playa at Burning Man. Though much of the art there is built for the festival, collectors and museums often buy it afterward to take offsite. Fergusons, a new cluster of art galleries and shops, features a massive stack of trucks curling in a circle toward the sky. Nearby, a towering, bright pink flamingo stands in the middle of a parking lot at one point used for a free, ongoing speaker series. A dog day care business featuring a giant yellow fire hydrant outside opened.

In front of Container Park, Tony installed his pièce de résistance, a forty-foot metal praying mantis trucked in from Burning Man. On most nights, employees of Container Park awaken the large, bug-eyed insect with a drum circle, inviting members of the crowd to take part. Soon the two metal antennas sticking out of the mantis's head shoot plumes of fire into the air in short, loud blasts, startling the visitors gathered around it. Some people clap and some laugh, while others are stunned into silence by the unusual spectacle. It is a surprising sight, even for Las Vegas.

Always looking for a close group of people to surround himself with, Tony took over two apartments in the Ogden, the luxury tower into which he had moved, one of the only nice buildings to live in in the area. The Ogden faces an empty parking lot, but at night, some residents stepping out onto their balconies have a clear view of the lights of the Strip.

Tony convinced friends and Zappos employees to move into his new building with him. Fred Mossler, his wife, Meghan, and their new baby joined him, as did many others. Eventually Tony would combine three large penthouse suites on the twenty-third floor. Plants filled one entire room to replicate a jungle. The "movie room" featured an expensive flat-screen TV. Energy drinks, including his favorite, Red Bull, were stationed throughout the space. He rented fifty additional apartments in the building, all of them filled with his friends, visitors, and coworkers.

One friend who lived there, Mimi Pham, had a markedly strong influence over Tony. With long black hair and a dragon tattoo on her right shoulder, Pham, who had met Tony at a shoe conference in 2005, had proven herself indispensable to every facet of Tony's life as his personal assistant. She got his meals and bought his clothes. She controlled his credit cards, and the two at one point shared an address on their driver's licenses. She doled out his tickets to Burning Man every year, a big responsibility and also an honor. Tony couldn't get through a day without Pham helping to organize some detail. When he ordered a last-minute, elaborate party, other Las Vegas employees would balk. But Pham would insist. She excelled at getting things done. With an investment from the Downtown Project, she opened a media production studio.

Even though they weren't a couple, she was extremely possessive of their special relationship. Tony's close friends knew not to mess with her. One friend compared her to a cat: "She'd be like the nicest kitty and then swipe you and cut your hand. And then she would just sit there, licking her paw." When Tony decided to tell a select few friends that he was going to rehab, one of the first he told was Pham.

Another friend who moved into the Ogden for a time was Suzie Baleson, a twenty-seven-year-old Texan who had recently quit her job as an accountant with the international consulting firm Alvarez &

Marsal to work with Tony's development fund in Las Vegas. Several of Tony's friends thought he might have a crush on Baleson, with her long blond hair and athletic body, but they weren't dating. Tony had girlfriends on and off, but at thirty-eight, he'd had no long-term commitments. Because of his unique ability to make everyone feel singularly special, women and men often hung around him. At Zappos, the company kept a file folder on his known stalkers.

Being a friend of Tony's meant learning to tolerate a lot of personality types, often in a good way—you met people you never would otherwise as a result of all the collisions. Tony wasn't discerning about who he chose to be his friend, and he sometimes trusted people too easily. "Tony collects people," one of his friends told the magazine *Wired*. "You almost don't even realize you're being collected."

Tony's interest in people often shifted like the seasons, but in a way that seemed to keep most people happy. Someone might be "in season," getting the lion's share of his attention, and then be out of season several months later, even though Tony still kept him or her close, inviting that person to events or parties or weekend trips. Though he might not spend every day with the friend anymore, he still found ways to connect and make him or her feel special. In that way, he accumulated an astonishing number of people who cared deeply about him and who turned to him for inspiration.

Still, for some people that approach to friendship created an intense longing. They missed the days and months when his spotlight had shone on them exclusively. Some friends spent years trying to regain his full interest.

Some of Tony's friends hoped that Baleson's season wouldn't last long. They found her to be something of a braggart, and she sometimes seemed to exaggerate her connections or accomplishments. She often talked about Deepak Chopra, the famous Indian American author and motivational speaker, whom she described as her mentor. "One can only imagine what sitting and chatting with Deepak for hours has been—it's beyond," she said in an interview for a podcast focused on female entrepreneurs. Even her descriptions of her after-college status as an international accountant, traveling through Europe and Asia to restructure companies, seemed inflated to some friends for one so young. She described Tony as a mentor, explaining in the podcast that "the most important thing he taught me was to surround myself with good people."

In 2013, after more than a year in Las Vegas, Baleson moved to New York City to start her own business, a health and wellness company called Wellthily. But like most people who collided with Tony, they stayed in touch. In a photo of the two of them on the subway in 2016, Baleson is smiling at the camera, her head resting on Tony's cheek.

In the spring of 2020, Baleson was still living in the West Village in New York, the US epicenter of the worsening coronavirus pandemic, when she heard about Tony's plans in Park City.

New York City residents were fleeing en masse. Baleson had earlier parted ways with her business partner and renamed her company the Wellth Collective. It had a grandiose, vague goal: "produce fitness and wellness-focused events around the world to introduce our tribe to the best in all things wellth," according to her website. The business, however, was somewhat reliant on travel, so it stalled as the pandemic unfolded. Baleson, single and thirty-five, had no reason to stay in New York.

She became one of an eclectic mix of friends and long-ago acquaintances that Tony began to assemble in Park City in the spring of 2020. Some moved there; others came for long visits. The group had few similarities except for their love of Tony and their lack of ties holding them back from joining him.

Tony was beginning to formulate a plan for Park City, one that had a two-pronged approach. First, he wanted to somehow help prop up the businesses that were suffering from Covid-19 shutdowns. Second, he wanted to create an environment where his friends could come and hang out without worrying about the threat of the pandemic, which, in only a month, had already completely upended the way the world lived. Tony wasn't particularly worried about the virus, but, always attuned to his friends' needs, he knew that some people would be more concerned about it than others.

To fulfill the latter goal, he decided to buy dozens of residential properties across town and turn them into Airbnbs. He already had shuttle buses to ferry people from Las Vegas to Park City, and now his friends would have a place to stay while they were there. He planned to turn over the properties to his friends, who could lease them out for some of the rental profits, with Tony taking a cut. Though tourism had come to a dead halt because of the pandemic—indeed, Airbnb itself was trying to raise private equity to stay afloat—Tony bet that it would eventually turn around. (It did, and Airbnb went public in December 2020, proving that it could navigate the pandemic.)

On the face of it, the plan didn't seem so unusual; at the start of Tony's development of downtown Las Vegas, even more bizarre ideas had been tossed around. The details weren't ironed out, but Tony rarely concentrated on those. He typically relied on trusted friends and employees at Zappos, or in downtown Las Vegas, to carry out his plans for him. He was the visionary.

Park City, with its neat rows of homey restaurants and retail shops such as Patagonia along Main Street, could not have been more different from downtown Las Vegas when Tony first took an interest in the area in 2011. Park City, in some ways, looks like Aspen, Vail, or any other American ski town: polished and neat, with few ragged edges. The pandemic, though, had changed the landscape, placing the city nearly on the same wobbly economic footing that downtown Las Vegas had been on a decade earlier. When Tony arrived in the spring of 2020, he thought it seemed just as needy.

The ski season had ended abruptly, and now the summer season was threatened as well. In early April, the organizers of the Tour of Utah, a bicycle race that passes through downtown Park City and draws thousands of onlookers, canceled the event. Next came the shutdown of what is known as the Silly Market, an outdoor festival filled with artists, entertainers, and food stands that typically takes place in the summer and fall. In 2019, the Silly Market had drawn nearly two hundred thousand visitors. The head of Park City's visitor center acknowledged that the city's tourism could be in "limbo" that summer.

Baleson and another Las Vegas friend of Tony's, Justin Weniger, began helping Tony with a quasi-business operation that everyone started calling "10X."

Weniger, a baseball cap–wearing event planner, had previously been at the helm of one of Tony's largest parties, an annual musical festival called Life Is Beautiful in the streets of downtown Las Vegas, which attracted more than 100,000 attendees in the early fall. Weniger, who speaks quickly, often mumbling, had helped organize the annual event for years but seemed to travel on the outskirts of Tony's main group of friends, never quite earning full admittance for reasons that are unclear. His status at Life Is Beautiful was thrown into limbo in early 2020 in part because of a possible sale of the event to *Rolling Stone* magazine. Life Is Beautiful looked likely to be canceled that year because of the pandemic, and Weniger was eager to help out with Tony's new business plans.

In addition to the separate, Airbnb portion of the business, the 10X scheme worked like this: Park City residents bought $10 monthly memberships that granted them access on a designated Sunday to unlimited food and drinks at a set list of local restaurants. Tony picked up the entire tab, supporting the local businesses in the process. The cost was offset—although not by much—by the $10 memberships.

The reason it was called 10X was that anyone who participated would theoretically get ten times the value of every dollar spent. Tony had tapped a local event organizer, Shaun Kimball, to work with Baleson and Weniger. Kimball, a surfer in his late thirties who lived part-time in Newport Beach, California, had met Tony several years earlier on a crowded day at Park City's No Name Saloon, a rustic bar on Main

Street featuring an antler chandelier and sparkling white lights hanging from the ceiling. The bar was packed, and Kimball and his date couldn't find anywhere to sit. Tony had observed their dilemma and invited them to join his table.

Kimball posted an advertisement on Facebook:

> Utah friends, anyone that knows me, knows I always GO BIG, for my next act, some will say "its too good to be true." Think Sundance in the Summer.
>
> You have the unique opportunity to participate in something truly amazing! Let me introduce you to 'The 10X-Experience.'

As many as a thousand people, mostly locals, purchased tickets. Covid restrictions were beginning to loosen, and more people were visiting Main Street again.

Some of Tony's friends were skeptical—and slightly confused—when he pitched 10X to them. How could a business make a profit from a customer who ate $100 in sushi and drank $50 in cocktails but paid only $10? The Airbnb portion of the plan also didn't add up.

For locals, the membership plan didn't make much sense either, but the benefits were clear; Tony was subsidizing their flailing businesses.

Tana Toly, whose family owns Red Banjo Pizza, the oldest business in Park City, had no idea who Tony was when she was pitched to participate, nor did she immediately know about his involvement in the plan. Her no-frills pizza joint with red-and-white-checkered tablecloths, founded by her grandparents in 1962, has remained mostly unchanged through Park City's evolution into a luxury destination.

The idea, local business owners were told, was that 10X would lose money at first, but increased membership pricing over time, from $10 to $100 to $1,000 or more, would eventually bring in a profit. The business would expand into other cities. Membership would also include experiences such as fly fishing, golfing, and horseback riding and eventually lodging.

"In all honesty it just—a lot of it didn't make total sense," Toly admitted. She agreed to participate anyway.

Businesses had been shuttered for nearly two months, and their owners were desperate. Even as Park City reopened in the spring and summer of 2020, event cancellations and the continued lack of tourism in general meant far fewer customers than normal.

Some of the business owners approached Kimball in tears, thanking the 10X organizers for the help. He accepted the gratitude on behalf of Tony, who rarely made a personal appearance at the Sunday events.

At Tekila, a two-story Mexican restaurant, Tony's 10X crew rented the entire restaurant for five weeks straight, from 5:00 p.m. until the bar closed, with Tony paying the bill. Members of his group piled onto the wide patio overlooking Main Street almost every night, drinking pitchers of margaritas and racking up tabs in the thousands of dollars. Most of the businesses had outdoor locations, and it was summer, so they weren't actively encouraging people to flout Covid rules.

Tony Hsieh was a mystery to Tekila's owner, J. C. Martinez, who met his strange new benefactor only once or twice, always in a crowd, and never for long. All Martinez knew was that Tony Hsieh was a godsend to his business.

It seemed like his whole mission, Martinez said later, was to "spread a lot of love all over."

CHAPTER FOUR

DELIVERING HAPPINESS

Las Vegas, 2010

If happiness is everyone's ultimate goal, wouldn't it be great if we could change the world and get everyone and every business thinking in that context and that framework?

—Tony Hsieh

In 2009, Tony Hsieh retreated to Lake Tahoe from Las Vegas with his longtime friend Jenn Lim, whom he called his "backup brain." In just eight days, they wrote the intertwined stories of Tony's entrepreneurial life and Zappos' bumpy rise to success. In a humorous, down-to-earth style, Tony told the story he'd been telling in pieces for years on the public speaking circuit.

The pair, who had met in their twenties at Tony's party loft in San Francisco, had flourished under pressure together before. They had summited Mount Kilimanjaro in Tanzania in 2002, reaching the 19,300-foot peak at sunrise after several days of hiking. Lim consulted for Zappos, including on workplace culture projects. Along the way, she had become a trusted member of Tony's inner circle.

In Tahoe, they worked on the book in twenty-four-hour stints with short naps, struggling to stay awake. They guzzled Red Bull and Tony's favorite drink at the time, vodka. "We tried coffee. And alcohol. And then coffee and alcohol," Tony told *Footwear News* in an interview. Lim added, "We actually put coffee beans in a vodka bottle."

Tony Hsieh's book *Delivering Happiness: A Path to Profits, Passion, and Purpose*, debuted at number one on the *New York Times* best-seller list in June 2010 and stayed on the list for twenty-eight consecutive weeks. Tony laid out how Zappos' purpose had evolved from building the largest shoe selection online in the startup days to a loftier goal by 2009: delivering happiness to the world.

Thousands of entrepreneurs and business leaders, hungry for a fresh start after the 2008 financial crisis and the long recession that followed, read about Zappos' ten core values, including what would become the most famous on the list, "Create Fun and A Little Weirdness." With the help of the book's publication, Tony Hsieh evolved into a happiness guru and Zappos' Las Vegas headquarters into a home for his apostles. Zappos had reached $1 billion in annual sales, so Tony's take that happiness leads to worker productivity and profits, not the other way around, carried new weight.

"So, in terms of this book, how is all this 'happiness' delivered? Just like everything else Hsieh has done: successfully," a reviewer for *Inc.* wrote. A *Wall Street Journal* review noted, "It is hard not to like a CEO who, without a trace of irony, says that his corporate mission has become 'delivering happiness to the world.'"

Inside Zappos, a world of pure positivity had been years in the making, starting with recruitment practices. "We only hire happy people and we try to keep them happy," Alfred Lin, the chief operating officer who left in 2010, once said. "Our philosophy is you can't have happy customers without having happy employees, and you can't have happy employees without having a company where people are inspired by the culture."

This radical approach was working. For seven years in a row, Zappos was named one of *Fortune*'s 100 Best Companies to Work For. Entry-level employees starting in the call center could rise to senior manager level within five to seven years thanks to a formal path Zappos had developed for moving up the ladder. The company required workers to take a four-week new-hire training course that averaged 160 hours and had additional hours of training for employees in the company's "core curriculum." Classes included "The Science of Happiness."

The starting pay at Zappos' call center, known as the Customer Loyalty Team, in 2010 was about $11, above Nevada's $8.25 minimum wage, and the company paid 100 percent of workers' health care insurance premiums. The starting pay has since increased to $15.75 hourly, compared to the state's $8.75 for companies that provide medical benefits.

Zappos was proving that shoes could be sold online at the same time as it was introducing its unusual culture of fun to the world. Getting a Zappos job became nearly impossible. Even before *Delivering Happiness* was published, the growing company had hired only 250 people from a pool of 25,000 applicants in one year. Prospective employees were picked up from the Las Vegas airport in Zappos' airport shuttle, and a job seeker was immediately disqualified if the driver reported that he or she was rude. An interviewee's technical skills and more subjective evaluation as a "culture fit" weighed equally in the hiring decision.

"Job interviews took place in a room set up as a talk show set," according to one case study by organizational behavior researchers. "Recruiters gave candidates creative tasks such as coming up with a design for Steve Madden shoes, and asked such questions as 'On a scale of one to 10, how lucky are you?'" The application forms included a shoe-themed maze and a crossword puzzle. The cartoonish vibe of the process obscured a possible hazard: the culture-fit question became a filter, one that appeared to favor the young, cheerful, and tattooed. Tony noted that his staff listed dog day care as their top request for the new Las Vegas campus—even more than child day care.

Tony's injection of playfulness into corporate life might not seem unusual today. Tech companies across Silicon Valley are known, if not lampooned, for their open-air offices featuring Ping-Pong tables, nap rooms, free meals, gyms, and beer and kombucha on tap. Such amenities might brighten the day or make employees' work life more luxurious. But it also has the effect of employees' staying in the office longer and working more hours. As a Google employee, for example, if you can do your laundry, take dance classes, and eat a gourmet dinner all on the Googleplex campus, why go home?

Tony took a different spin on companies' growing movement to make their offices "fun" and pushed it further. His vision was less about freebies and creature comforts (and getting employees to work nonstop) and more about embracing individuality and human connection as employee perks. He was trying to build a lifestyle. The company policy mandated employees' spending social time together. He introduced family picnics and all-hands happy hours that took place on a regular basis. Zappos encouraged managers to spend 10 to 20 percent of their time with team members outside the office, including at the ubiquitous gatherings at local bars and outings to local events. The ten core values included "Build a Positive Team and Family Spirit" and "Build Open and Honest Relationships With Communication." Tony even got himself approved by the county to officiate at employees' weddings.

"A lot of companies talk about work-life balance," he told the *New York Times*. "We're more about work-life integration. At the end of the day, it's life."

Though Tony's friends and employees never quite understood where his obsession came from, Zappos' new mission of delivering happiness was a composite of everything he had spent years working toward. Early on, he had thought that Zappos' mission could be "to inspire and be inspired," but others around him had wondered how a business could achieve that every day. It seemed more like a personal goal, something a human could strive for, not a for-profit venture. So he had begun to think more about the joy the company wanted to send in every box of shoes to customers: delivering happiness.

But Tony was also a shrewd businessperson, and he did not lose his drive for financial success. All of the warm feelings and camaraderie in the workplace culture were meant to lead to profits as well. Tony had realized years earlier at LinkExchange that investing in customer service, rooted in worker happiness, could be the key to growing the business. He had amplified that approach at Zappos, making it a core mission. It was, in fact, another of the reasons Jeff Bezos at Amazon wanted to buy the company in 2009. "I get all weak-kneed when I see a customer-obsessed company, and Zappos is certainly that," he said in the internal video to Zappos employees when Amazon purchased the company in 2009.

Every employee, no matter what his or her role, had to learn to answer phone calls from customers. Customer Loyalty Team members weren't judged on how quickly they could get off the phone or how much they could upsell a customer. Instead, Tony developed a new metric called Personal Service Level (PSL), which measured how well the employee connected with a customer. Zappos wasn't a shoe company, Tony liked to say; it was a service company selling shoes.

He fielded phone calls himself during the holiday rush, an annual two-week period at the end of the year known as "Holiday Helper," in which every employee spends ten hours on the phone. Sitting at his desk among his coworkers, Tony never introduced himself to customers but enjoyed getting into long conversations about obscure topics with them.

A customer in Florida called in and mentioned that he planted Christmas trees and raised cows. Soon Tony was in a deep conversation about how the customer had to castrate his cows. Another time, Tony answered the phone with a typical greeting: "Hi, welcome to Zappos, can I help you?" The customer replied, "Do you have any shoes that are like fall?" Without pausing, Tony patiently queried, "Do you mean like the season? Do you mean brown?" Before he could get to the bottom of it, the customer threw a curveball: "Do you know anything about quantum dynamics?"

At that point, a customer service agent at another company might have dodged the question and stuck to the script or simply hung up. But Tony got excited. Quantum dynamics, which describes energy at the atomic and subatomic levels, was something that he had studied casually. His curious mind frequently led him to research topics that had nothing to do with business. The customer had reached probably the only person at Zappos who would have known anything about it. Tony never mentioned that he was the CEO, even though they spoke for close to an hour.

Tony was the rare top executive who didn't care about titles, endearing himself to employees, who could also see that he authentically enjoyed being silly. It wasn't a gimmick. He loved board games, puns, dancing, and putting on magic shows. Most people thought he had the worst taste in music because he liked only songs that were upbeat, such as Mariah Carey's "All I Want for Christmas," any time of the year, or electronic dance music. He was constantly getting up to mischief and playing small tricks; he knew the entire secret menu at the fast-food chain In-N-Out Burger and claimed to be the only person to have ordered the now-discontinued "100 by 100" burger—one hundred patties stacked together.

He was also fond of robots and in 2013 was introduced through a friend to Alexandria "Ali" Bevilacqua, a twenty-seven-year-old actress and Las Vegas native who played a robot in the Blue Man Group. The first time they hung out together, Tony invited her to ride Razor scooters with him around his penthouse apartments at the Ogden. The two started dating shortly thereafter. Later, Tony decided he wanted to visit Santa Claus during the Christmas season, so he and Bevilacqua, along with Fred Mossler and another friend, joined a line filled with children and their parents waiting to tell the joyful man their holiday wishes. Spying a nearby playground, Tony and Bevilacqua, a small woman with short blond hair, left Mossler to stand in line while they pushed each other on the swings and took turns on the slide until it was time to see Santa. "He really didn't care what people thought," Bevilacqua said later. "It was like 'I'm going to have fun, and I'm going to do this hilarious thing.'"

Inside and outside work, Tony's thoughtfulness and generosity were unparalleled. He was the first to buy tickets to dance recitals or plays featuring his friends' children or donate to a school fundraiser. He remembered the music, movies, and bands each friend liked and introduced them to their favorite celebrities when they passed through Las Vegas.

When his friend Michael Cornthwaite's wife, Jennifer, was in labor at home with their daughter in 2013, Tony went directly from the plane after landing from Italy to be the first person to visit their new baby. Jamie Naughton, Zappos' longtime chief of staff, was having trouble getting out of a bad marriage in the early aughts. With no hesitation, Tony moved her, her baby daughter, and her mother into his own house in Henderson, Nevada, for several months.

He was hyperaware of what those around him needed. If anyone, even a low-level Zappos employee, wanted time with Tony, he personally handed over his cell phone to the person and instructed him or her to put the appointment on his calendar. At Burning Man, he noticed a woman in his group shivering and gave her a furry Technicolor jacket from his own stash to wear, making a new friend in the process.

At Zappos, his generosity came partly in the form of parties. They weren't just any parties, though; they were full-fledged events orchestrated over months, designed to give every worker an unforgettable experience, one he or she might not have had otherwise. Tony wanted to see what would happen when different people collided among the music and lights and other details. Zappos spent millions of dollars a year on the parties, "family picnics," and happy hours and employed an entire team of planners—the fungineers—to design them. The company regularly took over nightclubs and other venues across Las Vegas. Employees joked that "Party with your peers" was the unofficial eleventh core value at Zappos. Though Tony wasn't often involved in the planning, he stationed himself at the door to greet people when they arrived.

In 2015, Zappos rented out an open-air stage at the LIGHT nightclub at the Mandalay Bay hotel on the Strip. As music pulsed and lights flashed over the crowd, the Dancetronauts, along with acrobats from Cirque du Soleil, all dressed in space suits, flew over the massive crowd of screaming, cheering employees. At another point in the festivities, a haunting meditational song filled the giant space, and lit candles flickered along walkways. All at once, a procession of break dancers dressed as monks filed onstage from both doors, chanting to the audience.

The next year, for Zappos' annual vendor appreciation party, the theme was "Untamed Circus." More than 2,500 people poured into Drai's Beachclub and Nightclub at the Cromwell on the Strip, a 35,000-square-foot space with multiple roof decks. Zappos had turned the venue into an old-timey traveling band of oddities with an impressive array of clowns, stilt walkers, and ballerinas flitting around among the guests. Lion tamers and fire breathers performed for the retail industry crowd.

A giant red-paneled disco ball spun as the crowds danced and mingled; guests were served unlimited drinks from multiple bars and ate alcohol-infused cotton candy. At one point Tony stood onstage, attempting to juggle circus rings.

At one Zappos holiday party, a paintball warehouse was turned into an end-of-the-world scene, with zombies hidden around every corner, and a New York DJ, Jason Smith, who was regularly hired for Zappos' parties, organized sound effects, such as a plane crashing, from the top of a fake army tank. When attendees walked into the warehouse from the parking lot, they walked by a pretend CNN newscast about the end of the world playing on the side of the building. At another party, Tony dressed up as Morpheus in the movie *The Matrix* and handed out red and blue pills (really jelly beans) to attendees.

Smith, the DJ, was used to playing much tamer company parties and nightclubs in New York City. At Zappos, the work that went into the parties was beyond anything he had ever seen before. "They would make this really magical experience and transform the whole club," he said later. "It was surreal."

Taking care of others acted as a powerful salve to Tony. If his friends were happy, he was happy, too. He was like a mirror, reflecting those around him. "So if I am around an introverted person that is really awkward," he explained to the *New York Times* in 2011. "But if I am around an extroverted person I will be whoever they are times point-5."

Tony's employees and friends couldn't reciprocate his lavish gifts of time and money, and Tony expected nothing in return. He had an odd relationship with money. He didn't seem to take it seriously, but he also didn't flaunt it. Money would come and go. He used it only as a means to an end, and if his friends could benefit from it, why not?

His friends still found ways to show their devotion. For Tony's fortieth birthday in 2013, a group of people got matching tattoos of small circles—pixels, a nerdy computer joke—in his honor, surprising him at his party later in the night.

That stunt prompted questions from the local media about whether Tony was running a cult instead of a company, a half-joking question that had followed him since the release of *Delivering Happiness* in 2010. On *The Colbert Report* in 2011, Stephen Colbert asked Tony directly, "Is this a cult? Are you, dear leader, father of a cult? Do you have child brides? How much control do you have over these people?" Tony, dressed in jeans and a button-down shirt, his hair shaved close to his head, chuckled and quickly moved the conversation back to Zappos' ten core values.

Tony wasn't a cult leader, but it was true that he had attracted a legion of devoted followers who not only admired his business acumen but also his inherent goodness and ability to lift others up.

But Tony did a terrible job taking care of himself and tuning in to his own needs. Often he ignored them altogether. Devout people pleasers such as Tony generally worry that if they prioritize their own desires, they will ultimately end up alone. Why would anyone choose to stay?

One friend compared Tony to the children's story *The Giving Tree*, in which a tree gives and gives to the boy she loves, never receiving anything in return, until there is nothing left of her.

Tony's pursuit of happiness starting in the mid-2000s helped usher the burgeoning tech world into a broader movement that had been brewing in America for a few years already: positive psychology. Psychology as a science had focused on treating conditions such as depression and anxiety as described in a diagnostic manual. In the late 1990s, the psychologist Martin Seligman argued that that wasn't enough. Instead of focusing only on problems, psychology could also suggest how to live a good life—happy, healthy, meaningful—which, he argued, could be studied scientifically, too. By looking at geniuses and society's most accomplished members, psychologists could discover "the roots of a positive life," as he commented in his 1998 speech as president of the American Psychological Association. It wasn't an entirely new concept, as psychologists had been discussing a more humanistic and holistic approach to psychology going back to the mid-twentieth century. But in 2002, he went on to publish *Authentic Happiness*, which became a best seller. "Ideally psychology should be able to help document what kind of families result in the healthiest children, what work environments support the greatest satisfaction among workers, and what policies result in the strongest civic commitment," he wrote.

In the following decade, positive psychology took off among academics. Meanwhile, self-help books and consulting services by untrained gurus and life coaches also proliferated, fueled by the new scientific interest, offering the masses what the author, journalist, and activist Barbara Ehrenreich called "pop positive thinking," the linking of positive thoughts with good outcomes in life, in her critique of the field, *Bright-Sided: How the Relentless Promotion of Positive Thinking Has Undermined America*.

The lines between science and pop culture became blurred, at least from the consumer's perspective. The meaning of happiness remained up for debate. Pleasure, enjoyment, positivity, gratitude, purpose, well-being, and virtue, plucked from Western and Eastern philosophies, blended into a cultural movement. Positive psychologists tried to distance themselves from the pop culture of self-help but at the same time embraced methods echoing life coaching and motivation, including publishing books aimed at a general audience with "you" and "your" in the title and marketing to corporations interested in worker productivity. Simply being happy wasn't the sole goal, Ehrenreich noted; it was about happiness leading to improved health and success. "Happy, or positive, people—however that is measured— do seem to be more successful at work," she wrote. "They are more likely to get a second interview while job hunting, get positive evaluations from superiors, resist burnout, and advance up the career ladder. But this probably reflects little more than corporate bias in favor of a positive attitude and against 'negative' people."

In his journey into that world, Tony had discovered *The Happiness Hypothesis: Finding Modern Truth in Ancient Wisdom* by the social psychologist Jonathan Haidt, published in 2006, often recommending it to friends and in media interviews. The book argues that happiness can't be achieved by looking only outside oneself for fulfillment. Nor does it come only from within through a mindful, detached state of being. Instead, it "comes from between," from connections between yourself and others, in love and in work.

Tony might have been shy, but he never stopped wanting to connect with people. He saw himself as someone who could spread that philosophy. With *Delivering Happiness*, he could start from Zappos and launch a pay-it-forward happiness chain that could make the entire world happy. In doing so, he thought, he could be happy, too.

Tony dedicated the final chapter of his 2010 book to the concept of happiness, including graphs and charts that revealed his analytical mind in motion. In particular, he was fascinated by the idea that achieving a longtime goal or winning the lottery didn't provide lasting, sustainable happiness. He acknowledged that deeply human problem, but he didn't question whether the pursuit of happiness should, in fact, be the end goal. "The question for you to ask yourself is whether what you think you want to pursue will actually get you the happiness you think it will get you," he posited.

Tony believed that his brand of happiness could create the best business conditions. Workers could come as themselves and be accepted. Customers would be respected as individual humans with their own joy and pain, as well.

Lim, with the help of Tony, spun off *Delivering Happiness* into a consulting firm—what she and Tony called "a movement," capitalizing on happiness's moment in the corporate spotlight. Lim became CEO and Chief Happiness Officer. The consulting team would grow to include positions such as CoachSultant & Win-Win-Win Collaborations Booster, Culture Orchestrator, Global Happiness Navigator, and Happiness Owl. For years to come, Tony and Lim would relentlessly promote the book and its message, decorating a tour bus with a smiley face that they drove across the country, taking dozens of friends with them.

They were accelerating a trend across the United States, including on Silicon Valley's sunshine-soaked tech campuses. Companies had begun to embrace integrating the concept of happiness into the corporate structure, including more companies adding a "chief happiness officer" role. One of Google's first engineers, Chade-Meng Tan, took the title Jolly Good Fellow. He developed a mindfulness course for Google employees and wrote a book in 2012 about emotional intelligence called *Search Inside Yourself: The Unexpected Path to Achieving Success, Happiness (and World Peace)*. Tan began his speeches by asking the audience to do a thought exercise: "Imagine two human beings. Don't say anything, don't do anything, just wish for those two human beings to be happy. That's all."

Early on, in 2003, the now-common chief happiness officer role appeared as a marketing stunt. McDonald's named its mascot clown, Ronald McDonald, "Chief Happiness Officer" to generate some silly news stories. Today, the title has become accepted as a professional role at tech companies and other businesses for people who lead human resources or problem solving for customers. By 2014, there were so many happiness officers that the *New Republic* called it "the latest, creepiest job in corporate America."

Nonetheless, Tony's brand stood out. It seemed authentic and full of hope. Zappos' Las Vegas headquarters became an optimism mecca of sorts. Tony always promoted transparency—he published his daily email and meeting log online for anyone to see—and he threw open the doors to anyone to tour Zappos. Thousands of business leaders and entrepreneurs from retail companies, banks, and software providers made trips there, hoping to learn from Tony Hsieh, the man who was bringing workplace happiness to the masses.

One of them was Tony Gareri, who in 2010 walked the halls of the sprawling Las Vegas Market, a home furnishings trade show during which tens of thousands of retailers and suppliers browsing rugs, sofas, and bedroom sets typically fill up the expo center. Gareri was representing Roma Moulding, the Toronto-based picture frame company his father had founded in 1984. But that year, in the aftermath of the financial crisis, the trade show was nearly empty.

At a dinner with others in the industry, a woman handed him a copy of *Delivering Happiness*, which he finished on the five-hour flight home, reading the last lines with skepticism and a little curiosity. *Maybe it's a Vegas thing—good publicity*, he thought.

Back home, Gareri looked up Tony Hsieh and Zappos online, and on a whim, he put his name on a waiting list to attend a three-day boot camp at Zappos to learn all about the company's culture. The next day, Zappos called about an opening, and a week later, Gareri stepped onto a Zappos shuttle at Las Vegas's McCarran International Airport with other eager campers who'd just arrived. The days were an endless series of talks by quirky employees, tours of wackily decorated offices, and a field trip to downtown Las Vegas, to which Zappos planned to move its headquarters from the suburb of Henderson.

During a steak dinner at Tony's home, Gareri made sure to grab the seat across from the guru. He was now a changed man, wanting to institute a happiness culture at his twenty-six-year-old company. Initially, Tony told him that it wasn't possible. "You should shut down the company, go across the street, and reopen the company," he remembered Tony telling him, warning that a culture overhaul is a gargantuan task. If Gareri did try to instigate change from within, Tony suggested, it would be difficult and take a wholehearted commitment. That was enough for Gareri. "I needed to hear from him it was possible," he said.

Gareri knew that his company's culture had become toxic, a reality that had become clear to him while he was touring Zapposland. Roma Moulding's products were high quality, but Gareri had mentally checked out, waiting to decide whether to stay or go. Tony Hsieh gave him an answer and a newfound commitment to positive leadership.

Gareri got his father and other company executives to agree to try a Zappos-like culture revolution at the family-owned company. Starting with an admission to employees that the company had failed to put them first, he had begun to consider how the company could "blur the line between work and play." Roma Moulding started holding all-hands meetings, like Zappos' famous gatherings, with Gareri talking to employees with the zeal of a motivational speaker, that have continued for a decade and counting. Roma began promoting public tours to show off its own workplace culture as its business rebounded and thrived.

"Company cultures develop over time," said Gareri, who also launched a public speaking career. "It's not a three-month, one-year strategy. It's truly—as Tony stated—a five-minimum-to-lifetime strategy. The more love and the more attention you give it, I think it continues to pay dividends."

Happiness, though, can have a darker side. Psychologists have found that focusing on happiness can have the paradoxical effect of making people less happy by creating higher expectations. In one experiment, a group of people viewed a two-minute video clip previously proven to induce positive emotions about a female figure skater winning a gold medal and celebrating with her coach as the crowd cheers. Before watching the positive video, some participants read a made-up news article emphasizing the importance of happiness in life; others read an article that, instead of happiness, wrote about the importance of using "accurate judgment" in life. The group who read the article on happiness reported being less happy while watching the joyful video.

"These findings are consistent with the idea that valuing happiness leads to less happiness by setting people up for disappointment," the researchers concluded. Self-help books promote "a mindset to maximize happiness," they wrote, when, in fact, people might be more helped by the approach of the philosopher John Stuart Mill in 1873: Mill said that happy people are those whose minds are focused "on some object other than their own happiness."

In a separate study, researchers concluded that the pursuit of happiness can actually make people feel lonelier, because Western notions of happiness focus more on one's own feelings and do not take those of friends and strangers into account, which could possibly damage social connections with others.

Daniel Horowitz, a historian at Smith College, wrote about the rise of positive psychology and happiness studies in his book *Happier? The History of a Cultural Movement That Aspired to Transform America*. He traced how the positive psychology movement became big business in the 2000s, fueled in particular by the spread of messaging on social media and the popularity of TED Talk videos that feature snappy how-to-live-the-good-life content from witty, sometimes dramatic experts. Among the most popular TED Talks is "The Surprising Science of Happiness," by the Harvard psychologist Daniel Gilbert in 2004, which, as Horowitz noted, has been viewed almost 20 million times online. Meanwhile, tech companies and corporations as big as Walmart began hiring happiness coaches preaching themes similar to Tony's company-culture manifesto. Horowitz noted that the movement has attracted "a world of serial searchers" for life enhancement.

Horowitz pointed to a landmark work published by the social psychologist Philip Brickman in the 1970s. Brickman and a colleague published a paper stating that people can get stuck walking on a "hedonic treadmill," a futile search for long-lasting happiness. In fact, boosts in positive emotions as a result of good fortune or life events are only temporary. People adapt and soon return to their emotional baselines. The thrill wears off.

Unfortunately, Brickman committed suicide at the age of thirty-eight by jumping off an apartment building in Ann Arbor, Michigan. In an obituary, fellow psychologists wrote:

The best way off the hedonic treadmill, according to Phil's writings, is commitment—the almost magical mechanism that converts the inevitable pain and dissatisfaction in life into purpose and meaningfulness. Unfortunately, commitments can be very fragile. . . . His writings reveal deep feelings for the phenomena he studied; perhaps he had too much feeling and too much insight. These two things together are the mainsprings of unique creative achievement, but they are also the elements of tragedy.

Some research has linked the extreme valuing of happiness to an increased risk of developing mania as part of bipolar disorder and depression, and high levels of positive emotions can be associated with risky behaviors including alcohol and drug use.

The Nobel Prize–winning psychologist Daniel Kahneman, known worldwide for his happiness research, in a surprising 2018 interview said he had become convinced that people don't want to be happy— they're interested in life satisfaction, constructed by the memories of our lives and the accomplishments of our goals, rather than day-to-day happiness. "The question of whether society should intervene so that people will be happier is very controversial, but whether society should strive for people to suffer less—that's widely accepted," he said, adding later "in general, if you want to reduce suffering, mental health is a good place to start—because the extent of illness is enormous and the intensity of the distress doesn't allow for any talk of happiness."

In his own quest for peace and joyfulness, Tony struggled quietly.

He suffered from significant social anxiety, the unrelenting feeling of being watched and judged by the people around him, and also, likely, depression. Although he had never received a diagnosis of autism spectrum disorder, a developmental disability associated with difficulties in communication and social interaction, he speculated to some of his close friends that he was somewhere on the spectrum. It was easy to see why he thought so. In conversation, he often skipped small talk and asked something direct instead, such as "What would it take to reach your full potential?" Despite his limitless generosity, he was missing a level of empathy common in most people—and he knew it. He approached the problem as he had those of downtown Las Vegas and Zappos: by studying, reading books and articles about humans and their desires. He was brilliant—he could do complex mathematical equations in his head, and he told people that his mind was always working eight seconds ahead of everyone else's.

Unbeknownst to even some of his closest friends, Tony suffered from facial blindness, also undiagnosed, which sometimes made it difficult to identify the people around him. In an August 2010 essay, the *New Yorker* writer Oliver Sacks wrote devastatingly about the way his own inability to recognize faces and even familiar places had contributed to a lifetime of frustrating interactions: "On several occasions I have apologized for almost bumping into a large bearded man, only to realize that the large bearded man was myself in a mirror." It's unclear how severe Tony's affliction was because he told so few people about it. He once complained to a close friend that he might not recognize his own mother if she walked by him unannounced.

Tony developed workarounds by recognizing the voices of close friends or by asking a select group of people to help guide him through particularly difficult events with a lot of people. When someone entered a room, he might distract the person by offering him or her something—such as a meal—so he could leave the room and listen as the new person talked with others. Most of his friends assumed he was absent-minded or had memory problems because of his very busy lifestyle.

In one example of what was likely Tony's inability to recognize faces, Phil Plastina, the head of the Dancetronauts, who by that time knew Tony well, sat next to him at a bar for more than two hours one night in Las Vegas. Even though Tony turned to look at him several times, he never said anything, treating him like a stranger. Finally Plastina, who had been talking to someone else, took Tony's arm and said hello. Tony greeted him as if he had just arrived.

Each of Tony's health problems was an obstacle, standing in the way of the kind of life he wanted for himself, one filled with all different kinds of people and events. He refused to talk openly about any of his issues, despite the number of friends who surrounded him. He took Adderall, a medication generally associated with attention-deficit hyperactivity disorder, and Xanax for his social anxiety. He took Ambien to help him sleep. But that wasn't enough.

Earlier, when he had lived in San Francisco, he had discovered the pleasing effects of alcohol, specifically Grey Goose vodka, at the parties he had hosted at his loft during the years after the Link-Exchange sale. Alcohol was like a lubricant, enabling him to have the types of conversations and moments he wanted with the people around him. (It should not have been mixed with medications such as Adderall and Xanax, but he didn't appear to suffer negative effects from doing so.)

By 2010, what had been occasional drinking grew into a nightly ritual. Through the parties and events he threw at Zappos, he seamlessly infused it into the culture there as well. Though alcohol-heavy workplaces have often led to problems for companies, it seemed to work for the most part at Zappos, where so much prominence was already placed on "fun." It wouldn't be odd to see the CEO do a shot in the middle of the day or at a meeting. His employees worshipped him, and they joined in.

Drinking became a part of who Tony was, a feature of his character that everyone around him accepted, like his deep desire to have fun or his relentless determination to always be on time for everything, down to the minute.

To a few close friends, Tony admitted why he thought he needed so much alcohol in his life. He said he felt that he couldn't talk to people properly if he was sober. In other words, he had trouble forming connections, the friendships he cared so deeply about. Sometimes his friends would broach the subject with him, as in 2013, when his then girlfriend, Ali Bevilacqua, asked him, "What's up with the drinking? Why do you have to drink every night?"

"I have to drink," he replied. "It's the only way I can live in the now. It's the only way I can get out of my head."

Nothing cemented his drinking lifestyle more than the three-and-a-half-month book tour for *Delivering Happiness*, a cross-country road trip in 2010 on a large bus featuring friends he had collected over the years and whom he had invited to join him. The bus, colored light turquoise with the book's logo and a big, winking smiley face, stopped at music festivals, bars, truck stops, and more. On board, the bus had a full-time bartender, and it was a never-ending party, celebrating his successful book.

The group that followed Tony carried bright yellow HAPPINESS X-ING AHEAD signs wherever they went. Starting in Las Vegas, the bus drove more than three thousand miles across the country, stopping for sack races in Colorado, a happy hour with local residents in Omaha, Nebraska, and hula-hooping in Rhode Island.

In New Orleans, the tour bus drove through the Lower Ninth Ward, a neighborhood still devastated after Hurricane Katrina and the levee failures in 2005. Flooded-out houses were still marked with X's and numbers spray-painted by emergency workers who had recorded how many people or pets had been rescued or died. Tony's bus, usually filled with music and conversation, was silent as it pulled into the ward. Even years after the hurricane, the damage was startling to observe. Tony was emphatic about the group's visit, and he partnered with a nonprofit to spend two days repairing and rebuilding houses. He worked alongside everyone else. Other companies might have publicized that sort of "human" move by their CEO, but it would never even occur to Tony.

At the South by Southwest festival in Austin, the bus caught up with the actor and investor Ashton Kutcher, who later joined the bus trip for a stretch, partying with everyone on board. "Nobody in the bus had a personal agenda that they were trying to fill," Kutcher told Tony and Jenn Lim in a later interview. The pair often interviewed people for video postings online during the tour. "I think everybody's agenda was just to give and share happiness."

In New York City, Zappos employees rode in fifteen pedicabs through Times Square, waving HAPPINESS X-ING AHEAD signs and passing them out to tourists waiting to board tour buses or purchase cheap theater tickets. With big grins and shouts of glee, they shouted "Happiness!" or "Happiness crossing!" to mildly confused passersby on the sidewalks.

"But are you happy?" a bystander shouted at the miniature parade. No one seemed to hear or bothered to respond as the procession carried on.

PART II

CHAPTER FIVE

THE GHOST IN THE MACHINE

Park City, May and June 2020
Las Vegas, 2012–2016

*I think of my role more as being like the architect of the greenhouse,
where under the right conditions, the plants will flourish and thrive
on their own.*

—Tony Hsieh

In Park City, a blanket of wintertime snow hides a small lake on Aspen Springs Drive that disappears into the white landscape on the main highway into the ski resort town. But in springtime, the valley meadows thaw out, revealing verdant pastures traced by a few rusty fences and groves of trees. The sparkling pond reflects sunlight through the cathedral windows of what became known by Tony Hsieh and his friends as the Ranch.

Aspen Springs Drive, a residential road, passes the pond before carving through trees up the mountainside. The trees cloak luxury homes that are close enough to be considered part of a neighborhood but far enough apart that their residents can mostly forget about other people. Realtors marketed the house at 2636 Aspen Springs Drive—a nine-bedroom, thirteen-bathroom house on seventeen acres of land that also includes a horse corral, a tennis court, an indoor swimming pool, and waterfront lounge areas on a sandy beach with mountains in the distance—as Crescent Ranch. Sold for about $7 million in 2016, only four years later, the house was listed for $14.9 million in the rush for big houses and distant neighbors during the pandemic.

In late spring 2020, Tony toured the house and was immediately enamored. The house features tall windows, overlooking the private lake, the mountains in the background. Members of his entourage explored like kids, bouncing through the different rooms. Tony and his crew made the decision to buy it almost immediately. He offered to pay nearly $16 million, a million dollars over the asking price, if the sellers would not return home. They agreed.

Soon after, the sellers' real estate agent returned as movers were packing up the family's belongings. By then Tony had already placed hundreds of candles around the house. Lately, he had developed a fixation with fire. He "explained to me that the candles were a symbol of what life was like in a simpler time," the real estate agent said later.

Buying the Ranch was Tony's biggest step in what appeared to be a period of renewal in his life, despite the social distancing and doomsday atmosphere of the pandemic. Postrehab, he had embarked on a digital detox in an attempt to find clarity, turning off his two cell phones and answering only important emails related to his work at Zappos. He was still the CEO, but he was increasingly dropping out of online meetings. When he did show up, he often seemed unfocused, as though he were paying attention to something else. If any of his friends wanted to reach him, they had to email one of his assistants.

Despite being somewhat absent from work and hard to track down for friends, Tony seemed to be in the best shape of his life in early spring 2020. He wasn't drinking much and had even given up smoking American Spirit cigarettes for the most part, a habit he loved. He had made a pact with his Las Vegas friend Justin Weniger to stop taking ketamine, and staying off the drug seemed to be helping.

After he left rehab in late February 2020, Tony lived in the $4 million wood-frame house on Empire Avenue that he had initially planned for a vacation rental. The house was directly across from the ski slopes of Park City Mountain. In the spring of 2020, skiing was shut down because of the pandemic. But almost every day, Tony walked out of his house, crossed the massive, empty parking lot of the resort lodge, and picked one of the network of trails that weaves across the shuttered ski slopes, ascending the mountain.

The trails are strenuous, made all the harder by Park City's nearly seven-thousand-foot elevation, with hikes that can reach ten thousand feet. The high altitude can cause dizziness, headaches, or even an upset stomach in some people, especially those used to living at lower elevations, such as Las Vegas.

One of the more popular paths up Park City Mountain is the Armstrong Trail, a series of switchbacks on rocky terrain that passes through groves of aspen and pine trees, before eventually giving way to a panoramic view of Park City. At the cluster of boulders at the top, hikers can look out across the entire valley, the white letters *PC* carved into a hillside in the distance. But the view is achieved only after nearly four miles of straight uphill hiking, and assuming that one walks at a fast clip, the endeavor could take three hours or more. In the spring, the weather in Park City can be fickle, 70 degrees one day and 38 and snowing the next, with stretches of crusty snow lining parts of the trails shadowed by towering pine trees, making them even more treacherous to walk.

Weniger, a longtime trail runner and mountain biker, was a reliable companion on those hikes, but few of Tony's other visitors could keep up with him. Some dropped out of a hike before ever making it a third of the way up. On those long walks, Tony practiced a sort of heavy-breathing technique that he had read about in a book called *The Oxygen Advantage: Simple, Scientifically Proven Breathing Techniques to Help You Become Healthier, Slimmer, Faster, and Fitter* and that was supposed to boost his endurance.

Back at home, he lowered himself into icy baths at least four times a week, remaining five minutes or more, a method of reducing body inflammation and healing muscle aches. He also spent a long time stretching. Almost every day, he made soup. It was one of his favorite foods, and he hardly ever used a recipe, enjoying the act of throwing random ingredients and leftovers together to see what might work.

When Tony's longtime driver, Steve Moroney, who hadn't seen him for a month or more, came to pick him up at the Empire Avenue house in the early spring of 2020, Tony was standing in the kitchen wearing only sweats, his shirt off, drinking a glass of water. He was completely toned, his abs glistening.

"Wow," Moroney said. "You've really been working out!" Even when Tony had been on an exercise binge in the past—climbing California mountains or deciding to run a marathon—he had still usually had a little belly.

Moroney jokingly poked Tony's flat stomach. Like all of Tony's employees, Moroney's standing with his boss was more of a close friend than a paid worker, and he had been driving Tony and his entourage around since the Delivering Happiness tour bus a decade earlier. He viewed Tony as family. Tony smiled at Moroney and described his near-daily hikes.

Moroney, and others who saw Tony at the time, assumed that his new fitness routine meant he was better. He looked so good, so healthy, and there didn't seem to be drugs around. But other longtime friends such as Tyler Williams, his right-hand man and close friend at Zappos, saw something else when they watched him leave to hike miles up those mountains. They observed early signs of the manic behavior that he had displayed months earlier in Las Vegas, before rehab. Though drugs seemed to be out of the equation for now, he talked intensely about his big visions for Park City and 10X—not always coherently—while at the same time philosophizing about living a life free of constraints such as money and time. He didn't want to think about Zappos or even wear shoes.

Some of his new visions seemed to be instigated by his recent insecurity about what he had achieved in his career, compared with other chief executive officers. He didn't often compare himself to others, at least publicly, so that was a new phenomenon. In late May 2020, he had watched with rapt attention as the billionaire Elon

Musk's company SpaceX had launched two astronauts into space for the first time. Something shifted in Tony in that moment, and he seemed to question his whole approach to management, particularly developing people and urging them to learn through reading books on their own path. Though he wasn't necessarily discarding his overall quest for happiness, he wondered if he had taken the wrong way to get there. Maybe he shouldn't have been working at such a long, slow game, focused on building up the people around him to achieve greatness. Instead, and with an egotistical tone that was also unlike him, he wondered aloud if he had been doing it all wrong. Had he missed an opportunity to do something really big that could change humankind? He had to fix it—he had to fix everything *right now*. What exactly he had to fix was unclear to those around him.

That change in tone also accompanied his inexplicable new buying spree, starting with the Ranch. He was already talking about investing in other properties as part of his 10X plan. That was also very out of character since, until recently, he had lived in a small Airstream trailer, still preferred fast food, and, despite working at a shoe company, wore only black Asics.

Williams and others kept quiet about their suspicions about Tony's behavior because they initially didn't see any clear evidence that something was wrong. Despite his career-long focus on healthy relationships, which was a corporate value at Zappos, he had been hard to talk to about anything serious. He had walled off parts of himself and hated confrontation. It was part of the reason why getting him into rehab earlier in 2020 had been so challenging: his friends knew that he would react negatively to any questions, possibly telling them to leave Park City. They didn't want to leave. They were worried. Something was brewing.

By 2012 in Las Vegas, Tony had cemented his stardom with his success at Zappos and the publication of *Delivering Happiness*, but it wasn't enough to keep him still. He was an innovator, always seeking the next radical idea, the next promising discovery, while disdaining taking the easy route. His obsession with cities hadn't been quelled by his decision to personally invest $350 million into the one where he lived.

He began repeating a research conclusion that would become a mantra: when a city's population doubles in size, productivity increases by 15 percent. Corporations, though, get bogged down in bureaucracy and leave innovation behind while growing. "Cities have stood the test of time," he said. "They're self-organized. The mayor of a city doesn't actually tell its residents what to do or where to live."

Tony's thinking seemed inspired by researchers such as the theoretical physicist Geoffrey West, who applied scientific equations to the study of cities. His and others' work had found that as a city doubled in size, economic measures such as income, number of patents granted, and GDP went up by 15 percent—but so did the darker side of the equation, with a 15 percent rise in negative factors such as crime, traffic congestion, and certain diseases including AIDS. But ever a devotee of positivity, Tony focused on the good side of the equation as the foundation for his riskiest move yet.

Tony considered himself to be a "futurist," someone who studies and predicts what will happen a dozen years from now, or even fifty or a hundred years. He found that more than three-quarters of the businesses on *Fortune* magazine's first list of the five hundred biggest companies in the United States in 1955 had since failed. Zappos needed to ensure its survival in the long term. Tony had already rethought the traditional office and workday, even the role of the customer and the manager-employee relationship. Now he was eyeing something grander, questioning traditional hierarchy—as in workers managed by bosses overseen by more bosses—which dated back to the assembly lines of the Industrial Age. It felt nothing like the freewheeling office that was Zappos.

There was also Tony's role as CEO, a job that by 2012 he had held for more than a decade but didn't actually love. Unlike other business executives, who enjoy the power of overseeing a global enterprise, who work their whole careers to get to that point, he didn't like the unmanageable stress that came with it, and he especially didn't like telling people what to do. That was why he always recommended books or TED Talks to get his viewpoint across to someone. Often he would spend his mornings scouring the internet for interesting articles and information and then send them to the right people at the right time, usually when he wanted them to think about a new idea. Those missives were affectionately known as Tony's "data drops." "I think of my role more as being like the architect of the greenhouse, where under the right conditions, the plants will flourish and thrive on their own," he once said. Not only was he uncomfortable with the job personally, he questioned the role of CEO at any company—he found it to be a flawed title that caused nepotism and put the company at risk for relying so much on one person.

Instead he wondered how he could give more authority to the loyal employees he'd fostered for years. Eager to find a better way, he read about theories of self-management, which essentially does away with the typical company structure. It appealed to his desire for the next iteration of Zappos.

In October 2012, he traveled to Lost Pines, a resort about twenty-five miles outside Austin, Texas, the liberal tech hub of the South. He was giving a talk at the annual Conscious Capitalism CEO Summit, part of a movement started by Whole Foods cofounder John Mackey, where a group of about two hundred corporate leaders gathered each year. Americans weren't happy with the corporate greed that had been revealed during the 2008 financial crisis. Conscious Capitalism offered an answer by emphasizing a higher purpose alongside profits. Tony's presentation of Zappos' values and his interest in reviving downtown Las Vegas fit right in.

In the rotating cast of wealthy do-gooders laying out their plans, Tony paid attention when it was Brian Robertson's turn onstage. Robertson, with a goatee and a kind demeanor, has described himself as having a rebellious streak, questioning the status quo and authority from his school days into his professional life.

His life-changing invention, the reason he had been invited to speak at the conference, had come after he had nearly crashed a plane. He was flying solo with only twenty hours of training completed when a low-voltage light on his instrument dashboard turned on midflight. But Robertson ignored it because his other instruments, including the altimeter, appeared normal. He ended up flying through a storm and nearly losing control. He later thought about how humans in the workplace are a company's sensors and a lone worker can sometimes be ignored. "How do I build an organization where everybody gets to bring all of their wisdom, all of their gifts, all of their talents, and there's no risk that we outvote somebody that has some critical insight?" he asked at one TED Talk.

To the Texas crowd, he described the ability of his system of self-management for companies, which he had named *holacracy*, to flatten the hierarchy and ensure that all workers are heard.

Robertson noticed Tony in the audience because he wore a ratty T-shirt among the upscale crowd. He didn't know who Tony was, but he could feel him listening intently. Tony approached him immediately after the talk. "He came up to me and started just peppering me with questions, like really curious, a little skeptical," Robertson remembered. "I gave him all the answers I could."

Tony shared his favorite stat: "Research shows that every time the size of a city doubles, innovation or productivity per resident increases by 15 percent, but when companies get bigger, innovation or productivity per employee generally goes down." He added, "So, I'm interested in how we can create organizations that are more like cities and less like bureaucratic corporations."

Robertson said he thought he could help.

Holacracy is a form of self-management in which instead of a team of people reporting to a boss, who then reports to another boss, as in a traditional hierarchy, there are groups of largely self-managed teams. Workers fill "roles" within "circles." The circles are fluid; an employee can hold multiple roles. The traditional one-on-one meetings with a manager are replaced with "tactical meetings" "where all members of the circle are accountable to each other." Problems are called "tensions," and a tension is defined as "a gap between what is and what could be." The way holacracy spells it out, tensions are sensed intuitively by the body, rather than recognized only by the mind. Each circle holds governance meetings to "process" the tensions felt by circle members.

The name *holacracy* was inspired by the journalist and critic Arthur Koestler's 1967 philosophical psychology book *The Ghost in the Machine*, which explores the relationship between human consciousness and the physical body. Humans, Koestler said, are like "holons," things that are simultaneously independent and part of something bigger, connected by what is known as a holarchy.

"It captured the spirit we were looking for—governance of and by the organizational holarchy," Robertson blogged as part of the history of holacracy; "through the people, but not of or for the people."

After chatting at the conference, Robertson accepted Tony's invitation to visit Zappos in Las Vegas and talk about how holacracy could be implemented there. Then, in late 2013, Zappos began rolling out the new management structure. Tony expected a full transition to take as long as five years, with a basic framework in place within one year. He announced the change to holacracy at Zappos' quarterly all-hands meeting in November 2013. The event also included a *Lion King* performance and an employee climbing into a container of tarantulas for a $250 gift card.

Internally, Tony liked to tell people that Zappos was small enough to withstand the massive management overhaul that he was proposing, big enough to matter as the world watched, and strong enough to go through the pain.

On March 24, 2015, at 3:18 p.m., Tony hit "Send" on a 4,500-word email that would, for better or worse, make Zappos famous yet again. He instructed his employees to take thirty minutes to read the email. Zappos was shifting entirely to self-management, using the holacracy system, and as of April 30, there would effectively be no bosses. The company would become a "Teal organization," a concept introduced by the self-management guru Frederic Laloux, who wrote *Re-*

inventing Organizations: A Guide to Creating Organizations Inspired by the Next Stage of Human Consciousness.

Laloux created an overview of different business organizations inspired by levels of human consciousness through evolution. "Red" is "impulsive," with predatory leadership such as exists in street gangs; "orange" is "achiever," with goal-oriented leadership such as that of charter schools; and "green" is "pluralistic," with a focus on consensus building and values, such as Southwest Airlines. "Teal" is "evolutionary." A Teal organization has creativity and future potential, and "decisions are informed not only by the rational mind, but also by the wisdom of emotions, intuition, and aesthetics."

The announcement was like an earthquake that shook Zappos and its employees, who had grown used to their company's zany, everything-goes culture. Although it encouraged self-reliance, transparency, and autonomy, the holacracy structure was rigid, particularly at first. It came with a lot of processes and rules. As one executive put it, "It was like learning to write with your left hand." Some people broke down crying when they read Tony's email. At one of the leadership team's first meetings about integrating holacracy, with Robertson in attendance as the "facilitator," some of the executives were so shaken and upset that they opened a bottle of Grey Goose vodka to pass around,* taking shots while he was talking.

Tony's email had also included a fateful offer: the company would give any employee who didn't want to deal with self-management a severance of three months' pay. Those with at least four years' experience would get one month's pay for every year at Zappos. The offer didn't spell it out, but employees who chose to stay would implicitly be buying into holacracy. That was the tactic Tony often used quietly to persuade people to adopt his unusual plans, including in downtown Las Vegas, where entrepreneurs who accepted his investment money were also essentially signing off on his vision for the city.

---

* Zappos said that people who attended the meeting do not recall a bottle of vodka being passed around.

"Like all the bold steps we've done in the past, it feels a little scary, but it also feels like exactly the type of thing that only a company such as Zappos would dare to attempt at this scale," Tony's email said. "With our core values and culture as the foundation for everything we do, I'm personally excited about all the potential creativity and energy of our employees that are just waiting for the right environment and structure to be unlocked and unleashed. I can't wait to see how we reinvent ourselves, and I can't wait to see what unfolds next."

In early May 2015, Zappos reported that 14 percent of its workers—about 210 of its 1,500 people—had taken the buyout offer and left the company. That number increased to 18 percent by January 2016.

Tony felt frustrated that the media reports on the departures didn't focus on the other side of the equation: 82 percent of the employees had stayed committed to Zappos. If any other company had made that offer, he argued, the retention rate would have been much lower.

In 2015, the nonprofit arm of billionaire Richard Branson's Virgin Group invited Tony to speak at a small retreat on Necker Island in the British Virgin Islands. Branson, who has founded more than four hundred businesses worldwide, bought the seventy-acre, uninhabited circle of rain forest in the 1970s, turning it into his family home and a private getaway. Among celebrities and business executives, it's considered an honor to be invited, and sometimes attendees would come as part of a small conference or other event. As Branson observed in a 2014 YouTube video produced by Virgin, "The most extraordinary people come to Necker." He and Tony had crossed paths before, including when Branson had visited Tony in Las Vegas, touring Zappos and his other developments.

Tony, his hair shaved at the sides and styled into a tall mohawk, spoke about holacracy, detailing his efforts at Zappos. Afterward, he fielded questions from other attendees about the practice. By now he was an accomplished speaker and practiced at hiding any social anxiety he might have been feeling.

Soon a woman about his age, with long blond hair, standing in the back, began dominating the conversation, asking smart, open-minded questions about holacracy in a way that Tony had never heard before. He had been used to getting pointed questions from other business executives who missed the point of his new management system entirely. "I love you," Tony thought as the woman spoke, although he didn't say it out loud.

Afterward, as Tony stood around speaking to attendees, he was introduced to Jewel, who had skyrocketed to fame as a homeless folk-singer in the 1990s with songs such as "Who Will Save Your Soul" and "You Were Meant for Me." It was as though she and Tony spoke a secret language and she could translate his holacracy plans in a way that real people would understand.

Growing up in the backwoods of Alaska, Jewel Kilcher had relied on nature and the beauty of her surroundings to help her escape a tumultuous childhood, including an abusive father. She had ridden her horse frequently, and after she left home at only fifteen, she worked hard to remain true to those roots, even as she toured the world as a musician who had unexpectedly found fame.

She immediately saw that Tony was trying to build the company through holacracy like "a natural, living breathing organism," she later explained after Tony invited her to speak at a Zappos company event. Holacracy was all about "circles" of operation, and Jewel saw the body as a great metaphor: the kidney, liver, and spleen, all acting independently but still operating within the larger body system. "They're imprinted with the code, which is the values of the company," she explained. Because nature had been evolving and learning since the beginning of creation, to build a human system similar to it would be the most efficient and effective if a company cared about longevity, she reasoned, which Tony clearly did. Jewel didn't think about things such as "org charts."

Jewel had spent more than a decade working on mental health

issues affecting at-risk youth through her nonprofit, the Inspiring Children Foundation, and had expanded that work to helping school districts and companies. Tony was fascinated by her use of nature as a role model for grit and resilience. In 2016, he asked her to design a program at Zappos that would encourage employees to deal with stress and mental health and help turn them into resilient, self-starting entrepreneurs, which they would need to fit in the new holacracy system.

Alone and adrift at only fifteen, Jewel had herself struggled with mental health problems. Like Tony, Jewel is an introvert, but she had realized that her tactic of hiding in plain sight to keep herself safe was limiting her ability to experience connection and joy. She had set out to correct that by being vulnerable when she sang. She forced herself to maintain eye contact and be very honest about herself and her flaws. She found that the strategy worked: the feeling of connection was exhilarating and radical, and she knew she had stumbled onto something important. While she had been homeless, she had begun to study her anxiety and experiment with different techniques to help overcome it, including writing. She called her journal "The Happiness Project" and later wrote her own best-selling book, *Never Broken: Songs Are Only Half the Story*. Every time she wrote something down, she felt her anxiety lessen.

Tony and Tyler Williams worked with Jewel to develop an online portal at Zappos called "Whole Human," filled with mental health resources, one that could be used at other companies across the country. Jewel and her team created ten pillars of high-performance living, including emotional fitness, calm mind, physical fitness, and community and connection. They came up with dozens of tools to help employees when they felt overwhelmed, anxious, or depressed, including meditation and other mindfulness techniques.

As part of her work with Zappos, Jewel moved temporarily to Las Vegas, where the Inspiring Children Foundation is based. She became one of dozens of musicians and movie stars who flowed through the Airstream trailer park in downtown Las Vegas. Tony had moved there from the nearby Ogden apartment building in 2014 and now lived with thirty other friends spread out among twenty of the bullet-shaped metal trailers, along with tiny houses measuring only several hundred square feet.

The semiplanned community, which Tony referred to as "an urban version of Burning Man" and sometimes as the "world's largest living room," had a pool, a barbecue, and a campfire going every night. Five cats lived there, as did fifteen dogs and Tony's alpaca, Marley. Tony loved llamas and alpacas because they looked so silly. He also owned a small terrier mix, Blizzy, short for Blizzard, which he had spontaneously adopted at a Zappos pet event and whose stature in Tony's life warranted the establishment of Blizzy's own Instagram account. Sarah Jessica Parker posed with Blizzy for his feed, as did Britney Spears.

Jewel had been hanging out there one Sunday around 2017 for an informal weekly brunch Tony regularly held when two local musicians, a beat boxer and a rapper, also wandered in. That wasn't unusual. Sometimes there would be a high school kid playing a piano or a sixty-five-year-old playing the drums. Soon Jewel and the three musicians performed together for Tony and his friends, producing several new songs together on the spot. It was the sort of ultimate "collision" that Tony had always hoped for, and it was how Jewel was used to seeing him, quietly content and radiating positive energy from a perch nearby.

But as they worked with Tony at Zappos, Jewel and her team realized that there might be another reason he wanted them there: he was also struggling and clearly wanted to learn some coping mechanisms for his mental health issues from them. He was under so much pressure to perform for his employees and customers and even his friends. Jewel's team sensed that Tony was suffering from social anxiety, which he had told few people about, and they thought he had a sensitive personality. The latter attribute meant he would be hypersensitive to large groups of people and energy, a problem for Tony, who had built his life around being in groups. He hadn't learned how to manage that, or the constant stress of his life, in a healthy way. Working nonstop and traveling all the time—on business and road trips—were ways of self-medicating, as was his drinking.

By 2015, Tony's alcoholic beverage of choice had switched to the Italian liqueur Fernet, a weedy, herbal-tasting liquid that Tony liked to joke was his "Chinese medicine." He liked to pretend that it actually was medicine, a clear distraction from his reliance on alcohol, telling people it was a liqueur soaked in fourteen herbs and spices, that it was a digestive and helped with nausea. Don't judge it for sixty seconds, he would tell people. Allow it to coat your stomach like medicine. His friends would laugh along and gamely try the bitter liquid.

When Tyler Williams was asked in 2019 by a Medium writer about the things he wished someone had told him about Zappos when he first started the job, he said the amount of Fernet he would be drinking. "I wish someone had told me to build up my tolerance because seriously—we drink a lot of it," he said. Williams was the rare friend who could keep up with Tony's 24/7 lifestyle. He believed in Tony and the work they were doing at Zappos, and he didn't have any kids. His wife, however, put her foot down about living in the Airstream trailer park and also declined a job offer from Tony.

On some days, Tony drank throughout the day, but it wasn't obvious even to some of the people closest to him. During meetings throughout the day or at a Zappos event, he would have a shot here and a shot there, but there were different people attending the meetings, who saw him having only one or two shots at a time. When evening rolled around and the parties began, he would have several more shots or drinks over the course of the night. By the end of the day, he might have consumed as many as eighteen shots or drinks, and he was small. Despite the dozens of people around him all the time, very few of them—maybe none of them—would have witnessed the entirety of that consumption because they weren't with him all day long. Williams, who was about fifty pounds heavier than Tony, once tried to keep up with him shot for shot on a trip to Santa Fe. He passed out.

Tony easily explained away any concerns about his drinking, although there were very few people who tried to talk to him about it because of how resistant he was to any personal confrontation. He also seemed to have it under control. As a way of convincing his friends that he didn't have a problem, he took up smoking and said he would quit in six months to show them that he could give up anything he wanted. But when the six months ended, he extended that time frame to a year because, he said, smoking was "meditative" for him. He continued to smoke, and his friends stopped asking about it.

Once, not long after *Delivering Happiness* was published, a long-time friend who didn't see him regularly became concerned about his drinking. In a brief moment when the two were alone together, the friend asked him point-blank to give it up. Tony was quiet for a moment. Then he took the friend's hands and said, "I have a doctor, and he says I'm fine. If he ever tells me I'm not, I promise you I'll quit." A later court filing describing Tony's mental health issues during his lifetime seemed to indicate that Tony had consulted a medical professional on the matter, saying that "he understood the negative health effects associated with the prolonged use of alcohol and the prescription medication he was taking."

Tony's ex-girlfriend Ali Bevilacqua, meanwhile, tried to gently convince Tony to cut back on his drinking in a way she hoped he would be receptive to. Tony could be very stubborn, and he really didn't believe that anything was wrong. There was a subtle art to convincing him of things. Bevilacqua had moved next to Tony in the Airstream trailer park in 2018 when they were dating, and in the mornings, they had taken turns making each other breakfast. It was usually his most sober time of day. She would tell him, "I like you best when you're sober. Do you really need to drink?" Tony would shrug off the question. The problem was, he didn't like himself sober.

While Jewel was working with him at Zappos, Tony never outwardly asked her or her team for help with whatever he was struggling with, although he queried Jewel for book recommendations about mental health. He tried to take up meditation. When Jewel and her team held longer, deeper retreats or workshops in which Zappos employees had to discuss their personal struggles, he was conveniently not around.

When it came time for him to fully fund the "Whole Human" project, he declined, despite all the work put in by Jewel and her team to develop a prototype for the program. It's possible that Zappos just didn't have the funding. But Tony never explained why.

Tony's avoidance of discussing his own problems publicly isn't unique to him. The stigma around mental illness has existed for centuries. We have a history of locking people away in psychiatric hospitals, diagnosing people with schizophrenia, for example, while also categorizing them as ones to be feared and avoided. In the 1960s, society took a new approach: designed to deinstitutionalize the system and release people from deplorable conditions, a wave of hospital closures brought people back into communities. But outpatient treatment and community services have been underfunded and frequently ignored by political leaders. Many Americans, particularly racial and ethnic minority groups, have limited access to care, a crisis that worsened during the isolation and job losses brought about by the pandemic. Meanwhile, the news media and entertainment often portray those with mental illness as violent, unpredictable, and worthy of being blamed for their condition. The lingering bias that prevents people from getting help has been an ongoing, decades-long fight by advocates, who work to increase access to care in a broken, underfunded public system.

In recent years, the push to destigmatize mental health has gained steam with big celebrities taking up the cause or speaking publicly about their experiences. Amid the Covid-19 pandemic, Oprah Winfrey and Prince Harry launched a series on Apple TV+ devoted to the topic featuring celebrities such as Lady Gaga and other famous people. Kanye West, who was diagnosed with bipolar disorder, has publicly described his manic episodes, telling David Letterman in 2019, "You see everything. You feel the government is putting chips in your head. You feel you're being recorded. You feel all of these things."

In the business world, where a company's stock price flickers on just a few words from a CEO, mental health remains a taboo topic that is rarely discussed. Founders are synonymous with their companies; a public image of stability is crucial as they pitch for venture capital funding and make the rounds at networking events. Even those who are privileged to be able to afford the priciest private psychiatric care and have access to it fear the consequences from investors and customers, who demand a steady projection of confidence and infallibility in trying to grow a company.

One Sunday morning in 2017, Tesla founder Elon Musk tweeted to his followers—around 17 million at the time, now 60 million—about the reality of his life: "The reality is great highs, terrible lows and unrelenting stress. Don't think people want to hear about the last two."

In response, a Twitter user asked Musk if he had bipolar disorder. Musk replied, "Yeah," followed by a second answer: "Maybe not medically tho. Dunno. Bad feelings correlate to bad events, so maybe real problem is getting carried away in what I sign up for." When another follower said that a lot of fellow founders would want to hear about how he's dealt with the lows and stress, Musk responded, "I'm sure there are better answers than what I do, which is just take the pain and make sure you really care about what you're doing."

In 2021, Musk, while hosting *Saturday Night Live*, opened up further, announcing for the first time in his opening monologue that he had Asperger's syndrome, a form of autism.

Unhooking an entrepreneur's identity from the roller coaster of work is what Jerry Colonna, an executive coach, focuses on accomplishing with a blend of Buddhism and introspection. Colonna earned a reputation as the person "who makes founders cry" and promotes what he calls the "art of growing up." That involves radical self-inquiry, a process of a person confronting what they'd rather not see. Being a better human—in other words, growing up—is "hard because we're scared," he said. "Tony wrote a book on happiness," he said. "I wish he was aiming for contentment. . . . I am enough. I am enough just as I am."

Dr. Michael Freeman, a psychiatrist and clinical professor at the University of California, San Francisco, School of Medicine, noticed a pattern among the founders of smaller companies he interacted with in his career in Silicon Valley, which included his own entrepreneurial pursuits. Those company founders didn't sleep much. Some took imprudent risks and alienated their employees and colleagues, often blowing up their relationships. They had chosen a less stable professional life with long work hours and a high chance of failure. They were also often charismatic, bold, creative, and interesting to be around.

The links between artistic creativity—that of poets, musicians, and painters—and mental health had already been explored, including in the book *Touched with Fire: Manic-Depressive Illness and the Artistic Temperament* by the psychologist Kay Redfield Jamison. Dr. Freeman coauthored a study that continued the theme, and posed a similar question: "Are entrepreneurs touched with fire?"

What the researchers found surprised them. Nearly half of the study's entrepreneurs self-reported having at least one mental health condition, while one-third of people in a comparison group reported having a condition. Half of the entrepreneurs who reported having no mental health conditions said they had a close family member with one, compared to one-quarter of the nonentrepreneurs.

Across the United States, one in five people experiences a mental health condition each year. One in twenty experiences a serious mental illness such as schizophrenia or severe depression and bipolar disorder.

In Dr. Freeman's study, entrepreneurs were twice as likely to have depression, three times more likely to have a substance use disorder, six times as likely to have ADHD, and eleven times as likely to have bipolar disorder as were nonentrepreneurs.

In 2013, Aaron Swartz, a pioneer in online activism who created RSS when he was fourteen years old and cofounded Reddit, committed suicide at the age of twenty-six. He had written about depression in his blog. "I feel ashamed to have an illness," he wrote. "(It sounds absurd, but there still is an enormous stigma around being sick.) I don't want to use being ill as an excuse. (Although I sometimes wonder how much more productive I'd be if I wasn't so sick.)" He wasn't the only one; there was a rash of suicides among entrepreneurs at the time.

Dr. Freeman noted that many of the genetically inherited personality traits that are crucial for entrepreneurial success, such as risk and creativity, can overlap with mental health conditions like bipolar disorder and ADHD, when taken to the extreme or tested in stressful environments. Entrepreneurs, he said, "can be quite vulnerable."

Early June 2020, when Tony toured his new nine-bedroom mansion in Park City, should have been a hopeful time. The pandemic appeared to be winding down, with cities across the country tentatively reopening heading into the summer. Tony had been out of rehab and living in his new mountain town for more than three months. The plans for 10X seemed to be taking off. He was in the best shape of his life and had managed to stay off ketamine.

But lately it seemed as though he was losing his way again. Ali Bevilacqua, who was living in Los Angeles, had flown to visit him in Park City and had joined him and the rest of his friends for the tour of the new mansion, the Ranch. The two had broken up in 2014, in part because of Tony's alcoholism, and then gotten back together in 2018 for about a year. The last time Bevilacqua had seen Tony had been about six months prior at her own family's Christmas gathering in 2019, which he had attended in the past, even when they weren't dating. He had been acting strangely at the time, but she hadn't thought too much of it—there had been a lot of people there, and she was used to his awkwardness in groups where he didn't know many people. That was during the months he had been taking ketamine, but Bevilacqua said later that she hadn't known he was using drugs.

During her visit to Park City, though, Tony was not acting like himself. He told people that he had developed psychic abilities while living in Utah and could levitate. While Bevilacqua was there, he refused to eat or sleep and was paranoid and talking fast but not making much sense. He had taken a marker and scribbled over his entire body. On a boat ride with a group of people around nearby Deer Creek Reservoir, he sat huddled in a corner under a blanket. Bevilacqua had rifled through his things and found a vial of white powder: ketamine.

In a conference on the balcony of the Empire Avenue house—it was too soon to move into the Ranch, on the other side of Park City—Bevilacqua and Tony's other friends whispered about what they should do. Nobody knew, but everyone was worried. Bevilacqua eventually had to fly home.

Several weeks later, in late June 2020, Tony and his friends in Park City piled into Tony's main tour bus on their way to the unincorporated town of Bigfork, Montana, and the Flathead Lake Lodge, a family-owned, two-thousand-acre dude ranch. With sailing on Flathead Lake, one of the largest freshwater lakes in the West, horseback riding, and hiking, the lodge was a perfect getaway for the group, and Tony tried to go once a year for a week.

Tony's previous trips to Flathead Lake had been healthy and restorative, so his friends believed that taking him there would be a good opportunity to isolate him from some of his visitors, who were clearly supplying him with drugs. They thought the fresh air and change of scenery might help him.

The drive to Bigfork from Park City is almost seven hundred miles, winding through forests and mountain passes and through the state of Idaho. Steve Moroney, Tony's longtime driver, would be piloting. A group of friends joined them on the bus, including Justin Weniger and Tyler Williams. They planned to drive straight from Park City to Montana overnight, roughly nine hours or more, and stay at the dude ranch through the Fourth of July.

In a normal year, Bigfork is known for its Independence Day celebration, with myriad fireworks stands around town and a big parade winding through its main streets. Though the parade was canceled in 2020, Tony and his friends knew that the dude ranch organized its own private fireworks display on the lake. They could lie on their backs on the grass, watching the sky slowly get dark, the mountains in the distance, fireworks exploding in rainbows all around them.

CHAPTER SIX

A CREATIVE SOLUTION

Park City, June 2020
Las Vegas, 2013–2019

> *There is a difference between knowing the path and walking the path.*
>
> —Tony Hsieh, quoting *The Matrix*

In the darkened room where he was napping, Steve Moroney was shaken awake. Tony's longtime driver opened his eyes groggily to see his boss standing next to his bed, antsy.

It was late June 2020, and the crew had arrived in Montana only hours earlier to enjoy the Fourth of July there as a way to try to help Tony. After the long overnight drive from Park City, Moroney had been planning to take a substantial nap. What he hadn't known at the time, since he sat with headphones on in front of a curtain while driving so as not to be distracted, was that Tony had ingested a large number of psychedelic mushrooms while en route.

Tony had boarded the bus in Park City wearing only pajama pants. He had brought no luggage, except for a box of crayons. The tour bus was fifty-five feet long, and Tony had his own small room. He retreated there with the drugs that were somehow already on board.

As the group arrived in Montana in the morning, the mushrooms kicked in. Tony screamed to his friends, "Everybody get off the bus!"

and then began pacing up and down the aisles, shouting that there was an active shooter and crouching down between the seats to hide from the dangerous gunman. By that time Moroney had parked the bus at the Flathead Lake Lodge and gone to get a ride to his hotel nearby so he could sleep.

Tony's worried friends filed off the bus and decided to take turns going back in to check on him. Tony started to throw things around, trying to destroy the interior. The bus, which he had bought for about $2 million before he had moved to Park City, was one of his most prized possessions.

At one point, he shouted that his friends should join him in a suicide pact. Dying, he explained, was the best way to transcend human consciousness. He would burn the bus down, he told them, so they could all die together.

Of course he had no way to do it, but his friends were distraught. He was having a full-fledged breakdown, and he had never acted like this before. After several hours, he finally calmed down enough that he went to go find Moroney, leaving his friends at the lodge.

"Steve-O," Tony said. "I need you to wake up. I have a very important meeting, the most important of my career." Moroney sat up slowly as Tony relayed that they had to drive, right that minute, to go see Jeff Bezos, the founder and then chief executive officer of Amazon, for a meeting in Las Vegas. It was unclear why Bezos, who lives in Seattle, where Amazon is based, would be in Las Vegas, especially during the pandemic.

Tony apologized to Moroney. He was not usually demanding, and he cared deeply about his employees, particularly his longtime driver. The two had a special bond. He knew that Moroney needed sleep after the drive from Park City—but this was an urgent matter.

Moroney agreed to drive Tony the roughly fifteen hours it would take to get to Las Vegas, even though he had just driven all the way to Montana from Park City. He would end up driving more than 1,500 miles in two days. But first he went to look for a cup of coffee.

While Moroney got ready at his hotel near Flathead Lake Lodge, Tony disappeared. Soon after, in Los Angeles, Ali Bevilacqua, Tony's ex-girlfriend, answered a FaceTime call and saw on her screen that Tony was huddled alone. He was back on the tour bus. Right away she knew something was wrong. Tony spoke quickly again, saying that he was playing a game. He had texted several friends and offered to pay them handsomely if they could locate him.

"I'll give you a million dollars if you can find me," he told Bevilacqua, who had no interest in his money. It was clear that Tony was not himself.

Bevilacqua knew exactly where he was from an app that allowed them to share their locations, and she knew about his annual trip to Montana. She immediately called Tony's private travel agent and had him book her onto a private jet there.

It was hours after Tony had awakened Moroney when the driver finally started off with him. They left his friends, including Justin Weniger and Tyler Williams, who were aware of the change in plans, behind in Montana. Weniger would take a later flight back, while Williams and his wife stayed on for several more days. Instead of driving to Las Vegas, Tony directed Moroney to the nearest local airport, Kalispell, about half an hour away from the dude ranch.

There they picked up Bevilacqua, and they also picked up another friend who had "won" the $1 million reward for guessing Tony's location. And that friend had brought something for Tony: more drugs.

By 2019 in Las Vegas, Tony's drinking had increased enough that more of his close friends became concerned. He moved up evening bar meetups to the afternoon or even late morning. His face was puffy, and the whites of his eyes had turned a yellow hue. In 2016, he had gone through a stretch of working out and running, earning praise from his friends, but that period had ended. Now, at forty-five years old, he was hardly exercising and was not paying attention to what he ate.

The last five years had been challenging not only at Zappos but also at his downtown Las Vegas development project. Each problem represented a fissure, an accumulation of growing cracks in the fortress of happiness he had spent years building around himself and his friends and employees.

Tony had enticed roughly three hundred entrepreneurs to participate in the Downtown Project with investments from his commitment to spend $350 million, including a $50 million Vegas Tech Fund, $50 million on small businesses, and $50 million for arts and culture, health care, and education projects. His vision for Las Vegas was a continuation of what he had written about in *Delivering Happiness*: a new kind of Silicon Valley, one of joyfulness and community, that truly might help save the world. He wanted talented entrepreneurs who could fulfill that mission to relocate to the Nevada desert with him.

One of the first to move to Las Vegas was Jody Sherman, the cofounder and CEO of Ecomom, a website for healthy kids' products. Despite already having a network in Los Angeles, Sherman was attracted to Tony's vision for the area and Zappos' early success in online retailing. The Vegas Tech Fund was among the investors in Ecomom's $4 million fundraising round in late 2011, when Sherman relocated the company to Las Vegas. Much in alignment with Tony's beliefs, Sherman's vision for Ecomom included giving back. For Ecomom, that included an initiative to provide food to hungry children.

Just over a year later, in February 2013, Sherman died from a self-inflicted gunshot wound. He was forty-seven. It was revealed that the company had burned through millions of dollars from investors. The company management and board of directors, having uncovered the financial problems, shut Ecomom down.

"He was always very optimistic," Rob Skaggs, Sherman's brother-in-law, who worked for Ecomom in Las Vegas, said later. "There weren't signs that he was depressed or that he needed serious help that I could see."

The tech community mourned the beloved entrepreneur and called for a public mental health discussion on the pressures in startup life, including the high expectations to be—and appear—successful.

The following year, 2014, two other people associated with the Downtown Project in Las Vegas died by suicide. One was a young employee; the other was a barbershop owner with a store inside Container Park.

What leads a person to suicide is complex; the emotional pain that feels unbearable can have many sources, some unknowable from the outside. But the close-together deaths of those three men, who were closely attached to Tony and his Downtown Project, raised questions, most notably: If Tony's declared vision was one of happiness and community, how could those entrepreneurs have felt so alone?

The suicides were "a jarring moment of flesh-and-bone reality" for the downtown Las Vegas community, Vox wrote.

Meanwhile, questions emerged about how the Downtown Project was managing its investments. A high-profile win crumbled quickly in 2014. Jen McCabe, who led hardware investments for Tony's tech fund, had launched a manufacturing company, Factorli, in Las Vegas with a $10 million investment from the fund. Her company was even mentioned by President Barack Obama in a speech about the importance of American manufacturing to boosting job creation.

In an interview with Vox in 2014, McCabe described how she had been inspired by Tony. He had told her to spend three months doing nothing but writing down her startup ideas in a notebook. "I just trusted Tony," she said. "He looked at me seriously and unblinkingly, and when he laser-focuses in, when he speaks in that way, you absolutely know it'll work out."

Two months after Obama had mentioned McCabe, Factorli shut down. Downtown Project leaders, by some accounts, had simply lost interest in the company, and other businesses there were closing. One of the Downtown Project's successes, a robotics startup called Romotive, had decided to move away from Las Vegas to Silicon Valley.

Tony had picked up detractors: some Las Vegas residents bristled at the assumption that the city didn't have any arts and culture and that Tony Hsieh was going to swoop in and enlighten them. Others saw the redevelopment along East Fremont as an insular hipster-ville without consideration for the lower-income neighborhoods that had been there before Tony's arrival. The area was written up in Vegas tourism guides. But how many locals who weren't part of Tony's clique spent much time there? The facades of some of the shuttered businesses Tony had purchased were painted with brightly colored, funky murals even as the buildings remained unused.

Back in 2011, as Tony had been conceptualizing the Downtown Project, Brian "Paco" Álvarez, a Las Vegas native, cultural anthropologist, and well-known supporter of the local arts scene, had given Tony a tour of the small downtown arts district and its galleries. Two years later, Zappos had recruited Álvarez, convincing him to leave his government job as a curator of archives for the Las Vegas Convention and Visitors Authority, to manage art and goods for a Zappos gift shop, Z'Boutique, which sold company swag.

He wished that the city had been more critical of Tony's decision-making for the downtown area, rather than blindly offering support. "Do you need to invest $100,000 in a flower shop when there are ten other flower shops in the area?" he asked later. "Do you really need to invest in a donut shop that sells three- or four-dollar donuts with bacon on it in a neighborhood where the average income . . . is $32,000 a year?"

Phil Plastina, Tony's friend from the Dancetronauts who had also moved to Las Vegas, questioned him about that very aspect of his plans, telling Tony that he might have misjudged the kind of customers who would come to downtown Las Vegas and support the new companies. Plastina knew that some of the entrepreneurs were having trouble, and he could tell that they had no idea what they were doing. Some were blindly following Tony's vision.

"Listen, man," Plastina said to Tony one day in 2014. "There's something called 'demographic' that you're not paying attention to. These people that come here, they're from Middle America, they have NASCAR hats, and they drink. This is not the person that's going to buy glass art on a Friday night."

"This is an experiment," Tony explained.

"It's a pretty fucking expensive experiment," Plastina retorted. He did not care what Tony thought of him.

"Well, I have the money to see what happens here," Tony replied. That sort of thinking was common for Tony, who had always viewed money as a way to try new things, not as a status symbol.

In what seemed like a retreat, Downtown Project stopped using its much-touted "return on community" metric. In a firmly worded public statement, Tony reminded the public that his business venture was not a charity, nor could it solve all of Las Vegas's problems, writing:

> There are a lot of people that seem to expect us to address and solve every single problem that exists in a city (for example, homelessness, substance abuse, and mental health). . . .
>
> Downtown Project is a startup entrepreneurial venture that happens to also have good intentions. . . .
>
> We found that when we used the word 'Community,' there were a lot of groups that suddenly expected us to donate money to them or invest in them just because they lived in the community or because it was for a good cause.

The Downtown Project would shift away from a focus on "community" as a measure of success and instead turn to "Collisions, Co-Learning, and Connectedness," also known as "the 3 Cs." Tony had once again fit a real-world problem into a theoretical equation.

In September 2014, to cut costs, Downtown Project laid off thirty people to cut costs, about 10 percent of its employees, in what the *Las Vegas Weekly* called a "bloodletting." David Gould, a University of Iowa academic who had moved to Las Vegas and was Downtown Project's "director of imagination," declared in a public resignation letter written to Tony that the layoffs could be blamed on "a collage of decadence, greed, and missing leadership."

Throughout the turmoil and the scrutiny by the press, Tony remained coldly matter-of-fact. He seemed to be working to keep it all quiet or at least avoid it; Vox noted that there had been no large-scale supportive gatherings held or community resources established for the entrepreneurs in the wake of the suicides.

When the *Review-Journal* asked him about the shutdown of Factorli, once one of the Downtown Project's prized investments, Tony was clearly impatient with having to acknowledge what was going wrong. He wrote in response, uninterested in discussing a postmortem, even for an entrepreneur whom he had supposedly inspired, "I'm not on the board of Factorli and just like the vast majority of other investments, I'm not close enough to them to know the details."

Related to the deaths, he told Vox, "Suicides happen anywhere. Look at the stats. It's harder for people who are really good students in school. Then they move in to this, where there is no instruction manual, and you have to be MacGyver on your own."

Behind the scenes, Tony's close friends could tell that the problems at Downtown Project, especially the suicides, had affected him, but he just didn't know how to express it. He didn't want to talk about them in any depth.

At Zappos, he was dealing with another potential crisis. His leadership team was divided on whether holacracy was working or not. He faced particularly strong opposition from his chief operating officer, Arun Rajan. Rajan was focused on trying to run Zappos' bread-and-butter business, the e-commerce platform, and had little patience with Tony's management experiments or his happiness goals.

Holacracy had had some successes since Zappos had officially rolled it out in 2014, perhaps notably overcoming groupthink bias, the goal of allowing individual opinions to count. In one example, Zappos employees wanted to bring their dogs to work. Under the old management structure, Zappos' human resources director would have unilaterally made the decision and had declined several times in the past because she was allergic.

Holacracy didn't have a rule about dogs, so employees started bringing them in. Soon the employees who were opposed to dogs in the office brought up a "tension"—a holacracy term—to broker a peace deal. Through meetings guided by the new process, the employees agreed that the dogs could stay, as long as they used certain elevators and were approved beforehand.

Whether holacracy boosted Zappos' profits was less clear. Zappos' customer service department—the hallmark of Tony's "Delivering Happiness" mission—was suffering, with call center employees skipping out on shifts they didn't want and not enough resources being allocated to the team. Even as holacracy aimed to wipe out bureaucracy, meetings in each "circle" were overwhelmed by processes, with a long list of steps that a facilitator had to go through after someone brought up a "tension": an "amend and clarify round," an "objection round," "clarification of the tension and reactions," and finally the "closing round." The biggest problem for Zappos wasn't actually the meetings, though; it was the lack of accountability. If someone went against a policy, for example, it was often unclear whose job it was to reprimand or fire that person.

Even if Tony had wanted to (which he didn't), it would not have been easy for him to walk away from holacracy. Zappos had become the face of this new kind of management practice. Indeed, business leaders from around the world flocked to Las Vegas to learn about it.

The publishing platform Medium, one of the other high-profile companies to adopt the new system, had given it up by 2016, saying that it was "difficult to coordinate efforts at scale." Medium had also had trouble recruiting, which the company blamed in part on the public perception of holacracy, with media headlines such as "What Happened When This Major Company Got Rid of All Its Bosses" and "Here's How Zappos' Wacky Self-Management System Works."

On the hunt for a solution to solve the problems holacracy was creating, Tony read another book on company structure called *Organize for Complexity: How to Get Life Back into Work to Build the High-Performance Organization*, this time by an author who calls himself "an enemy of holacracy" but believes strongly in "decentralized decision making." Niels Pflaeging, a German management consultant, has staked his two-decade career on typical hierarchical structures at companies not working in today's complex market. In Pflaeging's decentralized approach to management, small teams of people, rather than a C-suite of executives, run the company, enabling true innovation to take place in smaller, less process-driven teams. But unlike holacracy's systems, with all of the meetings that Pflaeging, who counsels companies around the world, believes perpetuates command and control instead of overcoming it, his approach requires overhauling the company in favor of autonomous teams without the bureaucracy. "For an organization that wants to produce happiness, it's interesting Tony got hooked on such a technocratic, flawed thing," he said.

Hoping to make peace with his executives while also convincing them to stick with his management structure, Tony flew his leadership team to Berlin to meet with Pflaeging in late 2017, putting everyone up in suites at Das Stue, a five-star luxury hotel in the center of the city. He paid for the entire trip out of pocket, including every decadent meal, often ordered from the hotel. He encouraged his executives to bring their spouses, also paid for by him.

In return, Tony wanted his team to keep an open mind and read yet another book, a giant, complicated tome called *The Origin of Wealth: Evolution, Complexity, and the Radical Remaking of Economics*, by former McKinsey & Company consultant Eric Beinhocker. In many thousands of words, the book details the complications of markets and how companies need to be able to adapt.

Pflaeging found the whole visit slightly odd. He usually held workshops in conference rooms or offices; Tony's crew wanted him to come to their hotel suite. That was a normal practice for Tony; often at large events where he didn't know many people, he could stave off his social anxiety by renting a hotel suite and inviting groups there instead. At Das Stue, however, the suite had an open bathroom in the room where Pflaeging held his workshops, making it more awkward than usual.

In fact, in Pflaeging's view, Tony and his employees didn't seem to want to leave the hotel at all. Pflaeging recalled that at one point he had to convince them to go to another (nice) restaurant nearby. They ordered in Fernet. Pflaeging didn't like it. It was clear to him that at least some of the executives were frustrated with holacracy and trying to find a way out. "They wanted to move away from it silently," he noted.

Tony did ultimately change Zappos' approach to holacracy. He kept parts and added other features, most notably a term he invented, market-based dynamics (MBD), which he had already been working on before the Berlin trip. He had derived the concept from *The Origin of Wealth*.

Using market-based dynamics, each "circle"—at one point there were about five hundred at Zappos—ran like an autonomous small business, like a department in a typical company. The circles interacted with one another as they would with businesses outside of Zappos. Like small startups, they invested in their own projects and came up with their own budgets. At the same time, they were collectively responsible for delivering a profit for Amazon. For example, Zappos' IT department was its own circle and could charge for its goods and services if an employee needed a new laptop or help with software. But if someone within Zappos wanted to start an IT circle, he or she could do so, thus creating competition and accountability for the service. Tony wanted everything to be transparent, including each circle's budget. He also wanted to organize Zappos into a number of different "startups" to help drive innovation.

"If every circle by the end of 2020 increases revenue by 5% more than what it is now, without increasing expenses, that's $100 million to the bottom line for the company," he explained at a conference in 2019. "That's very doable for everyone."

Zappos was careful to note in an internal Q&A that "MBD is a layer we are building on top of Holacracy (not instead of Holacracy)."

Whether holacracy—or market-based dynamics—was a success by the start of the Covid-19 pandemic in 2020 depended on who at Zappos you talked to. In some circles, it worked smoothly, and the decentralized approach to management that Tony had sought had been achieved. Other circles, such as customer service, weren't using it at all. Market-based dynamics had been implemented at less than half of the company's units.

Some employees, particularly new hires, loved it. Others wished that Zappos had never changed at all.

Meanwhile, Amazon had started to exert more pressure on Tony and Zappos' executives.

By 2019, a decade had passed since Amazon had purchased Zappos, and its executives had been patient. As Jeff Bezos had promised, the company had largely left Zappos, and Tony, alone, a rare move that signaled his approval of Tony. Amazon had, in fact, learned from Zappos and its management experiments. At one point, Amazon executives had had preliminary discussions about integrating parts of holacracy into some of their other divisions. They seemed, on the whole, supportive. Still, Tony worried about what he and other Zappos executives referred to as "Amazon creep," the tech behemoth increasingly getting involved in Zappos' business. Tony wanted to protect his employees from Amazon's famously aggressive work culture and its layers of bureaucracy. Tony and his team were careful to call Amazon only if they really needed something. Sometimes even a simple question could turn into a conference call with half a dozen Amazon executives.

Tony reported to Jeff Wilke, then the head of Amazon's worldwide consumer business and one of Bezos's top lieutenants at the time. Wilke, then fifty-three, was widely seen as a successor to Bezos and the second most important person at Amazon. An email from him could be panic inducing—he dashed one off to his team anytime there was a shipping defect. He signed his emails with his initials, JAW.

The two, however, had a good relationship, and Wilke appreciated Tony as a business management visionary, often tolerating the antics he played in Zappos' internal reports to Amazon. Tony would sometimes try to avoid discussing dry business metrics by stuffing Zappos' updates with all the different management experiments the company was running.

Within the next two years, Wilke wanted Zappos to meet a series of business goals that had nothing to do with its culture or its management experiments. Rather, Tony would need to increase Zappos' profits and its customer base. It was a goal for all of Amazon's autonomous units; after a decade under the much larger conglomerate, Zappos should be meeting certain profit targets. It was now a "mature" company in Amazon's view, and it was falling short. Zappos was profitable, but it was hitting only about 30 percent of those targets and had no clear plan for improvement.

In typical fashion, Tony tried to think of ways he could meet the new business goals in a creative way, rather than just by selling more shoes. He started thinking about branching out into other business lines that could make Zappos more efficient and productive—basically saving money to make money.

He needed the next $1 billion idea.

To try to help boost his productivity, his solution was to hack sleep. In other words, he didn't sleep very much at all. He believed that rest should be measured by sleep cycles, not by hours, and he calculated that a person has five sleep cycles lasting about ninety minutes each in a seven-and-a-half-hour time period. As a workaround, he would sleep only six hours, or four and a half, representing four or three sleep cycles, at night and take a twenty-minute nap in the afternoon or evening, which he considered another sleep cycle.

"You're tired so you can go straight into REM sleep and kind of hack it that way," he told a blogger for the shared office space company WeWork in 2019. (The Centers for Disease Control and Prevention recommends that adults get at least seven hours of sleep a night.)

Tony purchased the Oura smart ring, popular in Silicon Valley, to "optimize" his sleep, allowing his concerned friends to access the data. They found that some nights he wasn't getting even four hours of sleep, more like two or three.

In 2019, worried about that trend and his increased alcohol use, some of his friends attempted to help him. Garrett Miller, a long-time Zappos employee and close friend, gave up alcohol himself in an effort to inspire Tony to do the same. Each night, he would try to get Tony to return to his Airstream trailer earlier than usual to encourage him to sleep. It was nearly impossible, though; Miller couldn't be around him all the time, and with Tony's entourage large and growing, he was always surrounded by people who wanted to meet him or musicians and movie stars passing through Las Vegas, as well as employees or friends out to party. At Zappos, Tony had long before integrated alcohol into the very fabric of the company, and there was no easy way to extricate himself. He had even built a bar called 1999, for the year Zappos was founded, near the lobby of the company's headquarters building, which also now housed a games arcade.

Tony's close circle of friends had shifted over the years, and stalwarts such as Alfred Lin, Fred Mossler, and Jenn Lim were no longer around as much. Mossler had left Zappos in 2016 to start his own high-end shoe company with his wife, Meghan, called Ross and Snow; they also had several investments around town, including the popular downtown Las Vegas eatery Nacho Daddy. Lin had left Zappos around the time *Delivering Happiness* had been published in 2010 to become a venture capitalist at Sequoia Capital in Silicon Valley, the banner firm that had long before funded LinkExchange. Even Phil Plastina, the head of the Dancetronauts, had stopped visiting the Airstream trailer park as much, as he was unfamiliar with the new, mostly younger group of Tony fans, a mix of Zappos employees and people Tony had met around Las Vegas.

Tony's longtime preoccupation with youth and surrounding himself with fun people had turned into something of an obsession. He began hanging out with a seventeen-year-old former waitress, Juliette Bajak, at the Airstream trailer park. Even though he explained to concerned friends that he was just mentoring her, it seemed like a strange friendship, even for Tony.*

Many of the people around Tony just assumed that it was normal for him to drink so much—hadn't he always? He tolerated alcohol well. He rarely appeared intoxicated and could have the same conversation at midnight that he had at 3:00 p.m. His energy and charisma also swept away most people's concerns.

Tony's fans latched onto his public persona, while his real self faded. In the last decade, he had become a sort of business god, known for his big ideas, eccentric lifestyle, and happiness mantra, and any character flaws weren't worth noting, or examining, by the people feeding off his wealth and energy. He was intensely idolized, and he was also beginning to believe in his own greatness.

At Cirque Lodge, the rehab facility that Tony briefly attended in early 2020, that sort of dichotomy is common. The team of therapists and pro-

---

* People familiar with Juliette Bajak said that she also viewed the relationship as platonic and Tony as her mentor.

gram leaders there are used to seeing clients such as business leaders, actors, social media influencers, and other public figures who work non-stop building companies or competing as high-profile athletes. The thought of slowing down feels like a threat. They are very smart, but they also have large egos. They rely on teams of friends or assistants to do everything for them; no one has ever told them no. When they have missed events or exhibited unusual behavior, their entourages have covered for them.

"They're insulated from a lot of the consequences that would hit the average person early" in an addiction cycle, said Aaron Olson, one of the therapists at Cirque Lodge. The rehab facility's high-powered clients, despite being surrounded by legions of employees and assis-tants, suffer from "an incredible loneliness," another Cirque Lodge therapist, Brian Tease, explained. "The public doesn't understand the shame, and this loneliness, that they have. In the end, what they really want is to be connected."

High-profile clients also face another hurdle to treatment, because they don't want to let down dozens of people who are dependent on them, whether those people are employees of a company, bandmates of a musician about to go on tour, or teammates of a professional athlete. Then there's another, more troubling and amorphous, layer around them. "You get a lot of people riding on coattails," Keith Fier-man, Cirque Lodge's intervention specialist, pointed out. Fierman keeps a Civil War–era ball and chain in his office at Cirque Lodge to symbolize alcoholism and addiction.

When Richard Losee, Cirque Lodge's founder, first decided more than twenty years ago to transition his new wellness facility into a rehab clinic, he'd had no formal psychological training. One of the questions he had thought about the most in those first few years was: When is someone an addict? There seemed to be no definitive answer, and it's one that society continues to struggle with, particularly when it comes to so-called functional alcoholics, a term some of Tony's friends used to describe him.

In her book, *Understanding the High-Functioning Alcoholic: Pro-fessional Views and Personal Insights*, the therapist Sarah Allen Benton cited research estimating that the majority of people struggling with alcohol abuse are actually high functioning.

Today, the National Institute on Alcohol Abuse and Alcoholism and other organizations don't even use the terms *high-functioning alcoholic* and *alcoholic* at all. The broad category is instead called *alcohol use disorder* (AUD), and patients are given a mild, moderate, or severe diagnosis based on a list of eleven symptoms, not on how much they are actually drinking. For example, its website asks whether you have "had times when you ended up drinking more, or longer, than you intended" or "spent a lot of time drinking." Answering yes to just two of the eleven questions means a person has a mild form of AUD.

Many people who abuse alcohol are what society might consider "functional," but they are privately, and quietly, ruining various areas of their lives. "How do we know they're 'functional'?" pondered Dr. George Koob, the director of the NIAAA. "They may be functional in the sense that they go to work every day, but are they making other wise decisions?"

The therapists at Cirque Lodge say that their clients often don't exhibit the classic signs of addiction touted in pop culture. Some haven't even been in trouble, never having received warnings for public endangerment or driving under the influence. Instead, in family pictures, it's often the addict who looks the healthiest. Everyone around him or her, meanwhile, suffers from the fallout of the loved one's disease. One therapist at Cirque Lodge, Francine Miller, said that her father had died of alcoholism when she was only seventeen. He had never missed a day of work in his life.

Cirque Lodge founder Richard Losee, who received his drug and rehabilitation certificate from the University of Utah, said he had found his best answer to the question of what constitutes an addict from one of his mentors in the field, who told him about a simple gauge: the addict doesn't know how or when he or she is going to stop. Other specialists say a person is an addict if his or her life has become unmanageable. (NIAAA's Alcohol Use Disorder spectrum questions are aimed at sussing out both these descriptions.)

One thing specialists seem to agree on is that every kind of alcohol or drug abuse is self-medication. As Fierman put it, it is covering up a larger problem that often hasn't been diagnosed. "You're uncomfortable in your own skin," he said.

In the latter half of 2019, Tony made a surprising proclamation to some of his friends. He had been looking for alternatives to alcohol and the medications he had been taking—Adderall and Xanax—to help his social anxiety and depression. He thought he had found a solution: he would cut back on drinking and ingest psychedelic mushrooms and ketamine instead.

Tony had recently tried ketamine at Burning Man with Tyler Williams, who was always game to experiment with his good friend, and he had enjoyed the intense feeling of happiness and spirituality that came with it. Ketamine, typically used by veterinarians on animals or during medical procedures, can cause mental detachment, almost as though a person is outside his or her own body, staring down. It can spark silliness. It can dull pain. Mushrooms are similar and can spark euphoria and happiness. But both ketamine and mushrooms can also cause panic and hallucinations, particularly if taken in large amounts or over a long duration of time.

The friends who knew how much of a problem alcohol had become for Tony were confused by his decision. He still took ecstasy on weekends sometimes and had done so at Burning Man, but otherwise he was not a habitual drug user. They were also relieved, though. Maybe he would really give up drinking, and his health would improve.

In late 2019, as proof that he was moving in the right direction, Tony showed some of his friends a TED Talk by Dr. Rick Doblin, the cofounder and executive director of the Multidisciplinary Association for Psychedelic Studies (MAPS). Dr. Doblin has crusaded against the criminalization of LSD and ecstasy by the US government almost since he was eighteen and experimenting with the drugs himself. He is well known in the field of psychedelics.

Early in his career, Dr. Doblin found that MDMA, otherwise known as ecstasy, in conjunction with intensive therapy, can be used to treat post-traumatic stress disorder in war veterans and survivors of sexual assault, and he spent more than three decades gathering enough testing data to prove his controversial point.

In April 2019 in Vancouver, Dr. Doblin, in the midst of his third phase of clinical trials, spoke about the promising results not only for sufferers of post-traumatic stress disorder but also social anxiety, substance abuse, and alcoholism. "Psychedelics are really just tools, and whether their outcomes are beneficial or harmful depends on how they're used," he told an audience that was clearly engaged and receptive, laughing at his occasional joke (LSD "let me have a spiritual connection that unfortunately my Bar Mitzvah did not produce") and clapping eagerly after he relayed his success in clinical trials.

What Dr. Doblin made clear in his TED Talk, however, is that psychedelics should be administered in a clinical setting as part of treatment that includes therapy with professionals. He also made another important distinction that Tony failed to convey to his friends. Rather than encouraging "microdosing," the en vogue practice, especially among the tech community, of consuming small amounts of drugs regularly, Dr. Doblin advised just the opposite: in his opinion, patients would benefit the most from taking several large "macro" doses of LSD or MDMA in a formal treatment setting with the oversight of a medical professional. Then they would stop using the drugs completely afterward. He believes that his approach addresses the root causes of a patient's problem, while microdosing is usually used more for inspiration.

"We'd rather not get people thinking they need a daily drug," he said in a question-and-answer session following his TED Talk. Indeed, ketamine is the most addictive of the psychedelic drugs, he said later. If you take it without therapy, you just keep needing more and more of it. When it wears off, it can be disorienting. When a user takes too much of the drug, "they can get this sense they're in touch with higher spiritual realms" and don't spend time coming out of that state, he said.

Tony was already using ketamine when he invited Dr. Doblin to Las Vegas in September 2019, but he had a lot of questions for the doctor about its use and how it could help him access different areas of the brain. He began talking to Dr. Doblin and his team about his making a large donation to MAPS (which never came through).

Dr. Doblin observed that Tony was constantly surrounded by a large group of people but also very shy. "It seemed like he was covering it up by always having people there," he said.

Several months passed, and then Tony again reached out, this time in February 2020, on the cusp of the pandemic. His mannerisms had changed. He seemed desperate, almost manic, Dr. Doblin thought. Tony told Dr. Doblin that he needed his help. He wanted him to create a study that he could participate in, in which ketamine could be taken legally to spark creativity. It would be a new use for the drug. He believed that it was helping him come up with new ideas, but his friends were worried because he was taking so much, Dr. Doblin recalled.

Dr. Doblin knew right away that what Tony was suggesting wouldn't work. He explained that it would take months to organize a study, and testing would be a massive barrier. How do you define "creativity," for example? He reminded Tony about the decades he had spent trying to create his own drug and therapy regime, which was still not available for use. He explained to Tony the myriad government agencies that regulated drug studies, including the Food and Drug Administration and the Drug Enforcement Administration.

Dr. Doblin believed that Tony had gained genuine insights from ketamine that were helpful, but he was obviously taking too much. During that call, he said, Tony was "trying to find a way to justify what he was doing."

By that time, February 2020, it had become clear to Tony's friends that his drug use was worse than his alcohol use. Tony told people that he was in a simulation created by artificial intelligence, as in *The Matrix*. By taking ketamine, he said, he could defeat the simulation to save humanity.

Tony believed that ketamine could make him grow taller or change his body into different shapes. At a wedding he officiated at in early February 2020, he twisted his body into yoga poses as if to prove his point.

Soon afterward, he went to Cirque Lodge in Park City for his short stint in rehab, never returning to Las Vegas, his home of nearly two decades.

In late June 2020, more than four months after his stay at Cirque Lodge, he arrived back in Park City in a limo with Ali Bevilacqua. The trip to Montana had been planned for a week; Tony had been there less than twenty-four hours. There had been no important meeting with Jeff Bezos. It seemed that Tony had made it up just to get Moroney to drive him to the Kalispell airport, part of his breakdown.

Moroney had picked up Bevilacqua and another of Tony's Las Vegas friends, at the Montana airport. Many of Tony's close friends knew by that point that the friend was Tony's ketamine supplier, and they had sought to keep him away from Tony. Moroney, however, may not have been aware until that night. On the drive back to Park City, they stopped for dinner at yet another person's place in Salt Lake City. At the house, there was a giant container of pills: crushed-up psilocybin, or psychedelic mushrooms.

Tony, only just coming off his trip from the large quantity of mushrooms he took on the way to Montana, grabbed a handful of the pills—about twenty capsules. There were so many in his hand that Bevilacqua was mostly joking when she asked, "You're not going to take all those, are you?"

Tony turned to her. He had never in his life been an angry person, only in a rare argument with a close friend, and until recently, he had almost never showed frustration, either. It was as if the drugs or his worsening mental health were exacerbating his worst traits. "Don't you ever tell me what to do, or I'll never take you anywhere again," he told Bevilacqua. He shoved the pills into his mouth and swallowed them all. A normal dose might have been one or two capsules.

Moroney had already left Salt Lake City to once again try to get some sleep, this time back at his hotel in Park City. So Bevilacqua and Tony rode alone the half hour back to Tony's wood-frame house on Empire Avenue in Park City in a hired limousine. As they drove, the effect of the large dosage of pills was beginning to take hold, and Tony talked nonstop, as if words couldn't pour out of him fast enough. He was no longer the quiet observer. Bevilacqua, beginning to panic about the situation, couldn't interrupt his stream-of-consciousness ramblings.

When they arrived back at the house close to midnight, the only person there was Juliette Bajak, who had moved to Park City to work as Tony's personal assistant. Bajak was older now, but she was the seventeen-year-old Tony had befriended in Las Vegas, and Bevilacqua knew her through him. Tony, clearly out of it, started to scream, and Bajak and Bevilacqua retreated to Bajak's room. They didn't sleep.

Tony's manic behavior progressed rapidly. Soon Bevilacqua and Bajak could hear him throwing furniture, dishes, and glassware around the house in a full-blown breakdown. Frantically, Bevilacqua tried calling and texting Justin Weniger and Suzie Baleson, but it was the middle of the night, and it was unclear if Weniger had yet made it back to Park City from Montana. Neither answered.

Bevilacqua finally called Moroney, waking him up at his nearby hotel. "If we try to leave, he's going to hurt us," she said urgently into the phone. In the bedroom, with the door locked, Bevilacqua and Bajak were trapped, with a man they didn't recognize, their beloved Tony, destroying the house around them. Moroney and another driver went to the house to try to help, but there was little they could do. Tony was in a state no one had seen him in before.

Finally, early in the morning of June 30, Weniger and Baleson arrived at the Empire Avenue house to help run interference with another friend. While Tony was preoccupied on the second-floor balcony, Bevilacqua and Bajak emerged from the bedroom and quickly ran toward the front door. As they hurried through the house, they saw the damage—furniture knocked over, massive dents and breaks in the walls. It seemed impossible that one person could have done it all.

Tony had recently started taking cold showers instead of baths, believing that each shower shaved off one hour of sleep he needed. He had left his cold shower running all night, and the stairs had turned into a gushing waterfall that was nearly impossible to traverse. They made it outside and scampered through several yards to reach the street, and another friend took them to a hotel. Bevilacqua flew straight back to Los Angeles.

Someone had called the police and told a dispatcher that Tony was "threatening to hurt himself," according to a later report from the Summit County Sheriff's Office. Five police officers and a fire truck responded to the scene. They found Tony on the patio of the house and were able to convince him to get into a waiting ambulance.

Several of Tony's friends, including Suzie Baleson, talked to the officers. It was morning now, around 8:00 a.m. At that point, the friends weren't concerned just about Tony's health but about his reputation. What if the media found out about it? It would be a disaster not just for him but for Zappos, Amazon, and Las Vegas. Tony's friends helped persuade police officers to take Tony to the hospital rather than arrest him.

That move ended up being a point of contention among some of Tony's friends who believed that an arrest might have provided a much-needed wake-up call. At the very least, Tony should have been shown the destruction he had caused in broad daylight, in case he didn't remember. Instead, the house was cleaned, and soon afterward Tony moved to his new mansion, the Ranch.

Later that night, hours after Tony had been taken to the hospital on June 30, Weniger called the police again, hoping that an officer could at least help keep Tony at the hospital. If he is released, Weniger told the dispatcher, "it will be a problem."

Tony left the hospital soon after.

CHAPTER SEVEN

THE FAMILY BUSINESS

Park City, July 2020
Marin County, California, 1970–1990

*People may not remember exactly what you did or what you said, but they
always remember how you made them feel. That's what matters most.*

—Tony Hsieh, quoting Maya Angelou

"Local Boy Has Got What It Takes!" read a December 1987 headline in the *San Rafael News*, a local newspaper for the Marin County bedroom community.

A grainy black-and-white photo featured a young Tony standing alone outside a post office, with bangs on his forehead and a poised smile, selling his latest business product. A ninth grader at the time, he had dozens of homemade graphic buttons for sale, pinned to boards for showing passersby.

Tony had launched a business with a $100 loan from his parents, Richard and Judy Hsieh, for a button-making machine. Kids mailed him photos to be turned into pins, and Tony mailed them back, for $1 each. Customers found him through a listing in a marketing book, *Free Stuff for Kids*.

What caught the local reporter's attention, though, wasn't the fact that Tony had racked up mail-order customers; it was that he was giving the profits to charity and wanted to contribute to a holiday party for his mother's patients at a dialysis clinic in one of her earlier work-places. He ended up raising $50. In the article, Judy Hsieh told the reporter that she wasn't sure what Tony would grow up to be. "But whatever it is," she said, "he can do it."

Richard and Judy Hsieh were exacting parents who wanted Tony and his two younger brothers to excel. The Hsiehs had left Taiwan and enrolled in a US university in the late 1960s, a decade when thousands of people arrived in the United States newly eligible under the historic Immigration and Naturalization Act. Before the 1965 law, the immigration system used country-of-origin quotas that banned or severely limited arrivals from Asian countries. In the early 1960s, less than 1 percent of the US population was Asian (compared to about 7 percent today).

Then President Lyndon B. Johnson, in a ceremony at the Statue of Liberty, signed into law a new policy eliminating the quota system. It set a cap of 290,000 annual visas, 120,000 for the Western Hemisphere and 170,000 for the Eastern. The new system had preferences for reuniting families and bringing educated, skilled immigrants to the United States.

With the door now open to Asians, students from Taiwan, including Richard and Judy, enrolled in graduate programs in the United States in search of better opportunities and an escape from oppression in their homeland, which was under martial law. The Hsiehs arrived at the University of Illinois at Urbana-Champaign during the height of Vietnam War–era political activism, including a nine-thousand-person demonstration at the university in 1969. Among the many groups being formed, Taiwanese students created the Taiwan Study Group to discuss the culture of the country on campus.

Richard, a tall, slender, gregarious man with a wide smile, graduated with a doctoral degree in chemical engineering. That December, Richard and Judy had their first child, a son named Anthony, whom they called Tony. Judy, more reserved than her husband, with long hair and a petite frame, graduated from Illinois with a master's degree in social work. She would later earn a doctorate in clinical psychology at California School of Professional Psychology Berkeley/Alameda in San Francisco.

Richard accepted a position at Chevron in the San Francisco Bay Area, decades before Silicon Valley's rise would make Marin County a sun-dappled playground for the rich and nearly inaccessible to the middle class.

The Hsiehs lived in a two-story, 1960s-style house halfway up a steep hill in the San Rafael community of Lucas Valley, then a working-class neighborhood filled with families. The community was tight-knit, and the dozens of kids living there had free range of the streets and the dirt trails that wound into the nearby hills.

Richard and Judy and their sons were known by the neighbors for their kindness. Though they kept to themselves somewhat, Richard always stopped to speak with anyone on the street and knew everyone's name. They hired a local babysitter, a teenager across the street. "They were so superfriendly," recalled Gloria Lightner, one of the neighbors, who still lives next door to the Hsieh's old house.

Lightner knew that Tony and his younger brothers, Andy and Dave, would receive a world-class education when they were older, because anytime she ran into Richard Hsieh, he would pepper Lightner with questions about the quality of the local high school, Terra Linda. Lightner had kids just a few years older than the Hsieh boys.

Later, when Tony sold LinkExchange to Microsoft in 1998, the whole neighborhood celebrated.

In *Delivering Happiness*, Tony called Richard and Judy "your typical Asian American parents" who, along with other Asian parents in the community, had high expectations for their three children. That included getting into a prestigious college, preferably Harvard; in adulthood, being called "doctor," whether through medical school or a PhD program; and learning to play musical instruments.

The Hsiehs socialized with other Asian families in Marin County at potlucks, where parents would brag about their kids. "That was just part of the Asian culture: The accomplishments of the children were the trophies that many parents defined their own success and status by," Tony wrote in *Delivering Happiness*. "We were the ultimate scorecard."

In middle school, Tony studied piano, violin, trumpet, and French horn and was expected to practice each for thirty minutes every weekday and one hour per day on weekends. To cut back on that rigorous schedule, he sometimes played tape recordings of himself practicing early in the morning, so his parents would think he was practicing while in fact he was still in bed.

"I always fantasized about making money because to me, money meant that later on in life I would have the freedom to do whatever I wanted," he wrote in *Delivering Happiness*. "The idea of one day running my own company also meant that I could be creative and eventually live life on my own terms."

Richard and Judy decided against sending the boys to Terra Linda and instead enrolled them at the Branson School, a renowned private college prep school for families living in the wealthy enclaves north of the Golden Gate Bridge. The wooded campus in the small community of Ross was a twenty-minute drive south on Highway 101 from Tony's house. Though the campus, with its manicured lawns and pale yellow buildings, isn't immediately impressive, it sits at the base of Mount Tamalpais, part of Marin County's lush nature preserves filled with redwoods and headlands overlooking the Pacific Ocean. Today, Branson charges students $52,800 a year.

Tony, who spoke Mandarin Chinese at home, studied Japanese, Spanish, French, Latin, fencing, jazz piano, and drawing, and he also joined the chess club and electronics club. He ran the light board at theater productions, turning that into a paying job operating a spotlight at a community theater. He got another paying gig at $6 an hour, testing video games such as *Indiana Jones* and *Maniac Mansion* for Lucasfilm, part of *Star Wars* creator George Lucas's media empire. Lucas's Skywalker Ranch property was just a fifteen-minute drive from the Hsiehs' home.

Despite his rigorous schoolwork, Tony was often silly, performing magic tricks, writing a Shakespearean sonnet in Morse code for a class assignment, and using the computer lab's dial-up system to call paid hotlines. He also launched small businesses, with varying degrees of success: an earthworm farm, which failed when the worms escaped into the yard (the Delivering Happiness bus visited a worm farm in honor of the childhood venture), manufacturing and selling a magic tricks kit, and his early button business, which received hundreds of mail orders a month, an early prototype of online retail.

All of those adventures became part of Tony's hero's journey. But underneath the quirky anecdotes, the pressure his parents imposed on him to achieve brought disappointment and loneliness. His childhood was not filled with much fun or freedom. He told some friends that his first memory was of learning how to swim as a three-year-old by jumping off a high dive at a local pool, which must have been a terrifying experience for such a young child. He missed his last dance in eighth grade because he was taking the SAT the next morning, years before students typically do in high school as a requirement for applying to college. The loss stayed with him many years later. In his senior yearbook, most of the graduating students had a personal page filled with photos and shout-outs to friends and family; Tony's was only a white page with doodles and random musings in black ink.

When the *New York Times* asked him for one of his childhood highlights, Tony recounted a seemingly inconsequential moment when some trick-or-treaters had shown up at his house on Halloween.

Later in life, many of Tony's friends believed that his childlike perspective and his obsession with parties and having fun were the results of missing out on so much while he was growing up. He pursued money early in life for the freedom it could bring him. It also had a side benefit: though he might not have become a doctor or a lawyer, no one—including his parents—could deny he'd achieved something big. And after becoming wealthy, he gave much of his fortune away, invested in the dreams of others and even an entire city, for the freedom he thought it could bestow on others.

What deeper emotional impact his upbringing might have had remained one of his secrets. Asian Americans are less likely than white people to use available mental health services, according to studies, even though they must often deal with high cultural expectations for academic success and careers and for fulfilling family obligations. The pressure of the myth of the "model minority"—the harmful stereotype of Asian Americans as a monolithic group with the same experiences who are all "nice," rule followers, and highly successful—can also take a toll on mental health.

As an adult, Tony alternated between ignoring his Asian American heritage and making fun of it, sometimes awkwardly. He called Fernet his "Chinese medicine," and referred to the bus that took him and friends on trips as "the Orient Express."

At one Zappos all-hands meeting, held at the Kà Theatre at the MGM Grand in Las Vegas, Tony stood onstage as the lights dimmed and pop music filled the cavernous room, which is typically used for Cirque du Soleil shows. Richard Hsieh came onstage in a full-body monkey suit. "It's the Chinese Year of the Monkey!" Tony yelled. Richard was helping Tony announce the grand opening of Zappos' office in China, and the Chinese New Year had taken place the previous week. (Other Zappos executives also wore monkey costumes.)

People who didn't know Tony well assumed that he was close with his parents, who sometimes took starring roles in his life. His mother, Judy, despite being educated in social work and psychology, managed a pan-Asian restaurant, Venture Frogs, that Tony opened in the Don Lee building on Van Ness Avenue in San Francisco after the 1998 sale of LinkExchange. The restaurant served noodles and dumplings with Silicon Valley references in the dish names, such as Palm Pad Thai and Founders' Ahi Tuna.

After Tony moved to Las Vegas, his parents would visit from their home in Silicon Valley, often speaking Mandarin Chinese with their son. They attended Zappos parties, and even Judy, who is more reserved than Richard, would dance and gamely wear disco clothing. Richard, who is more outgoing, often made jokes and texted separately with Tony's friends as a way of keeping up with his son.

Tony felt loyal to his family, but he did not frequently confide in them. He also truly trusted only a select group of Las Vegas friends, even though he had dozens of people around him. His family continued to have a hold on him deep into adulthood, even though they didn't play an outsized role in his daily life. He worried about making a good impression when they visited. Each year, the Hsieh family typically traveled to Mexico or Hawaii for Thanksgiving. During the trip,

Judy Hsieh would schedule an hour of beach time for herself with each of her sons individually, a move that Tony later told a friend was "very awkward." Even with his parents far away in the Bay Area when Tony was an adult, he worried that his mother would somehow find out that he smoked, a habit he knew she hated.

By the time he was in his thirties, Tony had realized that the typical American family setup was not going to work for him. As backup for his distaste for marriage, he liked to repeat the popular assumption: that 50 percent of marriages end in divorce. "I'm not opposed to the idea of marriage," he told the *New York Times* in 2012 when it interviewed him for its "Dating Profiles of High-Tech, High-Worth Bachelors" feature. "But statistically, if half of all marriages end in divorce, and of the ones that remain married many are unhappily married, the odds are stacked against you."

Tony did want to have deep, meaningful relationships; he just chose the option of having multiple connections simultaneously. The closest description of this is polyamory: having loving, intentional relationships with multiple people at the same time. The practice has become more mainstream in the last several years; Willow Smith, the daughter of Will Smith and Jada Pinkett Smith, for example, recently said she is polyamorous. "I think it's pretty hard to find one partner and call it a day," Tony told *Playboy*. "Using the analogy of friends, why not find just one friend and call it a day? The answer is because you get a different type of connection, different conversations, different experiences with different friends. I would say the same thing is true on the dating side."

Tony's long-term relationships didn't always overlap, and typically only one of his relationships at a time was serious. He often kept an ex-girlfriend tightly in his orbit long after a breakup. He had distinct levels of friendships, which he kept track of almost like a CEO evaluating an org chart (although he hated org charts): some good friends might not be long-term lovers but were snuggle buddies with no sex involved. Like the businessperson he was, Tony negotiated the terms of a relationship with a prospective partner in advance, making sure that whatever level the two would operate on, both parties agreed to beforehand.

Of course, some partners bristled at the arrangement—some women wanted more than Tony would give; committed girlfriends found it hard to watch him flirt with other women. Tony's magnetic joy, though, meant that most people accepted the deal, just to be near him.

By the summer of 2019, however, his pursuit of multiple relationships seemed to be isolating him. He was then forty-five, and many of his friends were married with children or at least had stable partners, and they couldn't keep up with his round-the-clock gatherings, often with new groups of younger friends. He had fallen out of touch with some longtime friends, including Nick Swinmurn, who had given Tony the idea of Zappos two decades earlier. The last time Swinmurn had seen Tony was in 2019, and Tony had asked him to rate his own happiness—a question he asked Swinmurn and other friends occasionally over the years. Tony seemed confused when Swinmurn answered that he was happy. Tony said that the majority of married people he had surveyed weren't happy. "He told me that his friends kept getting younger and younger," Swinmurn later wrote. "He seemed excited about this."

Possibly as an attempt to keep up with his friends, Tony began talking about having a child of his own, even offering to act as a "surrogate father" to one of his ex-girlfriends' children. But when it came time to watch the child on a trip to Hawaii, he let other friends take on most of the responsibility. In 2019, he embarked on a relationship, one of his last, with a married Zappos employee whom he fell for deeply. But the executive ultimately broke up with him, deciding instead to focus on her husband and children. She would later, however, help Doherty get Tony to rehab in Utah by flying to Park City with him.

Despondent over their breakup, Tony later in the fall of 2019 showed up at Ali Bevilacqua's house in Pasadena and told her that if she wanted to get back together for the long term, he would like that. She told him she would think about it.

After his psychotic break in Montana in late June 2020, Tony discovered that Tyler Williams, his longtime friend, had secretly been texting his drug supplier, begging him not to deliver more ketamine or mushrooms to Tony. Williams had even offered half of everything he owned in return for the supplier to stop.

When Tony discovered the text messages, he flew into a rage. He yelled at Williams and then told him he was not welcome back in Park City. It was the very thing that all of Tony's friends feared the most, and now it had happened to arguably the person with whom Tony was the closest. Everyone else around Tony witnessed his outburst or they heard about it later, and they knew that Williams had been banished. It was a warning shot.

While he was still in Montana, Williams called Richard Hsieh. Williams told him about the bus episode, explaining that Tony clearly needed help. Soon after, Tony trashed the Empire Avenue house, trapping Bevilacqua and Juliette Bajak inside. Tony's parents learned of that incident as well from another friend who called after it happened.

Tony's parents, now in their seventies, hadn't seen him since February 2020, when they had begun quarantining in the Bay Area due to the Covid-19 pandemic. California, among the states with the strictest Covid precautions, had advised travelers against leaving the state. But the Hsiehs, who were very concerned after Williams's call and the house incident, had to act.

In early July, they flew to Park City, along with Tony's younger brothers, Andy and Dave, to see the situation for themselves. Tony had calmed down somewhat from his breakdown a week earlier but was still not himself. He again had friends flying into Park City, but there was no mention of the June incidents by anyone around him. His closest gatekeepers, Suzie Baleson and Justin Weniger, didn't say anything to the visitors. Baleson was starting to plan a big 10X party for later that month.

The closest Tony came to acknowledging that anything was amiss after being released from the hospital was when he told one guest, angrily, that a rumor was going around that he was taking too much ketamine. He felt deeply betrayed, particularly after discovering Williams's texts. Tony couldn't see that his friends were trying to help him. Instead, he seemed to suddenly feel resentful of his decades of generosity. He had given everything he had to his friends, and now he felt that they were all turning against him.

The visitors in early July 2020 also didn't notice a big difference in Tony's behavior. Though he seemed a little on edge, his mood didn't seem out of the ordinary. But Richard and Judy Hsieh noticed. First of all, they saw that Tony had lost a significant amount of weight since February. He was acting slightly unhinged, climbing stairway railings to take photos and walking around barefoot. He chain-smoked constantly, even though he knew his mom didn't like it. Normally he would never have smoked in front of his parents.

One day, Tony announced to his parents and brothers that he was forming a new family business, one that would aim to improve their relationships with one another. The nature of the business was unclear. One of his brothers would be chief executive officer; the other would be chief operating officer.

At a private meeting, Tony asked his family to come up with ideas for how to raise a lot of money in three weeks. To save your son's life, he said. He left the room while everyone else worked on the assignment. The others waited several hours for Tony to return, but he never reappeared.

A couple of days later, Tony asked his mom a question: Did she want to be his friend or his family member? If she chose to be a nonjudgmental friend, he'd be open about his life. If she picked family, he would keep some secrets. Judy Hsieh, a trained psychologist, told her son she would be his friend, and in return, he told her about his drug use. She asked him to get professional help. Tony promptly turned the request into a negotiation, just as he had when Doherty had wanted him to go to rehab earlier in 2020. For every minute he went to therapy, Tony told his mom, she would have to agree to be immersed in an ice bath in exchange. It was clearly an impossible demand.

The next day, Judy Hsieh tried again. She pointed out to Tony his problems with memory and attention, a direct confrontation that sparked uncharacteristic anger in Tony. He told her that she wasn't his friend anymore and that the family was wasting its time. Then he stormed out of the house.

The episode divided the Hsieh family. Tony cut off his parents, telling his friends and assistants not to respond to them. The Hsiehs tried anyway. They asked for the people in his group to schedule regular Face-Time meetings with their son. Tony's assistants refused to respond. Dave Hsieh, the youngest brother, also went back home to Las Vegas. Dave Hsieh abhorred wealth and money and lived humbly with his girlfriend, preferring to stay out of Tony's and Andy's business plans over the years.

Andy Hsieh, however, returned to Park City ten days later, ostensibly to watch over Tony for the family. Tony agreed to pay Andy $1 million to stay.

Unlike Tony, Andy, who was younger by three years, had struggled since college to make a name for himself, always living in the shadow of his older brother's astounding success. He'd gotten bachelor's and master's degrees in industrial engineering from Stanford and then worked for a couple years as a consultant at McKenna, which appears to be a specialty food marketing company in San Francisco.

Soon after, he had left to take a general role at Zappos and moved with the company to Las Vegas. His LinkedIn profile still says he is a director there, nineteen years after joining in 2002. But he actually left the company more than a decade ago under circumstances that have never been established. There's suspicion that there was tension between the brothers at Zappos. The reason for his departure seems to have been kept a closely guarded secret.

Andy Hsieh tried his hand at launching his own startup, called Lux Delux, in 2011. It started off as an invitation-only membership platform, connecting the wealthy to high-end properties and clubs around the world, said David Louie, his former business partner, who is now a home mortgage consultant at Wells Fargo. Louie wasn't exactly sure who was funding the business but said that the whole Hsieh family seemed to be involved in some capacity, although he met Tony only briefly. The family flew him first class to London and other work locations on a private jet, an experience that Louie hadn't had before. "It was just the craziest being connected to them," he recalled. "They are such a smart family."

Lux Delux, however, was hard to scale, and Louie sensed that Andy Hsieh and his family wanted a change in direction. So in 2013, Lux Delux abruptly transitioned its business model to food delivery. Andy Hsieh and Louie created an app that let users order meals from their phone, hoping to capitalize on the wave of similar apps such as Seamless and Grubhub, which were gaining traction across the country.

Andy Hsieh and Louie focused Lux Delux in an area the Hsieh family knew well because of Tony: Las Vegas. Louie commuted back and forth from his family's home in San Francisco, all expenses paid. He and Andy Hsieh planned to entice restaurants around Las Vegas by promising them increased sales by allowing users to order their meals on the app with free delivery. (Lux Delux would take a percentage of a business's sales.) Ultimately they hoped to sign up many of the 150 restaurants then in downtown Las Vegas.

But Andy Hsieh couldn't get Lux Delux as a food app to take off, either. Louie eventually got tired of commuting from San Francisco and wanted to spend more time with his two children. He said that when he left around 2016, the business was still operational, and he doesn't know what happened after that. By 2017, though, it appeared to have been wound down. Louie's impression of Andy Hsieh was only positive: "supernice, superloyal, superhardworking," he said. "Just really good people, all of them."

As with the rest of his family, Tony wasn't close with Andy, who was more talkative and social than he was. When he went out in Las Vegas with Tony and his friends, it was always mildly awkward because no one knew him. Usually he wasn't around, though.

In 2019, Andy Hsieh again filed paperwork to start a new business, this one a computer technology consulting firm called Sweet Hall, located in Silicon Valley. He listed his parents' address in the incorporation papers. But it's unclear if the business ever took off. Unmarried and without immediate family, Andy seemed to have nothing to prevent him from staying in Park City.

CHAPTER EIGHT

UTOPIA

Park City, July 2020–August 2020

> *The wiser course is to think of others also when pursuing our own happiness.*
>
> —Dalai Lama

Tony Hsieh spent his whole career trying to solve for happiness. How could he lift up employees, empowering them to be their best selves? How could he create the ultimate, joyful workplace, where everyone would want to go? How could he deconstruct the very concept of a company so that there would be no confines at all? How could he create a city—downtown Las Vegas—where people would live and work in harmony, all within one square mile?

In the summer of 2020, Tony had an even bigger, monumental goal, one that would render his prior accomplishments narrow, even inconsequential. That new achievement would finally, once and for all, spread happiness to everyone he knew and loved, as well as to billions of people whom he had never met.

From his new home base in Park City, he wanted to create world peace. It sounded unbelievable, especially because philosophers, activists, lawmakers, and many others have tried unsuccessfully for decades, if not centuries, to achieve that very goal. But Tony was serious.

He would start by designing a model community in the small mountain town to show the rest of the world how it could be done. He would fill it with thinkers, artists, and scientists, who could help him build this new kind of utopia. The world's intellectuals would be free to run experiments, funded by him and his team, with the ultimate goal of achieving world peace. He dispatched one of his employees to begin researching what it would take to form a new nation and how to set up governance for it.

As with all of his previous big plans—the development of downtown Las Vegas, the culture and holacracy implementation at Zappos—Tony's vision was unfocused. He was only beginning to work out the details. But this would be his life-defining project, the culmination of decades spent trying to unlock the human spirit.

He labeled an orange sticky note "World Peace," with a drawing of the peace symbol, and stuck it to a wall at the Ranch. The multimillion-dollar, 25,000-square-foot mansion had become the epicenter of Tony and his employees and friends.

Another sticky note gave a date for implementing Tony's vision: New Year's Eve, 2020.

Surrounding those notes, Tony scribbled in black marker on nearly three dozen others, usually just one or two words, themes really, for how the group could solve world peace:

"NATURE"

"QUANTUM PHYSICS"

"MIND"

"BODY"

"SOUL"

"POLITICS"

The walls, windows, and doors of the Ranch were covered in thousands of other sticky notes unrelated to world peace, constellations of yellow, green, and blue. Tony had always loved using sticky notes, but this was a far more elaborate, disconcerting display. Some were arranged in long lines, large squares, or other shapes, such as hexagons. Others appeared haphazardly placed, as if written quickly and immediately posted to the wall. Not all the handwriting was the same.

The notes described the new plans Tony and his employees had for Park City, some of which were loosely tied to his new vision.

The 10X project had all but fizzled. Giving away alcohol for a fee—the price of the monthly membership—didn't comport with Utah's alcohol laws, which the organizers, in their rush to launch 10X, had learned only after the fact.

Tony's earlier plan to buy properties and lease them as Airbnbs had also shifted. The properties would instead be used to build a sort of compound where all the new intellectuals moving to and living in the community, as well as all the employees working on his new projects, could stay. By August 2020, Tony had bought nine houses around Park City, and sticky notes recorded more than a dozen other properties he hoped to buy for tens of millions of dollars. Some of the sticky notes briefly described plans for convincing homeowners who hadn't listed their properties to sell.

One of Tony's newest plans, part of his world peace vision, was to launch a TED Talk–style speaker series, funding new perspectives from people around the world and streaming their talks live on the platform Twitch.

One of the first to film a video for the project was Dr. Pravir Malik, a former Zappos employee, who had headed up the organizational sciences team when he was at the company. Dr. Malik, based in the San Francisco Bay Area, had a separate interest in light and how studying the properties of light can translate into running an organization. He has written ten books on the subject of light.

At Zappos, Tony was keenly interested in Dr. Malik's theories and usually met with him once a month to discuss his ideas and how they could be applied to companies. Tony encouraged Dr. Malik to distill his research on light into six maxims that all companies could use. Employees struggling with their managers should form a sphere of light around themselves and invite their boss into it, for example. "The employee's sphere engulfs the manager so that the manager is re-seen in light," Dr. Malik wrote in *Forbes*. "Visualize light flowing in and out of the manager. Such a re-seeing has to continue until the employee feels something in themselves has shifted."

When Tony reached out to Dr. Malik in 2020, Dr. Malik didn't relocate to Park City but decided to leave Zappos to focus full-time on the new streaming idea and other research work. "He wanted meaningful, deep content that could impact the situation around the world," he explained about Tony's invitation. He said he had been paid very well for his contract, more than he had been making at Zappos.

Tony also invited a Utah sculptor, Gary Lee Price, to make a TED Talk–style video in early August 2020. Tony had been walking through the Mountain Trails Gallery on Park City's Main Street one day and fallen in love with one of Price's pieces, a large bronze sculpture of Mark Twain sitting on a bench. He sent employees to purchase the statue for about $50,000 in cash and later moved it to the deck of the Ranch, overlooking the lake.

Tony reached out to Price, who told him the story of another piece he was working on, a 305-foot-tall monument called *Statue of Responsibility*, showing two hands intertwined. The piece is based on the 1946 book *Man's Search for Meaning* by the late author and Holocaust survivor Viktor Frankl. Frankl wrote that freedom should be balanced with responsibility and the Statue of Liberty should "be supplemented by a Statue of Responsibility on the West Coast."

Tony's crew filmed Price with a six-foot version of *Statue of Responsibility* near the lake at the Ranch, talking about his journey. (The real statue will be housed in California when it's finished.) Price, who was also interested in world peace, was fascinated by and enamored of Tony's earnestness in bringing about a seemingly impossible worldwide change. "It absolutely came from the heart," said Price, who had researched Tony's work developing downtown Las Vegas and his mission to spread happiness. "It all seemed congruent."

Price's wife, Leesa Clark-Price, was not as easily impressed as her husband. Though she admired Tony and his generosity, she noticed nitrous oxide cartridges scattered around the property and witnessed him, his employees, and his friends inhaling it. Her own son had struggled with drug addiction, and she recognized the signs.

When the Prices left after a two-day visit to the Ranch in early August 2020, Tony begged them to "bring a teepee and move onto the property," Leesa Clark-Price recalled. "They loved the idea of creating unique experiences." One of Tony's assistants later called to ask if she and Price could help them station his sculptures around Park City for a citywide scavenger hunt that would also include treasure boxes and magic. She said she would look into it.

To carry out his new plans, Tony needed more people to join him in Park City. As usual, he wanted to surround himself with an army of trusted friends, ready to assemble the necessary puzzle pieces to make his vision complete. The former collection of visitors in Park City, the ones who had gathered around him after rehab in February 2020, had largely dissipated after his June breakdowns. Only Suzie Baleson and Justin Weniger had stayed on.

Ali Bevilacqua, Tony's ex-girlfriend, had visited one last time after he had trapped her in the Empire Avenue house, trying once more to help him. But it had been almost impossible to find time alone with Tony among all his guests, and when she had, he had talked nonstop and refused to listen. Finally, she had tried to be mean to get through to him, telling him that he wasn't acting like himself and he needed help. She had thrown water at him. The two had screamed at each other.

Gone was the dorky boyfriend who had played silly games with her around Las Vegas, dressing up and taking pictures and playing his favorite board games. One time they had been in Mexico for vacation and had laughed so hard while hanging out at the beach that Tony had dubbed it "the beach of endless laughter." Bevilacqua believed that Tony had been truly happy during those times. He wasn't now.

Tony did end up quieting long enough to listen to Bevilacqua one last time. "But I had to leave him," she said later. It was the only thing she could do.

Tyler Williams had also been excommunicated after Tony had blown up at him. Tony had exiled his parents, and others who had visited in the winter and spring of 2020 also stopped showing up.

Tony called and texted more friends from different cities and stages of life. Others came invited by someone else in the group. It was deep into the pandemic now, and some people were tired of quarantining wherever they were and eager for something new.

Each new arrival laid his or her claim to Tony: through tales of epic parties attended together, intimate conversations, or because they were longtime friends. Some had been in the latest iteration of Tony's inner circle in Las Vegas; others reappeared after having moved to other cities and starting families. They were a mix of former Zappos employees, ex-girlfriends, artists, and drifters. Their connection, tenuous as it might have been, opened the gates to Tony's slice of Park City—and to his fortune.

The hodgepodge collection of Tony's followers had one thing in common: their utter devotion to him. Tony paid many of them handsomely, sometimes double their previous salaries, or in the form of huge commissions or subsidized rent, to join him on his journey.

Michelle D'Attilio, a former girlfriend in Las Vegas who ran Tony's social media accounts, relocated to Park City from Michigan. Daniel Park Elmhorst, a musician who had once lived in the Airstream park with Tony and competed on *America's Got Talent* in 2012, also arrived. Elmhorst, who goes by the name Daniel Park, now called a van his home and played music gigs on the road. A longtime friend, Victoria Recaño, an *Inside Edition* reporter, moved her family and young children to Park City from Los Angeles, renting a house nearby. Janice Lopez, an interior designer and childhood friend of Tony, had moved to Utah years earlier. Before that, she had cofounded and designed Airstream Park in Las Vegas. In Utah, she lived about seventy-five miles from Park City and showed up often, sometimes spending the night.

Two newcomers soon ended up with outsized roles. Rachael Brown, another former girlfriend and an early, influential Zappos executive, moved into the Ranch with Tony. She had begun working as a customer service agent at Zappos in 2005, one of the company's earliest employees, but had quickly moved up to training roles and become a confidante of Tony's. She had been organizing Zappos' all-hands events, the giant parties Tony loved, before leaving the company.

A cellist, Brown had trained at the prestigious Carnegie Mellon School of Music in Pittsburgh and played part-time with two groups in Las Vegas that had brought classical music with a twist to the Strip: David Perrico's Pop Strings Orchestra and Nina Di Gregorio's Bella Electric Strings ensemble. Despite living in Vegas for her music, she had been missing from Tony's inner circle for years. In Park City, she somehow emerged again, always by his side. Later, one of Tony's employees, Anthony Hebert, described her as Tony's "soul mate."

Brown hosted Tony and his friends at the house she had purchased in New London, Connecticut, more than two thousand miles away. The group drove buses across the country to get there in the summer of 2020, avoiding flying because of Covid. Tony preferred to travel by bus anyway. Brown's $1.3 million house is a stately property abutting the Thames River on the wealthy side of town. The well-manicured home has a rectangular pool set in a wide backyard patio overlooking the water. An attached shed holds pool equipment and beach chairs. The house is only fifteen minutes away from the smaller seaside village of Niantic, Connecticut, where Brown grew up, and her parents still live nearby, in a much less opulent neighborhood. She still planned to spend most of her time in Park City.

One of Brown's housemates at the Ranch, another newcomer, was a fortysomething cannabis entrepreneur and influencer named Don Calder, who runs a popular Instagram page, The High Society. His nickname in Park City became "Don Nipton"; before moving to be with Tony in the summer of 2020, Calder had tried to revitalize a tiny town on the California side of the Mojave Desert called Nipton.

Nipton, about an hour south of Las Vegas off Interstate 15, is miles from anything, an eighty-acre plot of land with temperatures that can soar past 110 degrees Fahrenheit in the summer. The town, which is like a real-life Schitt's Creek, has been owned for the last three decades by a California couple, Roxanne Lang and the late Jerry Freeman, who fell in love with it while prospecting for gold in the nearby mountains. Freeman bought it for about $200,000 on a lark in 1985, and he and his wife refurbished the small hotel and trading post on the property, added a grove of eucalyptus trees for some shade, and built five tiny cabins for tourists.

In 2017, the year after Freeman died, Lang sold Nipton in a seller financing deal to American Green, an over-the-counter cannabis company, which wanted to build a "cannabis oasis" and make the town famous. American Green sent Don Calder to live at its new property. Calder, tanned, with a wide forehead, and from Florida, heard about American Green's plans. He wanted to get involved and emailed the company out of the blue one night. He started organizing events, such as wellness retreats and a "sound bath" class, a meditative experience in which an attendee is "bathed" in sound.

American Green brought in art from Burning Man, including a giant circle of shopping carts, an eerie sight in the middle of the desert. The company built several tall teepees on the property, hoping to attract social media influencers looking for a good photo backdrop.

Calder met Tony when he was living in Nipton in 2018; Tony and his friends sometimes drove from Las Vegas in buses and stayed for a night or two. During one visit, as Tony and his friends ate at Nipton's small restaurant, the kitchen staff struggled to keep up with the orders. Without anyone's asking, Tony walked behind the counter, rolled up his sleeves, and started washing the dishes stacked in the sink.

That story about Tony is often repeated by the locals in Nipton, who revered him; they were less fond of Calder. Even though he lived in the town, which has a population of only twenty-five, they found him to be standoffish unless he needed something, such as to bum a cigarette. He often didn't turn up for barbecues. He smoked pot and took mushrooms.

Calder did, however, bring in a lot of visitors, increasing business, said Shawn Prophet, who worked with him at American Green during the time Calder lived there. "He turned the whole place around," Prophet said later of Calder's work in Nipton.

But then the pandemic hit in March 2020, and the cannabis retreats and other events in Nipton ground to a halt, along with the rest of the world. American Green had already missed payments to Lang for the financing she had provided to run the town. She tried to work with the company for months but was ultimately forced to foreclose. Eventually she put the town up for sale again. The restaurant and hotel closed because of the pandemic. The teepee coverings were ripped by the wind. Tourists still came through, but nothing was open. Calder tried to convince Tony to buy the town, but a deal never came together.

About an hour away in Tony's former home of Las Vegas, the economy had cratered as the casinos had shut down in the spring of 2020, and even after they reopened in early June, fewer tourists arrived. The unemployment rate in the metro area continued to be one of the highest in the United States throughout 2020, with out-of-work casino staff waiting in long lines for food. Down on its luck, with a lot of people suffering, Las Vegas wasn't an appealing place in which to start over.

By the summer of 2020, Calder had left Nipton and joined Tony in Park City.

Anyone in Tony's entourage who brought in business or a project to help with his vision was paid a commission, ultimately funded by Tony's fortune, estimated years earlier at about $840 million.[*]

As she had for much of the last seventeen years, Mimi Pham took care of the details behind the scenes, although she did not move to Park City. In 2020, Tony was paying her a huge sum to be his personal manager: $30,000 per month, or $360,000 a year.

In Park City, Pham was in charge of formalizing new business

---

[*] The origin of this oft-repeated estimate of Tony's fortune remains unclear. Estimates in news reports fluctuate from $780 million to "close to a billion," with sources unclear. In December 2021, a preliminary estimate showed his fortune valued at around $500 million.

deals, and she took a 10 percent commission on them, further increasing her income from Tony's ventures. For example, when Tony retrofitted his luxury buses for $3.68 million, she claimed $368,000.

Suzie Baleson handled some of the contracts through her business, the Wellth Collective, enabling her to collect commissions, and a string of sticky notes posted on one door of the Ranch confirmed that process. A contract would start with the Wellth Collective, move to two other employees for initial approval, and then eventually move to Tony for final approval. Baleson, who called herself Tony's business manager, moved her brother and sister-in-law to Park City as well, and her sister-in-law was also employed by Tony.

Connie Yeh, a cousin of Tony, was charged with transferring the money for the contracts, while Puoy Premsrirut, a Las Vegas attorney, typically drew up the necessary documents. Premsrirut, a friend of Tony, and Yeh had also worked with Tony on the Downtown Project in Las Vegas.

Weniger, meanwhile, now referred to himself as Tony's "bodyguard," ostensibly protecting Tony from others around him. As an organizer of the Life Is Beautiful music festival, he had also been tasked with developing several music projects.

Many of the group's plans were documented in daily online schedules kept by more than a dozen new employees and assistants hired by Tony, among them Anthony Hebert, Elizabeth Pezzello, and Brett Gorman.

Pezzello, a former competitive swimmer and Miss New York USA contestant, had followed Baleson to Park City as one of Tony's assistants. Though she had briefly worked as an executive assistant at the cloud storage company Dropbox in San Francisco, her last job had been as a YMCA swim instructor in Florida. Her fiancé, Brett Gorman, an investment manager in New York and graduate of Bowdoin College, tagged along. Gorman has a dog and loves to play golf, according to a series of sticky notes describing him at the Ranch: "Super athletic, healthy, have sense of urgency, hospitality focused" and "Love to make people laugh."

Pezzello's Instagram feed shows the courtship of the sun-kissed couple, both in their early thirties, over several years in New York, San Francisco, and Naples, Florida, where Pezzello is from: Pezzello, with long blond hair and flawless makeup, posing on the beach or on the ski slopes; Gorman, with a wide smile and an unshaven face, standing by her side or carrying her on his shoulders. Later the two would start a "vitamin-infused hydration therapy" business in Naples, delivering vitamins intravenously into people's arms.

In Park City, Gorman was assigned to write the group's newsletter, *Blizzy Ranch Daily News*, named for Tony's dog. For that job and several others, such as coordinating visitors, he was paid nearly $500,000 a year. The glossy newsletter provided weather and dining reports, with one issue chronicling a twenty-course sushi night "for the history books" that had included fish flown in from around the world and prepared by a local chef. "According to sources close to the Blizzy Ranch Daily News, there were rumors of crying babies falling asleep to the smoothness of Chef Ben's fish slice," the newsletter reported. Gorman sometimes added a line to his schedules: "Just trying to help/ensure Tony and Rachael have a great day!"

Tony's brother Andy was quickly swept up into the group's plans. Because he was a member of the Hsieh family, he was automatically accepted into the group, even though many of the others had never met him. He was assigned to line up a helicopter charter between Las Vegas and Park City and meet with tequila suppliers for a business he was planning, among other tasks outlined in the schedules. Some of the employees, including the house's main chef, began reporting to him, and he would send them on errands for Tony.

Tony's generosity had always been overwhelming, but in Las Vegas, his true friends had rarely taken advantage of it. None of Tony's longtime friends, the ones who had learned over many years how to tell Tony no to some of his most audacious and impractical ideas, who knew how to let him down gently, and who would never exploit him, such as the Mosslers, the Cornthwaites, Garrett Miller or Ryan Doherty in Las Vegas, and Alfred Lin in San Francisco, were involved in the Park City plans.

Instead, the new group of people didn't just expect his generosity, they adapted their whole lives to it. One string of green sticky notes in the Ranch spelled out "Tony's staff [whose] happiness depends on him." The list included Andy, along with Baleson, Weniger, and Pezzello. It wasn't clear who had written it.

As the group around him coalesced, Tony embarked on another hack, curious about what his body could live without. How little could he eat or drink? Could he stop urinating? How much oxygen did his body really need? Where would full control of one's body, defying nature, ultimately lead?

He was using a new drug, one that he believed could help him achieve his vision for world peace. Nitrous oxide, he decided, could perhaps spread happiness more effectively to everyone, helping him on his journey there.

PART III

CHAPTER NINE

GOOD AND EVIL RECONCILED

Park City, Summer 2020

> *Into this pervading genius we pass, forgetting and forgotten, and thenceforth each is all, in God.*
>
> —Benjamin Paul Blood, philosopher and
> nitrous oxide user, in 1874

The sound of running water with the faint singing of grasshoppers is audible as the documentary begins with a black screen. The sun edges out from behind an eerie dark planet, its bright light gradually overtaking the scene, as though it is opening a door into Tony's mind.

As rainbow-colored amoebalike forms explode across the screen, the calm voice of a self-assured guru begins to speak. "A revolution is happening within our hearts and on Earth to elevate us beyond illusions, fantasies, and social masks," the man says. "We are looking outside ourselves for fulfillment when the power to change is the inner journey."

The title emerges in white letters, "THE NITROUS OXYGEN ADVANTAGE," followed by "THE SECRET OF THE MAGIC BOX" and an explosion of small white hearts. Tony doesn't appear in the video, nor do any of his friends or employees, but he paid for its production in the summer and fall of 2020.

For the next thirty-five minutes, Tony's friend the *Inside Edition* reporter Victoria Recaño uses her soothing, trained voice to pull viewers through a galaxy of New Age images—flowers, mountains, and people hugging, crying, and meditating flash onto the screen—as she describes the properties and origins of a mystical drug, nitrous oxide. Inhaling the gas can alleviate depression and suffering and free humans from conventional thinking, she says.

Recaño was under contract through Suzie Baleson's business, Wellth Collective, to work on video projects for Tony in Park City, including one with a mutual friend, the singer Paula Abdul.

At times it feels as if the viewer is actually taking part in the video, flying through the farthest reaches of outer space, swimming through shimmering underwater caves, and running through the dark woods, as on a brief drug trip. The words "We must save our world" appear with images of modern horrors of war, floods, riots. CONSCIOUS LOVE flashes on the screen, followed by INFINITE ABUNDANCE, and COMPLETE SOUL-FREEDOM. The video often feels promotional, arguing in favor of the use of nitrous oxide.

"A lot of times on this little journey that you started, it gets really lonely," says one unidentified young woman in the video.

At another point, Recaño wonders, "To what extent are scientific beliefs conducive to human happiness?"

It's not until the end that she issues a sort of disclaimer: "It is important to emphasize that we are not advocating the use of general anesthetics as psychedelic drugs; rather, we're suggesting that the current description of cognitive effects of commonly used anesthetics is likely incomplete."

Tony had used nitrous oxide occasionally in the past, at Burning Man and a few parties. The drug had become more popular across Silicon Valley and among tech entrepreneurs looking for a new kind of high. Tony had also become curious about using the gas for his latest body hack: he was trying to see how much oxygen his body could live without, with thoughts of scaling Mount Everest.

He eventually linked the inhalant with his new mission of helping create world peace and produced three videos on the drug, "The Nitrous Oxygen Advantage" being the longest and most polished. Ultimately, Tony envisioned new arrivals in Park City, from friends and employees to intellectuals, watching them.

Nitrous oxide—discovered two centuries ago and also known as laughing gas, hippie crack, noz, and whippets—produces euphoria and sometimes leads to hallucinations in its pure form. The high rushes in in less than ten seconds; it fades away in a minute or two. To keep it going, a user must quickly inhale another shot.

The gas, administered through a mask, is sometimes used for medical procedures or dentist visits, to manage patients' pain and ward off their anxiety. Lower concentrations of nitrous oxide mixed with oxygen—25 or 50 percent—have been shown to alleviate the symptoms of treatment-resistant severe depression and labor pain. Nitrous oxide isn't addictive the way opioids or other drugs are, but its recreational use still carries risks. One pure hit can cause a calm, relaxed feeling, while a higher dose of two or more hits can make a person disassociate from his or her surroundings.

Tony's group liked whippets, a popular method of using nitrous oxide recreationally. Small cartridges are huffed through reusable commercial-grade cans used in restaurants for making whipped cream, similar to the refrigerated cans you might buy in a grocery store. The cartridges look like metal cylindrical bullets and fit into the palm of a hand. A user puts the spout of the whipped cream canister into his or her mouth and depresses the nozzle slightly, releasing a quick stream of gas.

Nitrous oxide has a long history of experimental use, with many people reporting a mystical, even religious, high from the gas. Perhaps best known among this group was the American philosopher and psychologist William James, born in New York City in 1842. James, who went on to become a Harvard professor, felt that the gas whisked him into another world, a shift in consciousness that, like a dream, slipped slightly out of his grasp once he was sober. "Nevertheless, the sense of a profound meaning having been there persists," he once wrote. He uttered or wrote streams of thought; in fact, he first used the term *stream of consciousness* while high on nitrous oxide. He recorded his nonsensical thoughts on paper:

> *What's a mistake but a kind of take?*
> *What's nausea but a kind of -ausea?*
> *Sober, drunk, -unk, astonishment . . .*
>
> *Good and evil reconciled in a laugh!*
> *It escapes, it escapes!*
> *But—what escapes, WHAT escapes?*

As Tony's video "The Nitrous Oxygen Advantage" details, nitrous oxide profoundly influenced James's thinking. In 1874, James, who suffered from bouts of depression, wondered whether nitrous oxide could unlock "the Secret of Being" after being introduced to the gas by another philosopher.

In the decades since, nitrous oxide has been embraced by the counterculture in the United States. In 1975, *Rolling Stone* profiled a group of nitrous-loving anarchists organized as the East Bay Chemical Philosophy Symposium, with the phrase "New hope for the silly 70's." The dozen members of the Berkeley, California–based group consumed 500,000 quarts of nitrous oxide between 1968 and 1970, according to the report, and were "trying to turn people on to it."

In the 1980s, the Indian guru Bhagwan Shree Rajneesh, whose cult built a compound on an Oregon ranch known as Rajneeshpuram, had a special dental room at his house. His dentist, a follower brought over from India, administered nitrous oxide and wrote down the meandering thoughts of Rajneesh, later known as Osho. He called the dental chamber "Noah's Ark," as heavy rains and floods left him isolated at his home.

Rajneesh's thoughts while high were later published as three books: *Notes of a Madman*, *Books I Have Loved*, and *Glimpses of a Golden Childhood*. He bragged of this work to his followers. "It must be absolutely unprecedented, because people are so afraid of the dental chair and the dentist, but I have enjoyed so much," he said in a recorded series of his talks to the group. "I can experience whatever is happening, even under a high dose of laughing gas. It was a beautiful time."

Infamously, in 1984, his followers committed the largest US bio-terrorism attack, poisoning more than 750 people in the small city of The Dalles by contaminating salad bars with salmonella. The FBI learned that they had been the source of the attack after investigating the cult for other crimes.

In the 1990s, law enforcement scrambled to deal with a new phenomenon: drug-fueled raves, such as the kind Tony had once attended. Kids high on ecstasy sucked on pacifiers, while others held balloons filled with nitrous oxide at parties that could draw tens of thousands of people to warehouses in seedier parts of cities. In 1992, three people died inside a pickup truck in the Los Angeles area after leaving the valve of an eighty-pound nitrous oxide tank open while huffing nitrous oxide from balloons. Fliers for raves were scattered in the cab of the pickup truck.

The drug became so popular that decade that in 1998 a video game developer released a spaceship racing game called *N2O: Nitrous Oxide*, with promotions that declared, "Get ready to go higher, faster than you've ever gone before" and "Never trip alone, always use 2 player mode." Figures wearing gas masks make an appearance, paired with techno music from the band the Crystal Method. Still, nitrous oxide wasn't taken seriously as a harmful drug.

The 1990s also brought the rise of Burning Man, so loved by Tony. Nitrous oxide cartridges are a frequent sighting around Black Rock City. One online nitrous oxide supplier offered an attendee discount for purchases: "Whipped cream and Burning Man?" the offer read. "Our nitrous oxide whipped cream chargers are the best quality and we have lots of inquires [sic] about delivering. We can typically get your N2O chargers delivered into a California or Nevada address within 2 business days, and we are excited to offer a number of exclusive deals especially for those customers."

The use of laughing gas as a recreational drug has been on the rise in the last two decades, particularly between 2014 and 2019, according to a study of federal data. The reason 2014 was a turning point is unclear. Investigators pulled mentions of nitrous oxide from emergency room and Food and Drug Administration reports, but the drug isn't tracked specifically.

In a survey of drug users from more than twenty-five countries, about 13 percent reported having huffed nitrous oxide in the last year, according to the annual Global Drug Survey released in January 2021, a rate that had doubled since 2015. Nitrous oxide use ranked higher than the use of heroin (1.3 percent) and meth (4.6 percent) but less than that of MDMA (38 percent) and LSD (21 percent). The Covid-19 pandemic is likely to have promoted the increase of nitrous oxide use, experts say. Drug overdose deaths surged by 30 percent in 2020 during the pandemic, preliminary federal data show.

Chronic nitrous oxide use can have devastating consequences. Nitrous oxide robs the body of vitamin B12, leading, in some cases, to spinal degeneration, weakness, numbness, and loss of bodily control. Inhaling too much can cause asphyxiation and lead to accidental injuries from tripping and falling. Tony was aware of the side effects as he started using nitrous oxide more heavily, and he wanted his friends to know about them, too. As always, he wanted them to come to a conclusion about a new viewpoint of his on their own. The other two, shorter videos he produced on nitrous oxide, both untitled, focused more on concerns people might have about using the drug. "How does it affect your health?" reads an interlude in one video. A different narrator from Recaño explains that the use of nitrous oxide can lead to a vitamin B12 deficiency and a host of other health problems, such as negative effects on a user's immune system.

The pandemic had made it hard for Tony to procure ketamine, which is often obtained illegally from veterinary clinics or other medical offices. Psychedelic mushrooms had also become harder to buy. But Tony and his friends quickly found that nitrous oxide was easy to get. At first, in the summer of 2020, they bought whipped cream canisters from local grocery or convenience stores. Tony would send his drivers or several of his new Park City employees to make nitrous oxide runs. Soon he was huffing it all day long, as many as fifty cartridges in twenty-four hours, making little effort to hide his habit. Spent cartridges littered his home in Park City among the candles and Post-it notes. Mimi Pham jokingly called Tony's huffing canister his "gun."

As the group's intake increased, they began ordering it easily online. One of their preferred vendors was Whip-It!, owned by San Francisco–based United Brands, which sells whipped cream cartridges on its website and through Amazon. Any user, without any identification or age requirement, can buy a pack of 24, 50, or 100. A case of 600 cartridges retails for about $500.

United Brands had been in trouble twice for failing to attach health warnings to its cartridges. In October 2020, as Tony and his inner circle were buying thousands of Whip-It! chargers from United Brands online, the company was ordered to pay a $50,000 civil judgment in San Mateo, California. The district attorney there alleged that United Brands had sold nitrous oxide cartridges online without verifying that the purchaser was not a minor and that the company had failed to attach the proper health warnings to the cartridges even after it had been ordered to do so five years prior. The action came after the Department of Homeland Security had identified United Brands as a seller of nitrous oxide in smoke shops across San Diego.

Nitrous oxide isn't a controlled substance such as ecstasy or heroin, so the Food and Drug Administration—not the Drug Enforcement Agency—oversees it at the federal level under its authority to crack down on "misbranding" of products. Some states, including Utah, have passed laws that deem it illegal to sell or use it for recreational highs or require a person to be at least eighteen or twenty-one years of age to buy it. But the fact that nitrous oxide can be obtained legally makes it very difficult for law enforcement to bring criminal charges. Utah law, for example, says that a person is guilty of nitrous oxide abuse when he or she possesses it with "the intent to breathe, inhale or ingest it for the purpose of causing a condition of intoxication."

Despite attempts by law enforcement to crack down, it's still a popular drug in Silicon Valley, where it's largely viewed as harmless. In downtown San Francisco, Dr. Paul Abramson, a family medicine and addiction specialist, sees patients, especially those who work in the tech industry, at his medical clinic who show signs of nitrous oxide use. They arrive suffering from the neurological symptoms of vitamin B12 deficiency. "I've gotten to the point where I see that, and I say, 'How much nitrous are you using?'" he said.

Some people using nitrous oxide show up for help from Dr. Abramson after being told by someone close to them, or even an employer, that they should see a doctor. Nitrous oxide, like ketamine, is a dissociative drug, making it "especially difficult for people to identify that they have a problem," Dr. Abramson explained. "It's very hard for them to see themselves from the outside and get help."

In Dr. Abramson's view, rather than criminalizing the gas, there should be more education in the medical community, including greater symptom awareness, which could lead more doctors to intervene and provide treatment.

At home in the Bay Area, Richard and Judy Hsieh had been worried about their son since they had left Park City in early July 2020. Trying to talk to Tony hadn't helped. Now they needed a more serious plan. They contacted two of Tony's former business partners and closest friends, Fred Mossler in Las Vegas and Alfred Lin in the San Francisco Bay Area, to discuss and form a plan. They also got Tyler Williams involved, and he agreed to travel back from Las Vegas to Park City for the effort.

The group found a private interventionist in Los Angeles who is an experienced drug and alcohol specialist, Dr. Elisa Hallerman, whose team, according to her website, "is exceptionally skilled at engaging in personal crisis management with the utmost discretion." Tony's parents hoped that the doctor's eclectic background would help convince him to speak with her. A former Hollywood talent agent, she is also a lawyer and developed what she calls "Soulbriety," the philosophy of soul-centered healing. She is herself a recovering alcoholic.

"If we were to reframe addiction as a crisis of meaning with existential and spiritual implications, could soul inform the recovery process? The answer is a resounding YES and then some!" Dr. Hallerman wrote on her website.

The Hsiehs also began gathering evidence of Tony's psychosis. They wrote a statement, later provided to police, outlining the interactions they had had with him during the July visit, including how he had asked his mom to take ice baths in exchange for his spending time in rehab. Ultimately, they hoped to convince a judge to award conservatorship—the legal process of placing a court-appointed guardian in control of Tony and his assets—to the family. Conservatorship has perhaps become best known in recent years because of the high-profile struggles of the performer Britney Spears, whose father held the controversial position of guardian of her roughly $60 million estate for thirteen years. She was freed from conservatorship in November 2021. Often, conservators are appointed for the elderly or those with developmental disabilities. The process is typically a last resort both for the courts and for family members, because it is incredibly invasive.

The Hsiehs hoped that Dr. Hallerman could convince Tony to be evaluated by a psychologist in Utah who would quickly recognize his precarious mental state and place him on a temporary psychiatric hold. During that time, the Hsiehs could file the legal paperwork needed to take control of his life and get him the help he needed.

In early August 2020, Dr. Hallerman flew to Salt Lake City and drove a rental car to Park City. She also enlisted a Summit County deputy sheriff she knew, Jon Evans. Because Tony lived in Park City and not Summit County, the Summit County Sheriff's Office didn't have jurisdiction over his address. Sometimes, however, deputy sheriffs freelance as security guards or do other off-duty work; in this case, Evans wasn't being paid.

In the weeks since the Hsiehs had left in early July, Tony had grown increasingly paranoid, a symptom of his drug use and his mental health breakdowns. He worried that Williams would suddenly show up at the house and try to take him back to Las Vegas. He was even more insistent that his parents stop interfering.

As part of his paranoia, Tony hired a local security company, Kane LLC, to staff the Ranch, stationing more than two dozen guards around the property and developing an elaborate security plan that included drones and cameras. He hired court reporters from another local firm, CitiCourt, to follow him around, typing notes on all his conversations with anyone who came through the house.

Dr. Hallerman arrived at the Ranch on a beautiful, sunny, hot summer day. Two sculptures had been installed in the yard, a giant orange-and-purple octopus that appeared to be coming out of the ground and a tall, blooming yellow flower. Tony had imported Burning Man to his new property, just as he had taken parts of it to Las Vegas. The sculptures stood out amid the natural landscape and muted-tone houses in the high-end neighborhood, and neighbors had noted their arrival.

With security personnel stationed in front of the mansion making it impossible for her to approach the house, Dr. Hallerman began questioning guests coming and going through the gates. She was aggressive, according to some people who witnessed her approach, asking them what they were doing, why they were there, and did they know what was happening inside? A man was dying, she told them.

One of the people she spoke to was Tony's ex-girlfriend, Michelle D'Attilio, who had recently moved to Park City to work for him. Startled by the direct approach of the apparent stranger outside, D'Attilio went back inside the house and told everyone, including Tony, what was happening. She warned them to stay away from the person outside.

Meanwhile, Justin Weniger told Tony's friends at the Ranch that he had the situation under control and had hired his own private doctor to help get Tony healthy.

Jon Evans, the Summit County deputy sheriff, took Dr. Hallerman, along with Tyler Williams, to the police department and conveyed her message to the officers there: a man was living in a residence in town who was using an incredible amount of drugs, and he needed help right away. Dr. Hallerman showed an officer, Sergeant Jay Randall, a statement from Tony's parents describing their son's troubling behavior lately, including the ice baths and confused speech. Randall reviewed the letter and agreed that it was worth checking on Tony. Dr. Hallerman wanted to go along, but Randall told her that wouldn't be allowed.

The police found Tony at his property across the street from the Ranch, a six-bedroom house inexplicably called "truffle shuffle" by Tony's Park City employees. Tony came out, apparently lucid. The officers told Tony that his parents were concerned about him and wanted the police to check on him. It was the worst possible thing to say to Tony, who at that moment was intent on banishing his parents from his life.

Tony assured the police that there was nothing to worry about. After speaking to him, the police agreed, deciding that he wasn't a danger to himself or others. They left less than half an hour after they had arrived. Back at the police station, Sergeant Randall found Dr. Hallerman, along with Williams, waiting for him. Refusing to give up even as the mission was falling apart, Dr. Hallerman asked to speak to the sergeant privately.

He refused, concerned that he was being manipulated and uncertain about the group's motives, especially because they declined to put him in touch with Tony's parents. The Hallerman group, meanwhile, found the police to be uncooperative and out of their league, unable to deal with the delicate situation.

Randall wrote in a later report about the incident, "I do not play that game."

The intervention failed.

CHAPTER TEN

SAVE YOUR SOUL

Park City, August and September 2020

Now, who will save your souls?

If you won't save your own?

—Jewel

I n mid-August 2020, Jewel arrived in Utah to visit Tony with the board president of the Inspiring Children Foundation, Ryan Wolfington, and another employee. They had planned to stay only a night in between other events that summer. An assistant of Tony's had called to invite them, ostensibly because Tony wanted to see Jewel.

Dozens of guests came and went on a daily basis that July and August, and sometimes Tony's mansion swelled with people. His employees, trying to maintain control of his schedule, meticulously wrote visitors' names on sticky notes organized in columns stuck to the walls of the mansion.

Some visitors were friends of Tony; others were friends of the growing entourage around him. Some people had been brought in to work on one of his myriad business development projects. Often guests were milling around who didn't know one another, perplexed by one another's purposes, almost "like a murder mystery party," Leesa Clark-Price, the sculptor's wife, had observed during her visit earlier that month.

The roster included an array of actors such as David Arquette and public figures such as the former Central Intelligence Agency agent Valerie Plame, who was there to give a talk on nuclear weapons.

Fresh off a plane or chartered bus, guests had to check in with the security personnel stationed in front of the Ranch, part of Tony's paranoia that his parents or unwanted others would somehow get onto the property. New visitors were expected to sign in, and a Polaroid picture was usually taken of them and hung on the wall, like a museum of mug shots. Their cell phones were collected by the staff. Outsiders were required to sign nondisclosure agreements, for reasons that were often unclear to them. The guests' visits were usually handled by Suzie Baleson and Elizabeth Pezzello, but Puoy Premsrirut, the Las Vegas attorney who also now worked in Park City, sometimes handled the legal agreements.

At the Ranch, security guards checked that each new arrival was "registered," meaning that he or she had been invited by Tony or another group member. The new arrivals were then given a rapid Covid test at a station out front—though some guests later learned that the swabs had been tested only for antibodies, not actual infections. The process, recalled one guest, was "very *Great Gatsby*": opulent but with strict, strange protocols.

A handful of court reporters were often there, following Tony and his guests around, transcribing their conversations. One time, for no apparent reason, they showed up dressed like characters from a medieval king's court. One of them, in a striped jester costume with a big, floppy hat, sat in a corner and smiled at guests as they arrived.

A month and a half had passed since Tony's late-June breakdown and hospital stay; his family's failed intervention attempt had taken place about two weeks earlier. No one had talked to him about either incident, and some of his new friends who had since moved to Park City hadn't heard about either one.

But his mental state wasn't improving. In recent weeks, Tony had developed a deeper fascination with fire. He liked fooling around with it and performing magic tricks. Fire was burning in the house all the time. Candles were sometimes perched dangerously on his bedspread, and he kept a small fire ring in his bedroom that shot flames into the air without any barrier.

When Jewel and her crew walked into the Ranch in mid-August, they were astounded. The house was dirty, with hundreds of candles dripping wax onto furniture, carpet, and countertops. Blizzy's droppings were scattered throughout the property, some covered in candle wax. Signs instructed visitors not to clean up the trash outside, particularly outside Tony's bedroom. At one point, Tony had told a visitor that to teach the world not to produce so much trash, it was better not to throw trash away at all. Showers and sinks ran constantly, unattended; the group was trying to mimic the sound of waterfalls. The house couldn't be cleaned because it was "nature." But that didn't stop brightly colored sticky notes lining the walls, the glass doors leading to the backyard, and the windows; the group was now using them to communicate instead of texting or sending emails.

Jewel and her team arrived during an unusual period of inactivity, with few other guests around. Baleson, Pezzello, and Rachael Brown greeted them at different times and introduced themselves, gushing thank-yous for visiting. But they had strange, blank smiles on their faces, as if they knew the situation was bad. Jewel and Wolfington immediately became uneasy. Jewel knew Tony's group of friends from Las Vegas, but she didn't see them around, nor did she recognize any of the new people. She inquired after Tony and was told that he was outside meditating in the "spa."

When Jewel walked out of the house, she found Tony sitting on a lawn chair in a corner by the small lake, wearing just his boxers. He was skinnier than she had ever seen him—emaciated. He was surrounded by whippet canisters. He lifted his thin arms to show her the inside of a small box, where he had inexplicably scribbled some barely legible numbers in columns. That, he told her, was the algorithm for world peace. "I'm going to start a new country," he proclaimed. He had stopped sleeping, he continued, because he had "hacked" sleep and his body no longer needed it.

Jewel was so stunned that she only listened. She was the first visitor to clearly see, or at least admit, what was really happening. Many of the other visitors hadn't known Tony that well, and sometimes the property was cleaner than it was during Jewel's visit.

But the sticky notes, the trash, even the random people wandering the mansion—they were all part of the vision of a man deep in the throes of psychosis. Tony's latest idea, his goal to achieve world peace, wasn't just impossible, it was the manic plan of a person who urgently needed help. Tony was in trouble. Jewel decided to extend her trip.

Familiar with mental health problems, Jewel had observed people combine them with drug or alcohol abuse to try to cover up their problems. As a child, she and her parents, who were also musicians, had performed in bars together around her hometown of Homer, Alaska. There she had frequently seen adults shutting out their lives by drinking. After her mother had left the family, her father, a Vietnam War veteran, had also struggled with alcohol, the only coping mechanism he knew, she later wrote in her book, *Never Broken: Songs Are Only Half the Story*. He had sometimes beaten her and her brothers. The experience had taught her that people inherit an emotional language, and unless someone teaches them a new one, they are powerless over the one they have learned.

"I saw that no one outran their suffering; they only piled new pain upon their original pain," she wrote. "I saw the pain pile up into insurmountable mountains, and I saw the price people paid who buried all that pain, and along with it their hope, joy, and chance at happiness. All because they were trying to outrun the pain rather than walk through it and heal."

At Tony's mansion, Jewel began asking the people around her, "What are you doing here?" "What is your purpose?" No one had a good answer. Most troubling—aside from the odd smiles and the appalling state of the property—was the apparent lack of concern about Tony's condition. Most of the people treated it as though it were normal, almost seeming to celebrate him. Tony had told his new employees that he was in a creative metamorphosis and would emerge soon. The last stage of the metamorphosis would be sobriety.

The one glimmer of hope Jewel found was Tony's brother Andy. She hadn't met him before that trip, but he seemed to be the only person to show compassion for Tony and his situation. He told Jewel and Wolfington privately that he was worried, but he didn't know what to do. His family had already attempted an intervention and failed. Afterward, Tony had banished his parents from the property and refused to talk to them again. To Jewel and her team, Andy seemed to be in a tough situation. He wanted to stay close enough to help his brother but also not be banned by Tony for speaking out too strongly, as had happened with Tyler Williams.

At one point, Baleson tried to explain the group's business plans to Jewel's team. She told them that if they wrote "$1 million" or "$2 million" on a sticky note and pasted it on the wall, Tony would be sure to fund whatever project they wanted to work on. Baleson said she ran each new sticky note by Tony in the evening.

Wolfington interpreted that as a bribe to ignore what they were seeing. "I'm not taking a cent from Tony in this condition," Jewel told her team after hearing about the conversation.

One night, Jewel played a private concert inside the Ranch in a cleaner upstairs area that her team had believed would be just for Tony and his friends. But some of Tony's employees had invited neighbors and other Park City locals—an attempt to make valuable connections across the wealthy city—so the event unexpectedly turned into a mini-concert. She sang her classics "You Were Meant for Me" and "Who Will Save Your Soul," a song she had started to write when she was only sixteen, a lost teenager in Alaska searching for a real home.

In the audience, Park City's wealthy residents and city developers clapped and sang along with her. Tony didn't make an appearance. Instead, he remained alone in his darkened bedroom at the bottom of the house, lit candles all around him.

Among the crowd was Teri Orr, the longtime Park City resident, arts leader, and former newspaper editor. In a newspaper column later recounting the party, Orr said she had heard Jewel sing "Who Will Save Your Soul" before, "But from the first notes that night there was something different. She was singing the song as a cross between a prayer and a plea."

The next day, Tony sat in a corner of the living room on a mattress with Rachael Brown and Justin Weniger, surrounded by candles. Some of the guests called it "the glowing room." The floor was covered by an inch or two of nitrous oxide canisters. A performance coach, Branden Collinsworth, also sat with them. He had been invited to town by Baleson, who wanted to work with him on several wellness initiatives in Park City. Collinsworth knew Tony from downtown Las Vegas; he had opened a gym as part of Tony's early development there. Like Jewel, Collinsworth had been shocked by the state of the Ranch and by Tony's condition when he arrived.

He had run into Tony earlier in his visit to Park City, and Tony had remembered him from Las Vegas. "I'd love for you to come here," Tony said. Before Collinsworth could answer, Tony had swooped in with what had become a common question for newcomers: "How much did you make in your highest-grossing year? I can double that, but you have to move here."

Tony's standard contract offer to new employees was double their best salary, but the staffers typically had to rent their accommodations from Tony, thus ensuring that he recouped some of the money. (Although sometimes the rent was also subsidized.)

Collinsworth declined. He had only just arrived, but he knew he wasn't moving to Park City.

When he went to visit Tony privately, with Weniger and Brown also in his room, he thought he had an idea for how to help Tony. His father is a biowarfare expert who lives in the Amazon jungle of Peru, and Collinsworth began to tell Tony about the sacred medicine men of that country and how a visit there might help him get healthy.

Collinsworth offered to play some of their tribal music, known as Icaros, for him. Tony demanded marijuana, so Brown went to get it and a Bluetooth speaker.

As Tony smoked his joint, first insect noises, then rough whistling, and finally the sound of a man chanting filled the room—the South American sacred tribal music.

When he was done smoking, he asked Brown for nitrous oxide, inhaling a new canister about every thirty seconds, one after the other after the other. Each time, he threw the empty canister somewhere in the room, and Brown brought him another one. Collinsworth sat by the window at a distance from Tony, worried that Tony might inadvertently throw one of the chargers at him.

After each nitrous oxide hit, Tony would roll on his bed, wriggling and writhing ecstatically, and sometimes he would get up and perform a "spirit dance." But he did not look happy; he looked extremely disturbed.

"That was fun," he proclaimed after the music ended. He turned to Collinsworth and asked if he could come back every day and play the music again. Collinsworth said no. He wanted to focus on Tony's wellness and possibly organize a trip to Peru to help heal him.

From the outside of the Ranch, Jewel had walked up to the window where Tony and Collinsworth were talking and where Tony had placed a surfboard, which acted as a ramp into the room. He didn't like to use the door. "This is really sad," she observed. "This is incredibly sad." She walked to the backyard and sat on the grass near the small lake with Weniger, who had left the room earlier. Soon Collinsworth joined them. "That's some heavy shit, man," he said.

Weniger agreed, "It's absolutely insane." He described how he had tried to get Tony off ketamine and how the bus trip to Montana had ruined everything. He didn't say anything about the recent failed intervention attempt by Tony's family that had taken place less than two weeks earlier.

"He is going to die," Jewel said bluntly. It wasn't the first time she had spoken those difficult words during that trip. She had been warning everyone at the Ranch who she thought might help, including Tony's security staff and his brother.

Before Jewel left, she told the head of security, Shawn Kane, "If he kills himself and everyone else in there from a huge fire, you can't say you were not warned."

Guests continued to arrive at the Ranch, and meeting after meeting chipped away at Tony's fortune, at least on paper. Tony's vision had been to solve world peace, but his dozens of side business plans and deals often had no relation to his broader goal.

One August afternoon, Mark Evensvold, a fiftysomething director of business development for the popular Las Vegas chain of restaurants Nacho Daddy, visited Park City. Tony had invested in the Nacho Daddy business along with one of its other owners, Fred Mossler. Evensvold had been warned by friends in Las Vegas that Tony was sick and that his extravagant business plans were covering up more serious issues. Still he went to Utah and sat with Tony on the lakeside beach.

As a court reporter listened in, Evensvold pitched that he bring his skills to Park City. Tony didn't need much convincing, agreeing to pay Evensvold $450,000 a year to operate the bars set up in various rooms in the Ranch, along with whatever else he wanted to do, under a project manager title. "Everyone is a project manager, and then you just work on whatever you feel like," he said.

As a signing bonus, Tony said, he would give up some of his investor equity in Nacho Daddy, of which he held 25 percent. Under the deal, Evensvold would take 20 percent, leaving Tony with 5 percent. Tony rambled on as they ironed out the deal.

Another new obsession of Tony's that came up in the meeting was the concept of time and how in today's society, people are forced to go from one moment to another constantly. In addition to world peace, he wanted to somehow achieve a state of "timelessness." "You're either living in this world, which has no time, no money in terms of what happens here," he told Evensvold. "But for anything that touches time or money or shoes is, like, not my world, so I don't care. I'm fine." Evensvold memorialized the terms of their agreement on a sticky note.

On August 24, 2020, a story appeared in the *Las Vegas Review-Journal*, only several hundred words. "Zappos CEO Tony Hsieh, Champion of Downtown Las Vegas, Retires," the headline read. The article contained little additional information, only a confirmation from a Zappos spokeswoman on the newspaper's scoop.

After his two decades at the helm of Zappos, forging through the dot-com bust, moving to and nearly taking over downtown Las Vegas, running one of the highest-profile management experiments on Earth, and rethinking the workplace around fun, collaboration, and happiness, no public company announcement went out about Tony Hsieh's retirement. No Zappos or Amazon executive gave an interview as reporters around the world jumped on the story, although Amazon later put out a brief statement.

The short *Review-Journal* story said only that Zappos' chief operating officer, Kedar Deshpande, would take over immediately as CEO. The newspaper instead quoted Las Vegas mayor Carolyn Goodman: "He's a modest person. He's not a braggart, but he loves to do things that are different and challenging. When everyone is swimming downstream, he is swimming upstream."

A longer follow-up story in the same newspaper two days later noted the $18 million in properties that Tony had purchased in Park City in the first half of the year, reporting that it was unclear what his plans were for the mountain town. The story quoted a spokesperson for the Downtown Project, since renamed DTP Companies, who said that Tony was "disconnecting" from tech for a bit and "just doing his retirement thing."

Tony had grown frustrated with Amazon since the company had issued the directive in 2019 about his needing to increase Zappos' profits. Tony didn't care that much about the numbers; he didn't really want to sell shoes. His goal was creating happiness. Before the pandemic, he had been asking his leadership team to think about the high performers at Zappos who might succeed him. Still, he had tried to come up with the next billion-dollar idea to help drive Zappos' growth, but he hadn't found it by the time the pandemic hit. Then he had moved to Park City.

In the first weeks after his short stint in rehab in early 2020, when he was still doing somewhat well, he had seemed a lot like his old self at work, directing Zappos' Covid response remotely with the same confidence he'd used to display. But in the early summer of 2020, he was again missing more Zappos meetings and falling behind on his work. Because of the digital detox he had embarked on, he wasn't responding to much email, either.

On a call with Jeff Wilke, the top Amazon executive Tony reported to, Tony proclaimed that he had made a groundbreaking discovery. He had solved the "traveling salesman problem": Given a list of cities, what is the shortest possible route that visits each city exactly once and returns to the origin city?

The question is infamously hard to answer. Believed to have been formulated in the 1800s, it is one of the most important unsolved theories in efforts to improve business optimization and logistics. It has vexed company executives and mathematical experts for more than a century, particularly those who are focused on logistics. The question has so many challenges: how to visit each city only once, for example. Some computer scientists have come close, deriving algorithms that seemed to find the best answer. But no one has yet to solve it.

Amazon, too, had employees working on the problem, and Wilke passed Tony over to the group. Once he was on the phone with them, though, it became clear that he didn't really have a solution. He wasn't making much sense at all. When the Amazon team questioned him in detail, Tony said they wouldn't understand. He had solved the problem in another language.

Wilke got back on the phone with Tony. He told him he needed to take a break. Take two months off, he said, and get yourself together. Tony wasn't on official leave, but Amazon wasn't going to wait forever. He needed to improve his leadership. Tony missed the informal deadline. In fact, he never really tried to meet it.

Though he wasn't technically forced out, Tony complained to some close friends that "retirement" had not been his idea, it had been Wilke's—and he would not have chosen to leave. On a series of sticky notes posted at the Ranch, someone had written the name of Deshpande, Zappos' new CEO, and added it to the list of people who were excommunicated from the group. Tyler Williams was also included.

If not for Covid, the party for Tony's retirement would have been epic. Instead, the company held a tribute to Tony during its virtual all-hands meeting in early September 2020. Deshpande sent out a short email to Zappos employees, announcing that Tony had decided to retire. "We want to thank Tony for his 20 years of work on behalf of Zappos customers and employees and wish him well in his next chapter," the terse note read. "As always, we are focused on wowing customers and the 10 core values that drive us every day." Tony didn't send out an email of his own, and Amazon provided the same statement to some reporters.

Having worked at Zappos since 2011, Deshpande was a fan of Tony's, having even visited him twice in Park City. But no one could be Tony, and Deshpande was far more serious than his famous predecessor. As chief operating officer, replacing Arun Rajan, who had defected to the Amazon subsidiary Whole Foods in 2019, Deshpande had been trying to run the core of Zappos, its e-commerce platform. He often didn't have time for the Zappos parties or the trips. With two daughters at home, he would sometimes fly to wherever Tony was for two hours, ask him for more resources, and fly back to Las Vegas.

Soon Deshpande emailed Zappos' 1,500 employees again. The email stated that employees in several divisions would be offered a buyout. Zappos would pay a month of full pay for every year that they had been with the company, with a minimum of twelve weeks' pay for employees who'd been there less than three years. The eligible divisions, clearly part of Tony's quirky leadership, included Brand Aura/Storytelling, Disrupt, Evolutionary Organization, New World Pioneers, and something called Sexy Infrastructure.

Deshpande knew that Zappos was a company of Tony loyalists, and he wanted people to leave if they felt they couldn't stay on without him. Deshpande also had a lot of work to do. From a business standpoint, the company was in chaos. Market-based dynamics was only halfway implemented, but the bigger problem was all the smaller, random businesses that had sprung up within the company through holacracy and did not add to the bottom line. Executives had identified more than a hundred company initiatives, and many needed to be defunded. The customer service division was struggling. Overall, Zappos was still not meeting its Amazon-mandated growth metrics.

Deshpande told executives that Zappos was going to "get back to basics," and focus on the e-commerce platform of selling shoes and customer service. But his email to employees and the buyout offer were badly bungled. Zappos' senior leaders, who reported to Tony, hadn't been told in advance. When the email did go out, it was unclear to some people whether the affected employees were being forced to take the buyout—were they losing their jobs? Some employees later got calls saying that their jobs were safe. Others didn't.

Zappos employees, still working remotely through the pandemic, took the offer hard. To many of them, it felt as though Deshpande was trying to get rid of Tony's people—that he was cleaning house. In one sign of that, Tyler Williams's group of dozens of employees, the "brand experiments" division running Tony's pet projects, lost most of its employees to buyouts. Williams, however, stayed on.

Tony had created a family at Zappos. Some employees believed that Deshpande was destroying the family.

Tony, who was aware of the offer at Zappos, recruited even more friends and employees to Park City, including Jamie Naughton, his chief of staff, who had worked at Zappos since 2004, and John Bunch, the senior director of business development, who had helped lead the holacracy rollout.

After a few weeks, about three hundred Zappos employees, about 20 percent of the company, had taken the buyout offer, more than had left after holacracy had been introduced in 2014.

In Park City, the small police department practices "community policing," a collaborative effort between officers and the town they oversee to solve problems. In ski towns such as Park City, officials sometimes refer to this as "resort policing," which often means that officers are more likely to give someone who breaks the rules a pass, especially if they're not a habitual offender. The goal is to keep the peace and maintain good relationships. In some communities, it's about building trust with police as a tool for addressing crime; in places like Park City, it can come off as policing for the privileged.

In 2017, Park City was ranked as the second wealthiest small urban community in the country, according to US Census data. More than 70 percent of the homes were second residences. The town's nickname is "party city," meaning that there is plenty of opportunity for leeway from community policing. Each year, the annual Sundance Film Festival draws a glitzy entourage of hundreds of A-listers, all of whom stay in second homes, swanky hotel rooms, or lavishly furnished Airbnbs. The ski season brings tens of thousands of tourists eager to have fun both on and off the slopes.

In a town full of wealthy residents who are constantly throwing parties, it's hard to stand out. By early September 2020, though, Tony and his entourage were heavily testing the Park City Police Department's patience. At Tony's mansion, a raucous party "had been going on for 40 days straight," one neighbor told the police department in a complaint. Tour buses and RVs lined the residential street, and music often blared late into the night, with dozens of people milling about the eighteen-acre property.

One night in early September, officers arrived at the Ranch to find dozens of lit candles scattered across the lawn and picnic tables, flickering dangerously close to trees and other brush. Glowing Tiki torches lined the walkway and the path around the small lake. A large, log-burning grill flung embers into the wind.

In the middle of the backyard, two giant wicker hot-air balloon baskets were improbably set up. As part of their new business plans, Tony and his group wanted to build a hot-air balloon monopoly, snapping up smaller companies across the country and expanding the business into Seattle, and Portland, Oregon.

In the backyard of the Ranch, guests were trying to recreate Burning Man, with a small wooden effigy burning nearby. The fire from the hot-air balloon baskets was visible to Tony's neighbors and from the street. Music blared, and dozens of guests and employees of Tony milled around the property.

Park City has very long, dry summers, and although the weather was growing colder, the fire hazard was particularly bad in the summer of 2020. The Park City Fire District had recently mandated that residents be allowed to use only barbecues or charcoal briquets—no open flames. So when one of Tony's neighbors saw the flying embers from the hot-air balloons and some smoke, they called the police. A passing motorcyclist saw a shot of fire and, concerned about its origin, also called in.

At the Ranch, police officers were given the runaround. Shawn Kane, the head of security, promised that he would deal with officers. Puoy Premsrirut also spoke to the police, claiming to be Tony's personal attorney but admitting that she didn't have a license to practice in Utah. "I'm applying for one," she assured them. When Andy Hsieh came out, he refused to give the officers his information, not even his full name. Tony never came out.

The officers left the group with a warning, but the next night, September 8, they were called once again by another neighbor complaining about the noise.

This time when Park City police officers arrived at the Ranch on a windy, uncharacteristically cold night, they insisted on speaking to Tony and if not to him, then to someone else who would be held responsible on Tony's behalf. Brushing past Kane's security team, they walked down the driveway to the massive entryway of the Ranch, a black and stone-columned affair with a red British telephone booth stationed beside the front door.

Directly inside, a whiteboard showed the faces and names of guests; as the police officers stood there, visitors came and went, checking out with security to board one of the tour buses waiting at the front of the property to go back to Las Vegas or wherever else they had come from. At one point, Brett Gorman appeared in a tie-dyed shirt and shorts to let his dog outside. "If you need to arrest the dog, feel free, I'll get a better sleep," he joked.

For more than twenty minutes, the officers waited outside, in the entryway. Tony never appeared. Instead, Andy Hsieh and Don Calder, another of Tony's housemates at the Ranch, finally stepped out of the glass front door, followed by Kane.

"We're looking for Tony, the homeowner," one of the officers, Corey Allinson, said. Again the police couldn't get a straight answer. Calder, wearing a thin long-sleeved shirt and baggy pants, told them that Tony was asleep, and besides, the house was owned by an LLC and Tony wasn't involved at all; it was actually owned by Mimi Pham and another member of their group. Because Pham didn't live in Park City, she wasn't always at the Ranch, but she helped orchestrate Tony's life from behind the scenes.

"We were under the impression that Tony was the responsible party for the home," Allinson pressed. "We were here twice last night for noise complaints and called again tonight. We keep going through Kane, and it's not fixing the problem. We want to know who's in charge."

Andy Hsieh, his black hair to his shoulders and wearing a white bandana around his neck, stood looking at the officers guardedly. He quibbled with Allinson about Tony's role, questioning him about what it meant to be the "responsible party." "What is the nature of the complaint?" he demanded at one point during the fifteen-minute conversation. "We only had one person singing karaoke."

Allinson again explained that the officers had been called multiple times before.

"Okay, but we're just talking about tonight," Andy said. "There was literally one person with his guitar. We could have him sing for you and you can judge for yourself. This is harassment now."

"We don't come here because we have nothing to do," the other officer, Leslie Welker, said.

"We literally have one guy singing acoustic guitar—it's not even plugged in," Andy Hsieh retorted. "It's literally absurd." (He was referring to the musician Daniel Park, who sang and played guitar wherever he went.)

Andy started to say that he was speaking only about the current complaint, but Allinson interrupted him, telling him sternly, "I'm not—I'm talking about how it didn't work out last night, too." He continued, "We're not here to say we're giving you a ticket. When we have a problem, who can we call but security? We're community oriented. We just want to have civil conversations.

"This whole deflecting around Tony, he's not the responsible party—that's fine, but we need a responsible party," he concluded. Someone had called Premsrirut, who showed up, looking disheveled, having just woken up. She described the litany of neighbor complaints as "unwarranted." "A little noise here and there," she countered.

The officers finally wrote down the names of Calder and Premsrirut and left yet again without citing the property.

Now the police department was on high alert, however, and its officers were frustrated. Internally, they emailed about all the incidents that had stacked up, noting from local property records the number of purchases in Park City that Tony had made since March: nine. The officers worried that Park City's council members might start asking questions.

After one of the incidents in September, a group of officers and fire officials left the Ranch and gathered in the street to discuss the problems at the property. Welker told a member of the fire department that Andy Hsieh was clearly obfuscating what was going on. "He's the brother of the knot head that owns this place," Welker said.

Another member of the fire department offered this description of Tony to the group: "He's a little eccentric, a little off his rocker, spending money hand over fist. He has all this crazy stuff going on." Rumors about drug use at the Ranch had reached the police department, although it wasn't on display when they visited the property, and they didn't go inside. Still, one Park City police officer in an undated text message asked another, "I wonder if DEA Vegas knows about this guy," referring to the Drug Enforcement Administration.

Around sunrise one September morning, as neighbor complaints reached a crescendo, Chief of Police Wade Carpenter decided to make a surprise visit to the Ranch, accompanied by a fire official. They asked a neighboring ranch owner for permission to walk through an adjacent field and up to Tony's small lake on the back side of the mansion. The chief had heard that many mornings, Tony cooked breakfast outside on an open flame, a concern given the nearby hayfields, which could catch fire during the drought.

That morning, smoke drifted off two or three firepits, rolling across the pond and across the canyon, visible as Carpenter approached. There were no flames, though, and no Tony; just the remnants of some overnight activities. One unidentified man floated on the lake in a kayak. In the backyard, the chief asked to speak to Tony, but he got the standard response: "Tony's not here."

City leaders wanted an end to the complaints from neighbors. Some had appealed directly to the mayor and other elected officials to intervene. Local politicians had begun quietly organizing challenges to the incumbent mayor, Andy Beerman, and city council members for the 2021 election. The goings-on at the Ranch added fuel to the political gossip around town. Tony's arrival had held promise; he was someone who might underwrite City Hall's cultural ambitions. But locals traded rumors of a darker side at the Ranch as some of them were hired for Tony's various projects, such as catering parties or procuring supplies throughout the day and night.

"We intentionally wanted to see what was going on early in the morning," Carpenter said later, referring to the fire hazard.

Though Carpenter's stealthy visit didn't result in a ticket, it got the attention of Tony's employees. Within a day or two, Carpenter was back at the Ranch for a meeting with them, led by Premsrirut, along with Kane and other members of the household whom the chief didn't recognize. Tony never made an appearance. The chief ticked through the list of fire and noise complaints.

"This is not a Burning Man community," he admonished the group, warning them about the open flames, heating lamps, and other fire hazards, along with the noise complaints. "That's not going to take place here." He noticed the hundreds of sticky notes on a board with various names, which he was told helped track Tony's visitors to his various Park City homes.

As far as Carpenter was concerned, the police had done their job, looking out for the immediate health and safety of the community. Tony could do as he chose with his own life, in his own home. "Adults are going to be adults, and people have their own free agency and make their own choices," he commented later.

After the meeting with the police, Tony's team members gathered to discuss who would be named the responsible party in the event the police ever returned. At first no one volunteered. Mimi Pham, who acted as a long-distance house manager and joined the meeting by video, refused to volunteer, saying that she did not want to go jail again for Tony. She was referring to her arrest after an ecstasy drug bust nearly twenty years earlier, before she had met Tony. Someone else would have to step up, she told the group. The team appointed the young assistant, Gorman, who was making almost $500,000 a year, in part to publish the *Blizzy Ranch Daily News*.

In response to the meeting, Tony's team made a sticky-note list of fire hazards that gave a "negative vibe": "open flame, fireworks, candles, tiki torch." Another list outlined a "positive vibe": "residential barbecues." A sound level above 55 decibels was a negative vibe; below was a positive vibe.

The group couldn't completely stop burning fire—Tony's obsession persisted. Instead, they planned to put in place a number of "mitigation tools" to help with the noise and open flames. They planned to hire a fire expert to be at the house all day and night, overseeing the group's use of it. A guard would walk the perimeter of the property and monitor the sound levels morning, noon, and night, working with Gorman to make sure the noise was at an appropriate level. The monthly cost of the two new employees would be more than $100,000.

Just one night after the police meeting at the Ranch, one of Tony's neighbors called the department, saying he couldn't sleep for fear that the propane heaters burning at the Ranch would spark a forest fire. Once again, the police showed up. "What are they up to here?" one of the officers at the scene asked Officer Welker, who had once again been called out to the Ranch, the third time in a week.

"Whatever the hell they want," she replied angrily.

This time, the police forwarded the resulting incident report for "illegal burning" to the city attorney to potentially issue a citation.

Soon after, the cold weather drove the parties inside and the neighbors stopped calling.

By the fall of 2020, Tony had become like an apparition, frequently holed up in his bedroom or flitting through the crowds of people at his mansion without stopping to talk. Sometimes he stood behind doors or partitions and observed a scene rather than interacting with anyone. He still spoke to his "core" group and the people who lived at the Ranch, such as Rachael Brown and Don Calder, but he rarely held meetings with guests or other employees. His entourage was steadily taking over his life and standing in for him when he wasn't around.

With Tony an elusive figure around the house, the group had solidified. No one had specific jobs or titles, but Andy Hsieh and Calder had risen to positions equivalent to leadership. Together, the two were trying to start a tequila business funded by Tony. Calder was now considered part of the "chief of staff team," along with Brown, Andy, Suzie Baleson, and Elizabeth Pezzello. Calder had several tasks assigned to him, some vague and some specific, including security and bringing in art. Pezzello, meanwhile, was in charge of all of Tony's outside communication, and she and her fiancé, Gorman, drove a Jaguar SUV they parked at the top of the Ranch's driveway, while Baleson drove a two-year-old Audi.

Soon Tony discovered about $500,000 in expenses that were unaccounted for. He asked Mimi Pham to step in and monitor spending.

Andy Hsieh was involved in a lot of the overall planning, orchestrating dozens of new employees and contractors. He was also in line for the same 10 percent commissions available to Tony's other employees. He helped convince an old friend, Tony Lee, a financial adviser and former banker, to join the team in Park City. Lee had long ago helped save Zappos after the dot-com bust by providing financing while he was at Wells Fargo, but he had long resisted efforts to get him to work for Tony. This time, Tony wanted him to manage the finances of his Park City ventures and scrutinize potential investments.

Andy and another of Tony's employees competed to convince Lee to work for him, to get the 10 percent commission. Lee eventually accepted the double salary offer of $1.5 million—of which Andy Hsieh would get $150,000.

At the Ranch, Andy often carried small liquor bottles in his pocket, handing out shots to employees and guests. He stored dozens of boxes of nitrous oxide canisters, ordered online from Whip-It!, stacked neatly on the shelves in his room at the Ranch, which was called "the treehouse" by the group. His sweatshirts hung on hangers nearby.

Brown acted almost like a spiritual adviser, recommending books to other employees to read. One she recommended, *The Untethered Soul: The Journey Beyond Yourself*, urges readers to journey into their subconsciousness and listen to their internal voices. "You do hear it when it talks, don't you?" the book's author, Michael A. Singer, asked in the first chapter. "Make it say 'hello' right now. Say it over and over a few times. Now shout it inside! Can you hear yourself saying 'hello' inside? Of course you can. There is a voice talking."

One pyramid of sticky notes described the group as THE CLAN OF THE WOLF HEART above Tony's name, in all caps.

"Intelligent wisdom," read one sticky note in the cluster.

"Do Not Silence," read another.

"Power of Inner Voice."

"Forgive and Encourage."

"Create spiritual boundaries."

"Master yourself!"

That set of sticky notes and another grouping appeared to be based on decks of oracle cards from the Australian spiritual teacher Alana Fairchild. Fairchild says she connects with the Universal Divine Mother through a "unique divine feminine energy work modality called *The Kuan Yin Transmission*," according to her website, which shows a picture of a middle-aged woman in flowing clothing half smiling with her eyes closed. Tony reached out to her twice to speak about his desire for world peace, inviting her to visit Utah to help accomplish the goal, Fairchild said later. "I would have liked to have known him better, and learn about his plans, and I may have been able to help him in some way, but none of those things eventuated." Still, Tony was a fan of hers and bought decks of her oracle cards, about which Fairchild explains in a video on her website that "each deck is its own spiritual practice."

The sticky notes described Tony and his group as "Earth Warriors, healers and transformation leaders":

"New way of
Thinking
Loving
Being"

"Our time has come!"

Blizzy, Tony's dog, whom Brown and Tony referred to as a "spiritual guide," had become almost a mythical figure for the group. The glass wall at the end of the dining room at the Ranch featured photos of Blizzy posing with celebrities. Everything carried Blizzy's name, including the newsletter that Brett Gorman produced, which also gave updates on the small terrier mix: "Blizzy had dog food for his first meal and decided to have chicken and rice on the side," read one story after Blizzy had returned from a trip with Tony. The group conceptualized a new property development called the Blizzy Hotel and Ice Bar. Soon most of the group referred to the mansion on Aspen Springs Drive as Blizzy Ranch. They planned to set up a livestream of the dog, to be called the "Blizzy Cam."

Though some people treat their pets like children, Tony's devotion to Blizzy was on another level entirely. Blizzy was his only dependent, his one constant, having been enmeshed in his life for the last five years. He had adopted Blizzy, who was now more than ten years old and had been sick and half blind for some time.

One day, the dog disappeared. The group went searching for him around the Ranch but couldn't find him. They assumed that he had gone off by himself to die. Tony was devastated. He and his employees began planning a special memorial befitting an animal of such stature.

Jewel continued to worry about Tony after she left, and she couldn't reach him. From Aspen, where she was staying for the summer, she sent him a two-page typed letter, alternating between serious concern and tough love.

"I need to be clear," she wrote. "You sound like a crazy person when you are talking and no one seems to be telling you. Its because you are also very smart. And they are used to you being eccentric. What you are saying isn't smart. Its mental. And very smart people see through you and know the difference. Your brilliance for creating connections is killed by the fantasy world you are living in. You can't even connect with me or anyone who comes to the house. It's sad. I find it incredibly sad, and I don't think this is your time to die."

She continued, "You need to ask yourself one question: do you want to die this year or next—Are you done helping the world? If you can die and not feel like you have failed, then I cannot stop you from slipping further into your self-made fantasy world until your organs fail. But if you have any hint that it would be an embarrassing waste of human talent to let yourself die in your underwear and on a ranch surrounded by 25 security guards and staff because your ego wouldn't let you see you need help, then let's turn this around before there is no coming back.

"Please get grounded," she wrote in conclusion. "If you want to save the planet, come back to earth and get to work in a way that will make a difference.

"I say this with love, and as possibly the only person in your circle who is not on your payroll."

Jewel worried that if she mailed the letter, someone in Tony's group would intercept it. She didn't trust anyone in Park City, but at least she and her team knew Justin Weniger, having worked with him previously in his role organizing the annual Life Is Beautiful music festival in Las Vegas.

When she had visited, Weniger kept assuring Jewel and her team that he was trying to help and that he was sticking by Tony to keep him safe from the others. Jewel's team sent the letter to him in Park City, with strict instructions to hand deliver it to Tony privately, when no one was around.

Jewel's letter ended up posted at the Ranch for all to see, on a window looking out into the backyard of the property. Someone arranged blue and pink sticky notes all around it and scrawled lines from the letter in bubbly handwriting. "I don't think you're well . . ." was written on one. "It was great seeing you!" said another and "I am going to be blunt." The group was mocking it.

CHAPTER ELEVEN

THE CULT OF TONY HSIEH

Park City, August–October 2020

Chase the vision, not the money, the money will end up following you.

—Tony Hsieh

It was November 2010, and Tony was on his Delivering Happiness bus tour, stopped in Los Angeles. His skin glowed, and his eyes were clear; his black hair was shaved close to his head. His body was a normal weight, and he wore his trademark T-shirt and jeans. He was surrounded by a small group of friends and employees, all of them relaxed and happy. In one corner of the large bus, a two-man band called Rabbit! had set up to play. Ashton, the guitar player, wore a furry hat that looked like a bear's head. Devin, who sang, held a small orange-and-white keyboard in the shape of a grinning cat. The keys were the cat's teeth, and pressing them produced a "meow" sound. "We hope you enjoy the meow-sic," Devin told Tony and his friends, who sat around the duo inside the bus.

Tony loved the band, which was like a cross between the children's musician Raffi and the comedy team Flight of the Conchords, because their lyrics were always positive and upbeat. Happy. He later used their songs for Zappos' customer service hold music.

That day, Rabbit! played a silly, catchy song called "Possibility" that Tony had actually helped write after Ashton had texted him, at a loss for a specific lyric:

We can go swimming on the moon
We could live inside a big balloon
Plant a garden underneath the sea
We could give our love and still be free
Everything's a possibility, when everything's a possibility.

Tony held a rattle in the shape of a bee—a baby's toy—shaking it as the musicians sang on the Delivering Happiness tour bus, smiling his mischievous grin, the one that meant he was happy. Everyone around him shook rattles, too, laughing and swaying to the music.

That memory of Tony is one that Mark Guadagnoli can still see clearly, as if it had happened the week before instead of a decade earlier. Dr. Guadagnoli, a longtime professor of neuroscience at the Kerk Kerkorian School of Medicine at the University of Nevada, Las Vegas, had been on the bus with his two children, who referred to Tony as their uncle. They all ended up in a video of the production by Rabbit!

Tony somehow always engineered moments like these—spontaneous minutes or hours of joy that would evaporate into the humdrum of everyday life but would always be remembered.

In the summer of 2020, Dr. Guadagnoli became one of several of Tony's friends outside Park City who say they called the local police, trying to get them to help Tony, as word of his worsening condition spread among his friends in Las Vegas. Several of Tony's friends had visited and found the situation very upsetting.

Dr. Guadagnoli had met Tony through Fred Mossler in the early 2000s. Mossler and Guadagnoli's sons were friends and had competed in a math competition together. At an introductory lunch with Mossler, Tony, and Alfred Lin, Dr. Guadagnoli told the group about his universal learning theory: if you studied or practiced something a certain way, you could learn things three or four times faster. Tony, keenly interested in his ideas, had promptly offered him a job.

At Zappos, then still located in Henderson, Nevada, Tony charged Dr. Guadagnoli with creating what was then known as Zappos University, an organization that would teach other companies about Zappos' culture and happiness mission, as well as fun classes, such as yoga and photography, for employees. Guadagnoli sat with Tony, Mossler, and Lin in an area of the company known as "executive row." Tony hated that name; it was far too corporate.

When Tony was grumbling about it one day, Dr. Guadagnoli suggested, "Let's call it 'monkey row' instead." Tony thought it was a great idea. Dr. Guadagnoli and another employee had netting strung above the row of desks and filled it with stuffed monkeys and other creatures. Tony later added more decorations, so it looked like a jungle. As a result, he bestowed the title of "head zookeeper" on Dr. Guadagnoli.

Dr. Guadagnoli stayed at Zappos only a couple of years before returning to the University of Nevada, Las Vegas, but he remained friends with Tony over the ensuing two decades. He occasionally did favors for him—coming up with metrics to measure the Downtown Project's success, working on the holacracy integration—but he never charged Tony. He believed that a person should just naturally help his or her friends, unlike some of the people he observed around Tony.

In mid-August 2020, ten years after the Delivering Happiness bus tour, Dr. Guadagnoli was living in the same house in Henderson, Nevada, when he called the Park City Police Department, around the time Jewel was visiting the Ranch. He hadn't physically seen Tony in months, but he knew something was very wrong with his old friend.

The problems had started in the spring. When Dr. Guadagnoli had texted Tony to say hi, as was normal, he had received responses that increasingly didn't sound like Tony. After two decades of messaging his friend, the new replies sounded as though they were from an imposter, and Dr. Guadagnoli began to suspect they had been written by Tony's new assistant, Elizabeth Pezzello.

Tony, about to embark on his digital detox, had introduced the two of them over text so Pezzello could arrange a visit to Park City for Dr. Guadagnoli. Because he had been separately texting her, he recognized the cadence in her replies from "Tony."

Every time Dr. Guadagnoli tried to plan his trip to Park City, he was told by the assistants that Tony was suddenly out of town. But he knew his friend would never be so flaky. He planned multiple trips, each one canceled at the last minute. He thought about just showing up without warning but shied away after other friends of Tony's in Las Vegas described confronting a "security force" at the Ranch that would likely block him.

He considered contacting Tony's brother, Andy Hsieh, whom he had worked with at Zappos nearly two decades earlier. But mutual friends of Tony told him that Andy Hsieh might not help, because they weren't sure if "he was part of the group," he recalled later.

Finally, from the bedroom office of his home in Henderson in August 2020, he called the Park City Police Department and implored officers there to make what's known as a welfare check on Tony.

Welfare or wellness checks are initiated by family members or friends of a loved one who are concerned about their well-being: an elderly relative is living alone and can't be reached; a parent is worried about an adult child. In other cases, loved ones are concerned that a person might be hurt by or hurt themselves or others. This is part of the routine work of the police force.

No federal laws govern how a police officer should respond to a welfare check request. Across the country, each police department handles them differently, explained Ron Bruno, a retired longtime police officer in Salt Lake City, who is now the executive director of CIT International, an advocacy organization for best practices in crisis response. The organization assists communities to develop programs to reform police response, including teaching certain patrol officers how to make welfare checks and respond to mental health calls.

Some police departments train every officer how to respond; others seek volunteers from among their ranks. Responding to a call relies heavily on the discretion of the officer who is dispatched, said Bruno. If someone has called in because he or she can't reach a friend or family member, one officer might undertake an extensive search of the premises, such as checking the mailbox for stacked-up mail or looking in windows, while another might knock on the door and leave if no one answers.

In recent years, some agencies have been considering building civilian task forces to handle the calls instead. In early 2021, the Summit County Sheriff's Office in Park City became among the first in Utah to launch a mobile crisis outreach team for psychiatric calls, putting the onus of response into the hands of trained mental health experts rather than deputies at the agency. Although deputy sheriffs go through training to handle the calls, "we're not the appropriate professionals to deal with a mental health crisis," said Lieutenant Andrew Wright at the sheriff's office. "Our role is to protect the public."

The sheriff's office had been limited to two options: taking a person to a mental health crisis unit at a hospital for a forced stay or to jail if there had been a criminal violation. The new team connected those in crisis with trained professionals who could stabilize people on-site and direct them to outpatient mental health resources. A similar pilot program offered in New York City in 2021 reduced hospitalizations, early data showed.

Even if Summit County's new team had been in place, Tony's properties fell under Park City police jurisdiction, so the sheriff's office would not have responded to any calls.

When Dr. Guadagnoli reached the Park City Police Department in August, he told an officer that he wanted them to perform a wellness check on a friend who lived there. The officer, whose name he wrote down and subsequently lost, first asked him a series of questions about himself before turning to Tony's situation.

Dr. Guadagnoli filled him in on his concerns, including that the people around Tony might not be helping him, and the officer agreed that the police department would do a wellness check, he recalled later. The officer promised to call Dr. Guadagnoli back in an hour, after it was done. Dr. Guadagnoli asked for his cell phone number so he could reach him more easily, but the officer said to call the main dispatch line instead. Still, Dr. Guadagnoli thought he might finally get some answers about what was going on with Tony.

An hour passed, then two. After three hours, Dr. Guadagnoli called the dispatch line again. When he was patched through to the officer, he learned that he had not visited the house in search of Tony. "I know somebody at the house, and they told me everything is fine," the officer told Dr. Guadagnoli, he recalled later.

Unbeknownst to Dr. Guadagnoli, the officer had called Suzie Baleson, who didn't live with Tony, but told him that Tony was going through some life changes and didn't want to be contacted, according to Park City police. Baleson assured the officer that Tony was fine and under the care of a doctor. He would be happy to meet with the police, she added.

On the call, Dr. Guadagnoli's frustration was mounting. "Let me get this straight," he told the officer. "You called somebody to talk to them about Tony instead of going there?"

"I know the person," the officer explained, "and I trust them, and they said everything is fine." The officer didn't give Baleson's name.

Irritated and concerned, Dr. Guadagnoli hung up to plan his next move. "That's when things got very weird," he said later.

Shortly after he hung up with the police department, Dr. Guadagnoli got a text from one of Tony's assistants in Park City. Suddenly, after weeks of trying to schedule something without success, Tony wanted to see him, and he was free that very weekend, the assistant wrote.

"Great," Dr. Guadagnoli typed back, ignoring the coincidence. "I'll be there Friday." Immediately the assistant texted that they would send a bus to drive Dr. Guadagnoli to Park City. He declined, not wanting to ride a bus with a lot of people during the pandemic, and said he preferred to fly. The assistant assured him that it would be a private bus that they would send to Las Vegas. They were insistent. (The group also took that strange approach with others who tried to visit Park City, regardless if the person was a longtime acquaintance of Tony or a newcomer.)

Dr. Guadagnoli had no idea why they would pressure him to take a private bus, but the whole episode made him very concerned that something nefarious was going on. It seemed clear to him that there was some kind of communication between the police and the people in the house. He certainly wasn't getting onto a bus alone at that point. It was starting to sound as though he himself might be in danger somehow. He stopped texting with Tony's assistant and called his personal attorney, outlining the events that had just transpired. His lawyer advised him, for his own personal safety, to stop engaging with the group. So he did.

The Park City police did end up going to check on Tony, according to the police department. Much as he had done during his parents' intervention attempt two weeks earlier, Tony assured officers he was fine. With his brother, Andy Hsieh, and his head of security, Shawn Kane, by his side, he complained about the police constantly checking on him and asked for privacy.

The Park City Police Department never told Dr. Guadagnoli that they had talked to Tony. As he spoke about the incident almost a year later, Dr. Guadagnoli said he felt physically ill recalling the series of events, and was sickened to learn the police department had never followed up with him. He felt he had never reached Tony.

By the end of the summer of 2020, Suzie Baleson was getting frustrated with the attempts by outside friends to try to reach Tony through the police. She explained to two of Tony's friends who were visiting from Las Vegas that the calls created more work for her. Every time someone called the police, she had to go over to the Ranch if she wasn't already there—she was living in one of Tony's rental properties nearby—and clean up the nitrous oxide canisters and trash. She also had to make sure that Tony was dressed, as he was usually just in his underwear now.

Meanwhile, Baleson was angling for projects with Park City leaders. Park City mayor Andy Beerman had heard earlier in the year that Tony had moved to town and was buying up properties across the city. Some of the business owners had told him about the 10X plan and how Tony was floating them. Especially in the midst of a global pandemic, a wealthy benefactor such as Tony could be a godsend to the small town.

Mayor Beerman, who oversees a liberal town in a conservative state, took office in 2018 after serving as a city councilor. A skilled rock climber, he had planned to summit Mount Aconcagua in Argentina if he didn't win. He and his wife, Thea, have lived in Park City since the 1990s and once operated the Treasure Mountain Inn on Main Street. Tall, with a shock of blond hair falling over his forehead, he is a longtime "Parkite," as the locals call themselves.

In Park City, the city manager actually runs the town, with the police department reporting to them. The mayor oversees the city council and the mayoralty is a part-time position, although it often becomes full-time work. The police department and other city agencies report to the city manager, who keeps the mayor and his office in the loop on important events.

At around the time Mayor Beerman heard about Tony in the summer of 2020, he was under fire after City Hall had subsidized artists to paint several murals including the words BLACK LIVES MATTER across Main Street. Soon after, vandals painted over the BLACK and the fist that served as the dot of the *i* in one of the three-hundred-foot-long murals, sparking polarizing, heated debates among community members during the ensuing days.

One of Park City's deputy city managers, Sarah Pearce, had been introduced to Mimi Pham by a Sundance Film Festival contact and wrote to her in late July, "We are thrilled to learn of Tony's interest in Park City and welcome an opportunity to engage with him. Mayor Andy Beerman is particularly interested in connecting."

Tony's group began inviting Mayor Beerman to the Ranch, but he demurred. "He's an enigma, and I'm playing a little hard to get," Mayor

Beerman wrote Pearce about Tony. "They've been trying to get me to attend parties, and I want a sit-down."

By the start of the fall, Baleson was working with the mayor on the wellness initiative that would get residents together to practice yoga at the town's wide, grassy square off Main Street. The community classes would be a mix of power yoga and something known as a "Wellth Session," named for Baleson's Wellth Collective. The classes would combine meditation and healing music and be led by Branden Collinsworth, the performance coach who had been in town in August 2020, at the same time as Jewel.

Mayor Beerman was enthusiastic about Baleson's plans. After a tour of the Ranch with his wife, Thea, he emailed Baleson in late September, thanking her for the tour and the visit. Clearly the Ranch had been cleaned beforehand. "It was nice to meet everyone and learn more about what you're doing," he wrote. "I'm excited by all [the] new and positive energy in such a crazy time. Your 'stoke' reminds us of why we are so lucky to live here."

Mayor Beerman invited Baleson to a fundraiser for his friend Congressman Ben McAdams, and Baleson promised that she and Justin Weniger would attend and contribute. He also invited her to his house for dinner with him and his wife. Baleson, meanwhile, called Mayor Beerman "very inspiring" and "an agent of change as both a citizen and mayor" in an email to him. Baleson and Weniger did attend the fundraiser for McAdams but do not appear to have made a donation to his campaign.

"We are all so grateful to be in a town led by people who care so much and put their heart into what they do," Baleson wrote to Mayor Beerman. "Thank you for spending so much time with us."

———

In private meetings about the group's business development plans in the late summer and early fall of 2020, Tony was often incoherent, detailing ideas that increasingly made little sense or agreeing to pay for other of the group's outlandish plans with no vetting. He was paranoid and spoke quickly. He thought his parents were watching him and feared that Tyler Williams was going to show up at the door.

Sometimes, usually when he wasn't doing nitrous oxide, Tony was sharp, like his old self. But those moments were becoming fewer and farther between. He still refused to sleep, and he continued to lose weight.

Tony had spent his whole life giving, often receiving nothing in return but love and friendship. It had worked for years, because he had usually been surrounded by true friends, people who truly loved him. Now his generosity took a darker, more sinister turn: he was being thoroughly exploited.

The plans detailed on sticky notes no longer had much to do with world peace, or if they did, the connection was a tenuous one. They also included ideas to supply Tony and his entourage with more alcohol and drugs, at a time when he clearly was using too much of both. Across Tony's fleet of buses, the group wanted to design a drone that could fly between the seats, carrying Fernet to passengers. Psychedelic mushrooms were harder to buy during the pandemic, so they researched how to grow and cultivate them at the Ranch using Uncle Ben's instant rice as a bed.

Their other ideas included procuring gold somehow, and in fact they had hidden gold throughout the grounds of the Ranch. The group wanted to set up a livestream of a goldfish in a bowl being fed. In India, they found a commune that seemed to operate with likeminded ideas about spirituality and drugs, marking it for a possible partnership. They targeted a geothermal site in Joshua Tree National Park in southern California for future growth. They made lists and lists of movie stars and directors who might somehow want to help build a movie studio: Keira Knightley? Jerry Seinfeld?

Tony had told some visitors that rather than just continue with his digital detox on his own, the whole group would go completely offline. No one would be able to reach them.

Inside the Ranch, the group installed mirrors everywhere and built a giant iguana exhibit, ostensibly to replace Blizzy. After disappearing earlier in the fall, Blizzy came back one day, sick and skinny, wandering in during the special memorial that the group was holding for him. Tony and Rachael Brown were thrilled.

At least some of the people around Tony seemed to realize how sick he had become. At one point, the group, at the direction of Justin Weniger, had tried hiring an in-house doctor for Tony. But, much as Jewel had, the doctor had warned that if Tony didn't stop taking drugs and improve his physical condition, he would die within months. Tony declined to follow his advice. The doctor quit.

Some members of the group, most notably those who had known him a long time, were caught up in Tony's charisma, and due to that and their devotion to him, they almost didn't seem to be able to realize the severity of the situation, particularly as he continued to claim that he didn't have a problem. His moments of clarity helped convince them that he was okay. This was a person they had idolized for so long and put on a pedestal. Tony kept reminding some of his friends that the last phase of his "metamorphosis" in Park City involved sobriety and they would have to wait only until he reached that stage.

Others, such as some of the new assistants and employees who hadn't known Tony previously, seemed to believe that everything around them was normal—it didn't, after all, sound much different to them than the stories they had heard about his early years in Las Vegas, including the sticky notes.

Everyone feared to some extent being exiled from the group, as Tyler Williams, Ryan Doherty, and even Tony's parents had been. Andy Hsieh's presence helped normalize everything. If Tony's brother was there, surely everything must be okay?

Tony used a rating system, tallied on sticky notes around the Ranch under each individual's name, to show who was in favor at the moment. No one wanted to fall short. There were scores for consistency, authority, and stress. "Job offer on hold for any new people until Mimi gives a score of 100," one sticky note read.

The groups closest to Tony made several attempts to try to help him, but each one was stymied by infighting among its members or by Tony's psychosis and drug addiction. No one really knew the best way to get through to him.

One morning in the late summer of 2020, Tony told Don Calder, who was living with him at the Ranch, that he needed to go to the hospital. But as Calder, Andy Hsieh, and the others sat in the waiting room, they suddenly saw Tony run out of a room, down the stairs, and out the front door. He had been fairly lucid going in, but once outside, he complained that the wait had been too long and he could design a far better hospital than the one they were at. He started listing all the design flaws of the building. He demanded that the group take a photo in front of the hospital and then take him home.

Meanwhile, Suzie Baleson believed that she could help get Tony back on track in a holistic way. She had decided to turn the ground floor of the Ranch into a wellness center with yoga teachers and meditation sessions, much like a smaller, more targeted version of what she was planning for Park City with Mayor Beerman. She tapped Collinsworth, the performance coach, who agreed to help plan the center for a consulting fee, not the outrageous salary Tony had earlier offered. He commuted from Las Vegas instead of moving to Park City. He began hiring high-end fitness instructors from around the country and organizing equipment: Pelotons, kettlebell sets, and an air compression device to help with blood circulation that cost nearly $1,000.

The costs stacked up, and the total price of the wellness center might have approached $1 million. Because the organizer of each of Tony's development projects received at least a 10 percent commission, Baleson was in line to collect as much as $100,000.

But then, just as the project was nearing completion after many weeks, it fell apart. Mimi Pham, still concerned about the roughly $500,000 in unexplained expenses, found out about the project and was angry that Baleson would receive the commission instead of her. The wellness center, an attempt to help Tony, was abruptly canceled.

Baleson and Pham often butted heads as they vied to be in charge of Tony's projects and the funding of them. One sticky note at the Ranch under "Tony want" advised, "Don't piss off Mimi"; another under "Suzie need" said, "Don't piss off Suzie."

Pham, who had worked closely with Tony for much longer than Baleson had, told Tony that he would have to pay a "disloyalty penalty" of $30,000 for every day that Baleson remained on Tony's properties. She began invoicing Tony for the additional money in mid-September 2020. After eight weeks, he owed her $1.8 million.

He ended up paying $420,000 for the right to keep Baleson involved in his plans.

Pham had her own ambitions during the summer and fall of 2020. In July, during the same week Tony's parents witnessed their son's manic behavior, Tony struck a $10 million movie deal on a Post-it note with Pham's boyfriend, Roberto Grande. Along with Tony's recent obsession over live video streaming, he wanted to invest in documentary filmmaking. He asked for a meeting with the leaders of a respected company in Los Angeles, XTR, founded by Bryn Mooser, whom he'd met at a downtown Las Vegas event years earlier.

Mooser's previous producing work included two films that had received Academy Award nominations for best short documentary. "Lifeboat" in 2018 had profiled volunteers saving North African migrants escaping from Libya by sea; "Body Team 12," released in 2015, followed a Liberian Red Cross worker tasked with collecting bodies during the Ebola outbreak.

Mooser and another XTR rep went to Park City to meet with Tony, Pham, and Grande to talk about the future of documentaries and how Tony could invest. Ultimately, Tony agreed to spend $10 million to support various films, along with the launch of a new streaming service, Documentary Plus. The deal was sketched out on a sticky note, including a $1 million commission to be paid to Grande.

Tony didn't know Roberto Grande well. Grande was a lawyer who had moved into entertainment marketing in Los Angeles, including cofounding a small firm in 2014 called Tier Zero Agency that offered "forward strategy and innovation" as well as some small-time movie producing. But a friend of Pham was a friend of Tony. Tony extended his trust in Pham to her boyfriend and also spoke about him heading up other projects in Park City.

Pham and Grande would later file a lawsuit over the XTR deal, involving the Hsieh family. Tony's family said later in court filings that she had "seriously overstated" her boyfriend's experience in the entertainment industry. By the fall of 2020, the investment agreement between Tony, Pham, and Grande had increased to $17.5 million—in turn increasing Grande's 10 percent commission to $1.75 million.

"Tony is one of the most visionary entrepreneurs of our time and we're thrilled to have his big ideas and passion at the table alongside us," Mooser said in October 2020 when announcing the deal to the website Deadline.

XTR and Mooser were unaware of his declining health and never had direct contact with him after the initial meeting. According to the Hsieh family, XTR held up its end of the investment agreement, while Pham and Grande provided few actual services, which the couple deny.

Tony had already spent tens of millions of dollars on real estate and investments in the roughly six months he had lived in Park City. By comparison, in Las Vegas, he had committed $200 million of his $350 million Downtown Project to real estate and urban development, and that amount was expected to last several years. In Park City, Tony's spending quickly escalated, with Post-it notes showing tens of millions of dollars more on contracts, hiring, and business ideas. For every new project proposed, it seemed, a new LLC was created and added to a complex web of companies associated with Tony's name.

In October 2020, no longer the CEO of Zappos, Tony bought the eleven-story Zappos headquarters in downtown Las Vegas—the former City Hall building—for $65 million from an ownership group that included other Las Vegas developers. They had bought the building from the city in 2012 for $18 million and leased it to Zappos. Among the owners was Andrew Donner, who also managed real estate for the Downtown Project and was a longtime friend of Tony. "Tony is one infectious guy," Donner once said. "I'm a believer."

The property had been listed for sale since at least April 2019, with no listing price. Tony paid nearly four times the price of the 2012 deal, and it's unclear why he agreed to spend that much. He told his friends in Park City that he wanted to buy the property essentially to stick it to Amazon. He was still upset over his breakup with the company, unable to see his own role in the situation. If he owned the property, Amazon couldn't really get rid of him; he would be the landlord of Zappos. That sort of vindictive behavior—buying a building to get back at someone—was unlike Tony, who wouldn't have considered a move like that even a year earlier.

The investment, on the one hand, could be viewed as a safe bet with a tenant such as Zappos, a successful company so intertwined with the building and with Las Vegas. But on the other hand, the US office building market was flailing in 2020 given the large number of employees working from home during the pandemic and companies suddenly reevaluating how much physical office space they really needed.

Still, Tony's $65 million deal was signed on October 20. By that time, he was almost entirely disconnected from his family and close friends in Las Vegas. Some of his friends who had moved to Park City but didn't live at the Ranch had trouble seeing him. Tony had long since stopped answering texts or emails, and Pezzello, who was in charge of his communications, often failed to do so on his behalf. At one point during the summer of 2020, Pham, increasingly frustrated with the situation and with Baleson, had insisted that Tony show up to regular FaceTime calls with her. He didn't often make those. She finally cut off the group's credit cards, which were funded by Tony, but still the spending continued. Even Tony's driver, Steve Moroney, who was still in Park City to work for Tony, had been shut out. He was living at the DoubleTree hotel, still being paid but with nothing to do.

As the weather turned cooler in October and the peak of the stunning fall foliage passed, Tony's group planned the kind of childlike events they thought would make him happy: pajama nights, comedy nights, and family sushi nights. There was a week of activities for Halloween, including pumpkin carving and trick-or-treating.

They planned to build Tony a soup bar. Tony had always loved soup.

CHAPTER TWELVE

THE SHED

Park City, October 2020
New London, Connecticut, November 2020

I have always felt that a human being could only be saved by another human being. I am aware that we do not save each other very often. But I am also aware that we save each other some of the time.

—James Baldwin

Andy Hsieh pounded on the door of the pool shed, trying to rouse his brother.

It was freezing outside in the middle of November 2020 in New London, Connecticut, and the backyard of the house at 500 Pequot Avenue was dark, the rectangular pool covered. The residential street abutting the Thames River was silent.

Tony had locked himself into the three-hundred-square-foot shed attached to the house with only a thin blanket and a propane space heater to keep him warm. He nestled among a jumble of lawn chairs, beach floaties, and pool toys, his whippets lying next to him. He lit a candle.

The Hsieh brothers, along with Daniel Park, Elizabeth Pezzello, and Brett Gorman, were staying at Rachael Brown's house, leaving for Hawaii in the early morning of Wednesday, November 18. The Mercedes vans hired to take them to a nearby airport were waiting outside on the dimly lit street. A private jet stood by to fly the group to Maui.

Tony had not wanted to go to Hawaii, an odd departure for him.

Hawaii was one of his favorite places, and he usually went several times a year. But when Pezzello and Gorman had pitched the trip in Park City in the fall of 2020 with a cute PowerPoint presentation explaining why a group trip would be a good idea, Tony had been skeptical. He had asked them how much it would cost. He, of course, would be paying. About $250,000, they told him. Possibly this was another attempt, however expensive, to get Tony out of Park City, where he might start to recover in a different environment. But whatever the reason Pezzello and Gorman wanted to go, Tony told them no.

The discussion might have ended there, but then Brown had taken up the case, telling Tony that she wanted to go and that they all needed a break from Park City. Grudgingly, Tony had agreed.

Because of his resistance, the previous day at Brown's house had been tense. Brown and Tony had bickered nonstop until finally, late at night, their annoyance at each other had erupted into a full-blown fight. Brown was also annoyed about the state of her house. She preferred it clean and was upset that Tony left candles, trash, and nitrous oxide canisters everywhere he went.

The New London Fire Department had been called in the middle of the night earlier that week in mid-November 2020 when a fire alarm had gone off, triggering an automatic call for help from Brown's security system. Eight firefighters, including the battalion chief, two fire engines, and an ambulance had been dispatched to Brown's house—a typical but very resource-intensive response. At the door, one of Tony's employees traveling with the group had assured them the alarm had been due to a cooking accident and they didn't need assistance.

Then, within an hour, the alarm had gone off again. This time the firefighters had insisted on going inside, despite the group imploring them not to investigate. In the basement, firefighters had found "a slight smoke condition," they later wrote in a report of the incident. Light smoke had filled the air. There was melted plastic on the stove top and cardboard that was hot to the touch. Firefighters had noted an unattended candle in "an unsafe location." They had put it out.

As the homeowner, Brown had been forced to deal with the situation in the middle of the night. She had worked with the firefighters to cool all the hot objects in a bucket of water.

All of that might have been tolerated at the Ranch in Park City, but this was Brown's personal space.

Finally, as night fell on Tuesday, November 17, she ordered Tony out of her house. Tony told Brown that the beach wasn't part of her property, and she couldn't make him leave. So he wandered outside the fence from Brown's backyard to the small beach abutting the wide Thames River. At night, it would have been almost pitch black, the moon a thin sliver in the sky.

Andy Hsieh and Brett Gorman tried to mediate the fight. One of them suggested that Tony stay in the shed for a few hours until it was time to go to Hawaii. Tony sometimes used it as a space in which to meditate.

At about 3:30 a.m., after Tony had been in the shed for several hours, Andy Hsieh went to check on his brother for the last time. Tony told him that he needed five more minutes before they left for the airport. Andy Hsieh agreed and went back into the house. Soon he came outside again with Gorman and began walking across the yard toward the shed. Suddenly a strange hissing noise filled the darkness, like a valve releasing pressure. A nearby carbon monoxide alarm started beeping. They ran to the wooden structure and tried to pull the door open but found it locked. They needed a key code they didn't have. They yelled for Tony, but he didn't answer. Andy Hsieh dashed back into Brown's house, trying to find a heavy object to help get inside. Smoke poured through the cracks in the shed door.

Next door, one of the neighbors on Pequot Avenue, Patricia Richardson, woke up when she heard screaming outside. "Tony!" her neighbors yelled. "Tony! Tony!"

A month earlier, in late October 2020, Tony had decided he wanted to fly to Alaska. A friend of his, Brock Pierce, was campaigning for

US president in the upcoming national election as an independent, and Tony told his employees in Park City that he wanted to go help him. Pierce is a former child actor, appearing in both *Mighty Ducks* films in the 1990s and starring alongside Sinbad in *First Kid*, where he played the rebellious thirteen-year-old son of the president. Later in life, Pierce had invested heavily in Bitcoin and cryptocurrencies, appearing at one point on *Forbes*' list of Cryptocurrency's Wealthiest People, with an estimated fortune of $1 billion.

Pierce had met Tony years earlier and had sometimes visited him in Las Vegas. The two shared a love of Burning Man. After moving to Puerto Rico, Pierce had aspired to help the US territory recover from a debt crisis and the damage caused by Hurricane Maria. A 2018 *Rolling Stone* profile took a more whimsical view of his plans, saying he wanted to build a "Burning Man Utopia," a characterization Mr. Pierce disagrees with.

Much as Tony had done in Las Vegas with entrepreneurs, Pierce enticed crypto startups to move to the Caribbean island.

"In nearly 10 full days together, I rarely saw him sleep in a bed or eat a full meal," the *Rolling Stone* reporter observed of Pierce. "He crashed on random couches, in the back seat of cars, on tables at bars. He gave away necklaces, bracelets, food, money, time, tequila, you name it."

He and Tony, Pierce said later, were kindred spirits, "visionary pioneer types." "We don't see the world for what it is, but what it can be," he observed. They also seemed to share the same childlike optimism about the people around them. Pierce told *Rolling Stone* that he didn't know some of the people he invited to join his business ventures. "If you are making that effort, I'm gonna trust you," he said.

Pierce's quixotic campaign, in the midst of the contentious race between Donald Trump and Joe Biden, barely made headlines. Later Pierce explained that he had run as "an exploratory mission to understand the mechanics of our political system."

With his shoulder-length blond hair tucked under a trucker's hat, Pierce based his campaign on a platform of crypto, criticism of the two-party system, greater use by government of technology, universal basic income, single-payer health care, and the legalization of marijuana. He drove a tour bus through Iowa and to Cheyenne, Wyoming, and across the country to New York City.

"I'd start by pardoning and expunging every person in our criminal justice system for nonviolent cannabis-related crimes," he said in one campaign video on Instagram.

Tony heard what Pierce was up to and told him on a phone call in the fall of 2020, "I want to come see that." In October, he and several members of his Park City group flew to Anchorage, where Pierce was in town for a few days. They followed him on the campaign trail, where he was pulling eighteen-hour days meeting with locals and legislators. Pierce said that Tony and his group hadn't technically helped him campaign and had been more of a distraction than anything else.

Along the way, Tony's group took hits of nitrous oxide, even in public at a restaurant. At one point, Tony visited a rabbi at a nearby synagogue for reasons that were unclear. Pierce didn't think that Tony's drug use was the cause of the problems he was facing, but the result. Instead, he thought, Tony wasn't "grounded."

"People like Tony, they're surrounded by people who are generally lying to them because everyone wants something," he said later. "So you start to become disassociated from reality. I deal with this as well. It's very easy to be disconnected when you're not grounded. He didn't have a clear vision of what his next thing would be."

Riding on a bus with his entourage and Pierce one day, Tony stood up and proclaimed that he would give them all $1 million each. It didn't sound like his normal generosity, though. It sounded more like the stunt he had pulled in Montana, when, high on mushrooms, he had texted his friends and offered them a $1 million reward for finding him. In Alaska, some of his employees looked pleased at the offer. Pierce brushed it off. "Aww, man, I don't need your money," he said, laughing. Tony, though, kept a straight face.

The visit lasted only a few days, and then Pierce headed to New York. He knew he would see Tony soon, though; he had just invited the group to his fortieth birthday party in Puerto Rico, in a few weeks' time.

Since Jewel had left the Ranch in August 2020, she and her team had stayed in touch with Andy Hsieh. Calling quietly from his room or an empty bus, Andy Hsieh secretly delivered updates on Tony. As experts on mental health, Jewel and her team wanted to help the Hsieh family try to figure out what to do about their son.

Jewel's team decided to revive the efforts the Hsiehs had gone through over the summer to initiate a conservatorship. The new plan relied heavily on getting Tony to a hospital under the guise of another issue, at which time a mental health professional could evaluate him. They hoped that the issue would arise organically, because Tony typically refused any medical help at all. Because he always walked around barefoot, maybe he would step on a piece of glass, cut himself, and need to get treated, for example.

As in the Hsiehs' plan from early August, when they had attempted the intervention that had failed, Jewel's team counted on putting Tony on a temporary psychiatric hold, at which point the family could file paperwork for a conservatorship and Tony could get the treatment he so clearly needed.

It was hard to pin Tony down, though, in the fall of 2020. He suddenly seemed to always want to travel, as if he knew there was a plan to intervene. During the second wave of the Covid-19 pandemic emerging across the United States, Tony's group flew mostly on private jets, lessening the risk somewhat. After the Alaska trip, they planned to fly from Park City to Rachael Brown's house in New London, Connecticut, then to Pierce's house in Puerto Rico and then back to New London in mid-November. From there, they would go to Hawaii. Tony usually went somewhere warm such as Hawaii for his annual Thanksgiving trip with his family, but he still wasn't speaking to his parents.

Andy Hsieh, Park, Pezzello, Gorman, and Anthony Hebert flew to Connecticut and then Puerto Rico in early November. The rest of the group stayed behind in Park City. In another last-ditch effort to help him, Don Calder, Tony's housemate at the Ranch, had recently convinced him to try another biohacking regime called NAD therapy. The expensive therapy, not approved by the Food and Drug Administration, involves intravenously receiving nicotinamide adenine dinucleotide (NAD), a compound found in living cells. The treatment is supposed to help drug and alcohol users especially, because their natural level of NAD is depleted. Tony had begun the therapy just before he left Park City, so the group hired a traveling nurse to go with him and continue providing the IV infusions.

As he was leaving Park City for the last time, to go to the airport, Tony FaceTimed Calder and his childhood friend Janice Lopez. Lopez, devastated by Tony's deterioration, had been unsure of what to do and how to help him.

In recent weeks, Tony had become suspicious of some of the people around him. He had hired the court reporters to make sure he had records of what was happening. Tony Lee, the former banker who had been brought on over the summer in Park City by Andy Hsieh, had been reviewing Tony's myriad new deals: the hot-air balloon business, the Zappos headquarters deal, the leasing of the tour buses, and the recent plans to procure gold. Andy also asked Lee to help identify and remove people in Tony's inner circle who were taking advantage of him. It's unclear if anyone was removed.

It still didn't seem like enough. At some point, the group had actually moved Tony out of the Ranch and into his mansion across the street, the "truffle shuffle," to try to get him away from some of the employees and contractors he had hired.

During the FaceTime call, a strange look came over Tony's face. Then he warned Calder and Lopez, "Don't trust anyone here."

In Puerto Rico, Pierce—known locally as "Mr. Bitcoin"—planned a big celebration for his birthday in mid-November, with dozens of friends, some of whom had also flown in. Tony didn't make it to the party, though. He had been in San Juan only a couple days before Blizzy, who always traveled with him, grew even sicker than he had been in the previous months. He and his group cut their trip short and returned to the East Coast instead.

Once back at Brown's house in New London, one of the assistants took Blizzy to a nearby vet, where he had to be put down. Tony was despondent. He believed he had lost his one true partner. Earlier in 2020, he had interpreted his friends' efforts to help him as abandonment after his years of giving to them. Now, as his mental health struggles and drug issues reached another peak, he seemed to feel there was no one left who loved him.

The group buried Blizzy in Brown's backyard and placed a stack of white rocks on top of the grave and an arch decorated with fake flowers between the rectangular swimming pool and a neighbor's fence.

In Las Vegas, Phil Plastina was among the group of Tony's longtime friends who hadn't seen him during the pandemic. For most of 2020, Plastina and his Dancetronauts group had been sidelined as all their performance venues were shut down. Burning Man organizers canceled that year's event. Plastina's art car, the one with the electric siding and the jack that lifted the stage into the air, had been parked outside his house in the Las Vegas suburbs, unused.

Consumed by his own situation, Plastina knew that Tony was living in Park City but hadn't been able to visit him. One of the last times Tony had texted him had been on July 4, 2020, only a few days after his breakdown at the Empire Avenue house. Plastina had had no idea that Tony was struggling or that he had just been in the hospital. Tony hadn't told anyone.

"When are you able to travel?" Tony texted Plastina. "We are throwing a big $1 million Covid safe party tomorrow 10 a.m. to midnight in Park City across multiple venues if you're able to make it here tonight or tomorrow morning! Do you guys want to perform?" It was very common for Tony to text friends shortly before a party or trip, hoping to whisk them away at the last minute.

"Oh geez, that sounds amazing," Plastina texted back, although he demurred, as he was visiting relatives in Florida. He texted Tony a selfie by the pool.

In response, Tony sent Plastina a giant spreadsheet detailing his plans for the earlier Airbnb scheme that had since gone nowhere. It was one of the last times Plastina heard from him.

Months later, in mid-November 2020, Plastina received a startling call from a mutual friend. "Tony is in trouble," the caller, another old friend of Tony, told him. He explained what he knew about Tony's mental state and his heavy drug use.

Not knowing that Tony was actually in Connecticut, Plastina's friend advised him to go to Park City right away. "He needs to see a familiar face," the caller said.

Plastina immediately texted Tony and waited. No response. He texted a different number he had for him. Still no response. He tried Tony's email address. He sent several more emails. Tony had never in his life been unreachable to his friends.

Plastina never heard back from him.

⸻

From Brown's house in New London around the same time, Andy Hsieh frantically called Jewel's team in Las Vegas. Tony was extremely paranoid, he told them, and was acting self-destructive. The group, after leaving Puerto Rico early, would be in Connecticut for a few days in mid-November 2020. It would be the opportunity to implement their plan to get Tony real help.

Jewel's team had been in touch with a doctor she knew, Blaise Aguirre. Dr. Aguirre is a child and adolescent psychiatrist at McLean Hospital, a nationally recognized Harvard-affiliated psychiatric hospital outside Boston. Dr. Aguirre, who typically works with highly suicidal patients, is a friend of Jewel. The two had spoken on a virtual mental health panel hosted by *Time* magazine three months earlier, in August 2020, just before Jewel had visited the Ranch for the first time, and they also knew each other from other events.

Dr. Aguirre hadn't met Tony, but he knew that Jewel was very worried about him and agreed to help as a favor to her. He is often asked to intervene in similar situations, when a patient seems to have lost touch with reality or is possibly suicidal. Jewel's team thought that Dr. Aguirre could go to New London, Connecticut, and use his expertise to talk to Tony at Brown's house, to help calm him down. He could then facilitate Tony getting to a hospital nearby, where an emergency room physician could place him on a temporary psychiatric hold. Dr. Aguirre couldn't do that himself because of his out-of-state medical license. While Tony was in the hospital, the family could file for conservatorship.

The Hsiehs had much of the paperwork ready and were working with Jewel's board president, Ryan Wolfington, to find an attorney.

"The brother was beside himself," Dr. Aguirre recalled later. Andy Hsieh believed that Tony was deteriorating quickly and was very concerned about him.

Soon after, in the early morning of November 18, 2020, Tony's employees took turns checking on him in the shed. He had moved out there around midnight after fighting with Brown all day. The Mercedes vans were scheduled to drive him and his entourage to the airport several hours later, around 3:30 a.m.

Through the shed door, Tony requested that items be brought to him: water, pizza, cigarettes, a protein shake, more whippets. The employees, primarily Brett Gorman and Anthony Hebert, went back and forth constantly throughout the night, padding across the dark lawn from the house, taking Tony the food and water and drugs he wanted. Each time they checked on him, they wrote the time on a sticky note and posted it on the shed door. Sometimes, for reasons that are unclear, he locked the door after they left.

A New London police report would later note the apparent normality of the strange scene: employees being asked in the middle of an East Coast winter night to deliver items to their wealthy benefactor who was staying in a storage shed. "There appears to be no concerns between Hsieh and his employees," the report said.

Tony used the propane space heater in the shed despite the objections of some of his employees. The space heater, two large, round coils attached to the propane tank with a hose, was clearly intended for outdoor use only. At one point, Anthony Hebert noticed a candle burning near Tony's blanket. The blanket looked charred and was smoldering.

"You're going to smoke yourself out," he warned Tony about inhaling the fumes. "That's poison."

"It's poisonous, but I used it to light a fire," Tony replied. He did extinguish the candle, though.

Around 3:15 a.m., Tony peered out of the shed. No one was around. For several minutes, he was alone in Brown's backyard—all of his employees were inside the house. He wheeled the propane heater out of the shed, perhaps finally acknowledging that it was a danger to use inside. But the long hose of a pool cleaner that was also in the shed had become wrapped around the outside of the propane heater, making it hard to maneuver. As he opened the door of the shed, wisps of smoke drifted into the air, and it appeared that a small fire was burning behind him. Tony tried to close the door of the shed, but the pool hose prevented it. So he dragged the propane heater back inside. Once he was back inside the shed, the door clicked. Tony had locked it again. To get in, someone would need the code. Later, rescue officials would say he had been "barricaded" behind the door.

Andy pounded on the door several minutes later and told him it was time to leave for Hawaii. He didn't see any smoke, possibly because Tony had shut the door tightly. Tony told his brother that he needed five more minutes.

Andy and Gorman were again walking toward the shed after giving Tony the time he requested when they heard the hissing noise from across the yard around 3:30 a.m. Now smoke was pouring out of the cracks around the door. They raced to get into the shed. They called Tony's name over and over, but he didn't respond.

From inside the house, Hebert smelled burning plastic and ran outside. He tried to pull open the shed door himself, but this time, the handle came off. From inside the structure, he could hear groaning noises. Tony still wasn't responding to the group's calls.

Meanwhile, Elizabeth Pezzello, who had been inside the kitchen getting ready for the Hawaii trip, heard Andy Hsieh calling his brother's name outside and then saw him run into the house, looking for something to pry open the door of the shed with. She called 911.

"911. What's the location of your emergency?" the dispatcher asked her.

Pezzello, who hadn't yet been outside, sounded calm as she gave the address and explained the problem: "We need help as soon as possible. Someone is locked in a room with a fire."

"There's a fire?"

"Yes."

"500 Pequot Avenue, and they're trapped in a building?"

Suddenly there was a burst of commotion on the line as inside the house, Pezzello called for Brown and asked her for the code to the storage shed. Because everyone there except Brown was an infrequent visitor, no one else knew how to operate the lock. "We really need help," Pezzello told Brown as the dispatcher listened in. "Tony's locked in there." Shouting erupted in the background.

The dispatcher interrupted the exchange: "Where in the building are they? Where—"

"We just need you to come quickly," Pezzello interrupted, her voice rising with panic.

"They're on their way," the dispatcher assured her, but Pezzello had turned away from the phone and was shouting the code of the storage shed door to everyone outside.

"Is it 514?" the dispatcher asked, confused. He thought Pezzello was calling out the address of the house.

"No, no, no, 500 Pequot!" Pezzello shouted into the phone.

"Can you get the other people out of the house?" the dispatcher asked, his voice intensifying as well. The situation was quickly becoming desperate. He asked, "So how many people are trapped?"

"It's a storage unit outside of the house," Pezzello replied. Outside,

Tony's employees and his brother pushed the numbers of the code over and over, but the door still wouldn't open. Police later found that the right code might have opened the door, but it was hard to tell with so much damage to the shed. The group might have entered it incorrectly in their rush to get to Tony.

Pezzello again shouted the code to the group trying to get inside the shed: "1014! 1014! 1014!"

"500 Pequot Avenue, structure fire, report of a person trapped," the 911 dispatcher said, speaking to rescue units in the background.

"Tony!" someone screamed in the background of the 911 call. And then: "Get the shovel!"

"They're on their way," the dispatcher reassured Pezzello, who was still on the line. He asked her name.

"Elizabeth," she told him and spelled her last name.

Still on the phone, she walked down to the basement on the ground level, where sticky notes covered the surfaces like wallpaper. The shed and the basement shared a wall with a window facing into the basement, although it did not provide a view into the shed. It faced only Sheetrock. Pezzello shouted to the others, "Can we go through this way?" and then "Guys, there's a window, there's a window here!"

Daniel Park, who had run downstairs, found a brick and threw it at the window, breaking the glass and the Sheetrock. Fire shot into the basement. Park found a fire extinguisher nearby and sprayed it over the flames, mostly putting them out. Still, he couldn't see Tony through the smoke.

A chorus of voices screamed, "Tony! Tony! Tony!" There was complete chaos now.

"Elizabeth," the dispatcher asked sternly on the 911 call, over the din in the house. "The person barricaded themselves?"

"Yes," she said, frantically. "Yes, yes, yes."

"Why did they barricade themselves? Are they trying to harm themselves?"

"I don't know, I don't know, I don't know."

"How old is the person?"

"Um, about forty-five years old," she said, missing Tony's age by a year.

"Please hurry up, please hurry up," she implored desperately. "This is urgent, this is really urgent." She broke down and started to cry, wailing into the phone.

"This is so bad, oh, my God."

Within minutes, the New London fire and police departments had arrived at the house. They descended on the scene, quickly taking charge. They bashed in the door of the shed using special tools that weren't available to Tony's employees and kicked a propane heater out of the way to reach him. He was lying on his back, his right arm draped over his chest. He was surrounded by whippet chargers and small bottles of Fernet. A charred plastic bag of sticky notes lay nearby.

The fire in the shed was not devastating, and the firefighters put it out quickly. Soon, Vernon Skau, the fire marshal, would take pictures of everything inside: the propane heater, the candle wax, and the whippets. The shed was charred, many of the items still smoldering.

Tony was unconscious but not badly burned. The firefighters quickly pulled him out. He was loaded into an ambulance and transported to the Lawrence + Memorial Hospital, just minutes from Brown's house. Andy Hsieh jumped into the ambulance with him. Soon after, a helicopter flew Tony to the burn unit of Bridgeport Hospital, about sixty-five miles away from New London.

In the days that followed, some of Tony's friends in Las Vegas heard what had happened, but it hadn't yet been made public that the former Zappos CEO had been involved in a fire. Even though Tony remained unconscious, many of his friends expected him to recover, in part because he hadn't been badly burned.

Mark Guadagnoli, the longtime friend who had tried to initiate a welfare check with the police in Park City over the summer, heard that Tony's condition had improved from critical to stable and for the first time felt hope. He thought that maybe the fire would finally be the wake-up call that Tony needed to get better. He would be extricated from the hangers-on around him. "He's going to be forced into recovering," he thought.

Other Las Vegas friends thought the fire was a fake story, made up by Tony's entourage in Park City. They believed that Tony had actually overdosed and the group was covering it up.

At Brown's house in New London and in Park City, Tony's followers continued, unabated, with their plans.

One entry from Hebert's schedule noted, "Cleaned after the fire, dealing with police and fire department. . . . Priorities this week: getting a quote on wrapping the tree on the patio with LED lights, would really add to the space."

For nine days, Tony lay in a hospital bed at the Connecticut Burn Center at Bridgeport Hospital. He had been hooked up to a ventilator, and he appeared to be sleeping. His injuries were not severe. He was still for the first time in years.

His family—Richard and Judy and his brothers, Andy and Dave—surrounded him, but no one else was there. They kept vigil during his long sleep.

The smoke, soot, and fire had caused a cerebral edema, in which the brain swells, causing pressure. Brain edema can sometimes be treated, but it can also cause irreversible damage. Tony Hsieh, the beloved man who had tried so hard to bring happiness to everyone around him, would never wake up the same.

On the ninth day, November 27, 2020, Richard and Judy Hsieh opted to remove the ventilator. Tony was gone.

EPILOGUE

In the end, it turns out that we're all taking different paths in pursuit of the same goal: happiness.

—Tony Hsieh

Forty-nine days after Tony's death, the Hsieh family held a private Buddhist ceremony for their oldest son.

Tony was also Buddhist, a fact not many people knew about him. He wasn't devout. But he ended *Delivering Happiness* with a quote from Buddha: "Thousands of candles can be lit from a single candle, and the life of the candle will not be shortened. Happiness never decreases by being shared."

In Samsara, or the cycle of reincarnation, a person goes through an intermediate stage between death and life. While waiting for rebirth, a person's spirit can be frightened by apparitions that slow down the path to enlightenment. People pray for their loved ones to realize what's not real and move on to their next place in the universe, a transition that can take up to forty-nine days in some Buddhist traditions. For Tony, that day of rebirth was January 15, 2021.

On that day, with the pandemic still ongoing, the Hsiehs held the memorial online. Tony's mom, Judy Hsieh, performed a traditional Chinese dance for her son, who had always loved to dance. She also sang a song from *The Phantom of the Opera*, "Think of Me." She is not a formally trained singer, but her prerecorded rendition was haunting.

Tony's cousins spoke, as did his best friends from high school and other close friends from over the years. Judy Hsieh was the only immediate family member to do so. She hadn't seen Tony alive and in person since early July 2020, six months earlier. At the memorial, she kept referring to him lovingly as "my boy."

From around the world, memorials poured in during the days and weeks after Tony's death. Hundreds of Tony's friends, politicians, business leaders, actors, and an endless number of fans wanted to honor the beloved entrepreneur through videos, songs, letters, and social media posts. It was a collective outpouring of grief that connected loved ones from all different backgrounds with a new, shared mission: remembering Tony. He would have been proud of the synergy, even though he had hated being the center of attention.

His death was publicly announced the day he passed away, November 27, 2020, in a public statement by Zappos CEO Kedar Deshpande. "The world has lost a tremendous visionary and an incredible human being," he wrote. He offered few details about how the forty-six-year-old had died.

On Instagram, Amazon's then chief executive officer, Jeff Bezos, wrote, "The world lost you way too soon."

"I treasure every conversation I ever had with Tony Hsieh," former president Bill Clinton, who had met Tony years earlier at a speaking engagement, tweeted. He had immediately reached out to the Hsieh family after Tony's death to offer his condolences and later also spoke at the family's private memorial. "He was fascinating, brilliant, and inspiring, and his unwavering efforts to spread happiness—and enthusiasm for mentoring young entrepreneurs—touched countless lives for the better," he wrote.

Ivanka Trump, fresh off her father's loss in the 2020 presidential election, offered her praise of Tony, sharing photos of them together over the years, including on the Delivering Happiness tour bus. In one, Tony is stiffly dressed in a suit and tie, his hair cut short, standing in front of the White House with Ivanka, wearing a half smile. In another, he grins from the middle of a group of people, including Ivanka and her husband and former White House adviser, Jared Kushner, in what looks like a casino. "Tony was a deeply original thinker always challenging me to reject conformity & follow my heart," she wrote.

Many of the hundreds of messages received by the Hsieh family came from Tony's fans who didn't know him personally. They often began, "I'll never meet Tony, but he's had a major impact on my life," as Alfred Lin, Tony's longtime business partner and good friend, recalled in his own public letter to Tony. "As you watch the world turn from above and debug some metaphysical anomaly that you've just observed, I hope you also notice the impact you've had on so many lives," Lin wrote.

Fred Mossler, who had been friends with Tony for more than two decades, recalled the unusual way Tony had viewed his business rivals in an interview about his friend's death with an industry trade publication, *Footwear News*. If the competition copied Zappos' model of free shipping, Tony believed that could only be a good thing. "It was never about what was best for Zappos," Mossler said. "It was about what was best for the human condition."

In his tribute, Tony's former business partner Nick Swinmurn described Tony's odd practice of rating his friends' happiness on a scale of 1 to 10 and wrote briefly about how he had drifted apart from his old friend in recent years because of their different lifestyles. "He was a complex puzzle," he wrote, "much too complicated for me to completely understand, which I felt was exactly how he wanted it."

In Las Vegas, on East Fremont Street, a board appeared outside one of the Burning Man art sculptures Tony had imported, the tower of twisted semitrucks in front of the Fergusons Downtown art complex. On it, people posted dozens of sticky notes with messages remembering Tony, checkering the board with faded neon squares:

"Will do my best to continue spreading empathy and delivering
     happiness now that you won't be around physically."

"Your obsession with post its always annoyed me but your inspiration
     could never be contained to one idea (which I love)."

In front of the Downtown Cocktail Room, where Tony's plans for Las Vegas had begun to percolate a decade earlier, the Cornthwaites, who had long before introduced Tony to downtown Las Vegas, hung a poster of his grinning face and one of his favorite questions: "What if?"

Zappos also unfurled giant wraps over two sides of its downtown office tower with a photo of Tony and the words "THANK YOU, TONY." Internally, Zappos, whose employees were still working remotely, held an online memorial, including a video curated from thousands of hours of footage of their chief executive officer that the company had collected over the years.

Tony's name and photo appeared along the downtown section of Las Vegas's Fremont Street lined with old casinos and tourist attractions. Months into 2021, many of the businesses and street signs still featured remembrances for Tony: painted portraits of his likeness, silly llama drawings, or his most inspiring quotes on billboards: "No matter what your past has been, you have a spotless future."

A petition appeared online calling for a street to be named after him. But Las Vegas mayor Carolyn Goodman, a longtime fan of Tony, didn't like that idea. At a city council meeting just days after his death, she told the public that his memory shouldn't be confined to a boring roadway. Instead, his ethereal being should be celebrated through naming a park after him or through a public artwork, such as a piece of sculpture that moves. "A street is so perpendicular and horizontal, that's so un-Tony," she said in a radio interview. (As of September 2021, a memorial had not yet been established.)

Several months after his death, one of Tony's longtime friends told us about a dream they'd had about him, one of those dreams that is so clear that it appears to be happening in real life. In it, Tony was checking on his friend, and he asked about everything that had happened since he left. As usual, even in death, he was more concerned about everyone else than about himself.

The friend talked about how Tony had died and how all his friends had been so devastated—and still hadn't recovered. They described the gaping hole that all of them walked around with, that would never be filled. Still, Tony was laughing in the dream—that infectious laugh of his—and he hugged his friend. He appeared happy.

On December 1, 2020, Jewel turned on the camera and stared at the lens. She wore a colorful shirt and a cowboy hat, a piece of fabric patterned with flowers and animals draped behind her. She held her guitar.

"Hey, it's Jewel here," she said. She smiled, but there was sadness behind the smile, her eyes tinged with red. The hat was the same one she had worn when she had played the private concert at the Ranch in Park City several months earlier.

She told the audience on Instagram that she had sat for a while before pressing "Record," trying to find the right words to describe her good friend Tony Hsieh and her feelings about his death. "For somebody who writes for a living, and is fairly verbose, I didn't really know what to say," she said. She paused. "I don't think anyone knows what to say at times like this."

The world didn't yet know about Jewel's efforts to save Tony and how close she had come to reaching him. Perhaps if he had entered the shed in New London, Connecticut, one night later or delayed his trip to Hawaii for some reason, the doctor whom Jewel and her team had recruited might have been able to convince him to go to a hospital. The Hsieh family could have finally intervened successfully.

Instead, in her elegy, she recounted how she had met Tony on Necker Island in 2015 and how she had been riveted by him and his ideas for holacracy. "That's never happened at a company that I'm aware of," she said. She described his great ability to empower everyone, even her. "And I'm a folksinger!"

Tony had once posed a question to Jewel that he liked to ask people: "What's your definition of success?" Jewel couldn't recall her own answer, but she remembered Tony's. "His answer was the willingness to lose it all.

"I guess that's what it really takes—because you have to put your whole heart into something you believe," she told her audience. "To believe with that much conviction is a rare gift—to give yourself to it. That really is a beautiful definition and that really is how I think of Tony—very brave."

She began to sing a rendition of "Somewhere over the Rainbow," her deep, soulful voice emanating from the screen. After a few minutes, she stopped in midlyric. Her eyes filled with tears, some streamed down her face, and she had to pause for several moments before continuing with her elegy.

Before she turned the camera off, she spoke to her friend for the last time: "Tony, may you be over the rainbow with the bluebirds, and your worries far behind."

In New London, Connecticut, the fire and police departments immediately launched an investigation into the shed fire. The fire department was overwhelmed with worldwide media attention once the news broke that Tony had been the unidentified man pulled from the shed and that he had died in a nearby hospital. The attention was so intense, with reporters camping out at Rachael Brown's house at 500 Pequot Avenue and Fire Chief Thomas Curcio fielding dozens of calls weekly, an enormous number for a small department, that the fire officials organized a meeting with New London's mayor. They discussed not only how to handle the constant requests for information but also how to proceed carefully with their examination into what had caused the fire. No one famous had ever died so publicly in New London before.

City, police, and fire officials all agreed that their internal inquiry would be no different from the many others they had conducted over the years, regardless of Tony's stature. There would be no leaks to the media, no preference given to any party as information was uncovered. Vernon Skau, the longtime fire marshal, remembered thinking he had wished that that much attention would be bestowed on the many problems city officials faced in the poorer neighborhoods of New London.

Skau headed up the joint investigation, an effort that would take the better part of two months and fill a thick binder. All fires are similar, he said, but each examination comes with different details, twists and turns that will reveal themselves over time. "Every fire investigation— you have a different flavor," he said later.

On the night of the November fire, he and members of the police and fire departments had taken dozens of pictures of the inside of the shed and everything that could have caused it: the whippets, the Tiki torch fluid, the candle and its wax, the propane heater, and Tony's cigarettes.

The shed was filled with so much beach equipment and other house junk that it was hard to sort through the wreckage. One photo showed a jumble of paint cans and rollers, fold-up beach chairs, and stacks of soda boxes, much of it charred from the fire. In another, a ball of extension cords and foam rollers for the pool crisscrossed a smoke-stained white blanket. One of the photos would end up framed for a time at the fire station, where photos of some of New London's most famous fires hang on the walls.

Skau and his team spent the next six weeks analyzing the many shed photos, trying to find the potential cause. He returned once more to the house at 500 Pequot Avenue to examine it, as well as to study the door-locking system that Tony's employees couldn't get to work. He walked around the outside of the building, noticing every detail. He analyzed grainy footage from Rachael Brown's home camera system, which faced the yard and the shed, to piece together the last few hours of Tony Hsieh's life.

He and his team saw the multiple trips that Tony's employees had made to take him nitrous oxide, pizza, and water, and he saw the wisps of smoke escape the shed when Tony had opened the door around 3:15 a.m., what looked like a small fire burning behind him. He couldn't tell what was fueling it. He watched as Tony dragged the propane tank with the vacuum hose wrapped around it outside the shed and then back inside, his last moments in the outside world, alone. It was hard to tell from the videos if Tony had been acting strangely in any way. (Investigators never figured out why Tony had dragged the heater outside and then back in.)

Skau heard the door lock behind Tony for the last time.

In partnership with the police department, the New London Fire Department had interviewed everyone at the scene, taking detailed statements from all of Tony's employees who had been there. Only Andy Hsieh's statement was missing; he had jumped into the ambulance with Tony directly after the fire, and Skau felt they already had enough witnesses.

Skau had thought the Mercedes vans outside of the house at 500 Pequot Avenue were bizarre, but the employees who had been waiting inside the vehicles carried the same expressions he was used to seeing after an emergency: disbelief and shock.

When interviewed, Anthony Hebert told police that Tony was retired because of mental health concerns and a "midlife crisis," although he said he was not aware if Tony had been diagnosed with anything. He said that Tony had been "distraught" over the death of Blizzy three days earlier.

That was a familiar theme; the nurse who had recently been traveling with Tony to give him the NAD infusions also noted that he had been depressed over the death of Blizzy, as did Brett Gorman. Tony had been "despondent," Gorman told police.

By the end of January 2021, Skau and his team were ready to release their findings. Already, the Connecticut Office of the Chief Medical Examiner had ruled the death an accident following an autopsy, saying that Tony had died of complications of smoke inhalation. The office declined to release the autopsy or specify why it believed that the death had been an accident. In dozens of interviews with Tony's close friends for this book, very few believed that Tony would have intentionally hurt himself.

The New London fire and police departments released witness

reports, videos, photos, 911 calls, and incident notes from the scene. Together, the records painted a heartbreaking, detailed picture of Tony's last hours, including his friends' and brother's last attempts to save him. Over and over, they had tried to get into the shed but couldn't reach him. But Skau ultimately couldn't pinpoint the exact cause of the fire, in part because there were so many objects in the shed that could have caused it. The joint report was inconclusive.

Skau wrote that it was possible that the heater had come into contact with some sort of combustible, such as a piece of paper, that would have started a fire. Then that fire would have heated the propane tank, triggering a release valve, causing gas to rush—likely the hissing noise Andy Hsieh and Brett Gorman had heard when they were walking across the lawn to the shed. Possibly that was why Tony had tried to roll the propane heater out of the shed earlier in the night. Still, there seemed to have been a small fire burning in the shed already, so Skau wrote that there was a "low possibility" that the portable heater had caused the fire.

Another option was that Tony's cigarettes or marijuana—a pipe was also found in the shed—could have caused it, but the report concluded that that was also unlikely. "A lighted cigarette will only occasionally set fire to dry fuel," it read.

Having observed several candles in the shed, Skau wrote that it was possible that using them in an improper way could have started the fire. The candles "could not be eliminated as a cause of this fire," he concluded.

The report noted all the objects around Tony, including Fernet bottles and whippets, which led investigators to believe that he might have been "impaired or intoxicated" at the time of the fire.

"It is possible that carelessness, or even an intentional act by Hsieh could have started this fire," Skau wrote. There wasn't enough evidence to state that conclusively, though.

At a press conference at the end of January 2021, Skau, Chief Curcio, and Captain Brian Wright from the New London Police Department fielded dozens of questions from reporters about their findings. Many asked about Tony's mental state at the time and what had led him to be in the shed. Officials hewed closely to the findings in their report.

The police and fire departments had determined that it was not a criminal act—that none of Tony's employees, or Tony himself, was to blame. Skau said that there were no other state or local agencies looking into the events of that night, as far as the New London Fire Department knew. At the time of this writing in September 2021, there were still no government agencies examining the fire or the events leading up to it in Park City, Utah, or New London, Connecticut.

Skau was asked at the news conference whether the fatal fire could have been avoided. "Any situation such as this," he replied, "things can be prevented."

The battle over Tony's fortune began swiftly afterward.

Tony died without a will, a startling fact that was revealed in court filings in Las Vegas just a few days after his death. He had left no plan for his vast estate, which had become convoluted in the last year of his life as he had spent money rapidly in Park City, often through dozens of other friends, employees, and contractors.

Many of the contracts were written on the thousands of multicolored sticky notes stuck to the walls and windows and doors of the Ranch, many signed like contracts. Tens of millions of dollars in real estate—the houses and other properties in Park City and Las Vegas—were shuffled among limited liability companies and held by shell companies. The transcripts produced by the court reporters held more verbal contracts initiated by Tony, sometimes as he was clearly not in the right state of mind. All of that would have to be unwound.

"You're going to have to look at each specific sticky note and decide if it's a contract—is it binding?" one attorney, Justin H. Brown, who deals with estate planning, told us in December 2020. "Was he in the correct state of mind—did he have the capacity to even enter a contract?"

At the heart of Tony's estate resolution was one crucial question: How much was he actually worth? No one seemed to know, not even those closest to him.

What was known was that Tony had earned $32 million from the 1998 sale of LinkExchange to Microsoft for $265 million. He had then catapulted further with the $1.2 billion all-stock deal to sell Zappos to Amazon in 2009. He had owned Zappos shares along with an interest in his venture fund Venture Frogs, which also owned shares in Zappos after investing in the company long ago. Estimates of Tony's fortune have varied over the years,[*] with some journalists using $840 million as his net worth. Some friends estimated that the figure was likely much higher because he had a number of other investments, some undisclosed, including a stake in Elon Musk's SpaceX.

Tony hadn't lived an opulent lifestyle, at least not before moving to Park City. But he had committed to spending huge sums of his fortune, such as the $350 million promised to downtown Las Vegas. His mission to spread happiness often manifested itself in spending on others, a pattern throughout his life. In Utah, he had bought about $70 million in real estate. Wealthy elites were scrambling to leave crowded coastal cities in the pandemic for spots such as Utah's mountain towns, driving up prices. And Tony hadn't been afraid to spend even more to get what he wanted, particularly in his diminished state. He had been running through his cash on hand.

Within days of his death, Tony's father, Richard Hsieh, and brother Andy Hsieh were appointed special administrators and legal representatives of Tony's estate, by a judge in Las Vegas. The judge found that Tony's personal and business affairs "require immediate attention to prevent loss to the estate," the court records disclosed.

As part of their legal team, the Hsiehs hired Vivien Thoreen, a Los Angeles attorney who also represented Jamie Spears, the father of superstar Britney Spears, in the #FreeBritney movement over her con-

---

[*]   We found various reports ranging from $780 million to nearly $1 billion as Tony's net worth, though the figure used most recently was $840 million.

servatorship. They began the process of trying to untangle Tony's estate right away, traveling to Park City. They asked friends and employees staying at the Ranch and Tony's other properties to leave.

The move by the court to appoint Andy Hsieh in charge of his brother's assets was intensely controversial among some of Tony's close friends. Andy Hsieh had lived at the Ranch with Tony, directing dozens of contractors and employees, eventually rising to become part of Tony's "core" group. He had been forming his own business, a tequila company, funded ostensibly by his brother, while Tony had clearly been deteriorating. All of that had taken place after his own family's failed intervention attempt in August 2020, when Tony had exiled his parents and agreed to pay Andy $1 million to stay, despite his persistent abuse of nitrous oxide. Andy Hsieh had himself stored whippets for Tony in his room. He had worked to keep Park City Police Department officers off the property. Years before, he hadn't spent much time around Tony and his old group of friends.

But Andy Hsieh had also quietly remained in touch with Jewel and her team, a fact not many around him knew, keeping her up to date on Tony and trying to form a plan with her to save him. Of the many people around Tony in August 2020, he appeared to Jewel's team to be the one with the most compassion. Andy Hsieh had told some of Tony's friends and employees that he stayed close to his brother to make sure he was safe.

In early 2021, Mimi Pham sued Richard and Andy Hsieh as the administrators of Tony's estate who now controlled Tony's businesses and filed claims for payments with the estate. As Tony's longtime assistant, she claimed that she was owed more than $90 million from various ventures remaining from her long friendship with Tony. That included an estimated $75 million for what she said was the anticipated profit from documentary movie streaming deals. She claimed another $7.5 million from a project in Park City to revamp an old lodge.

To mount the legal fight, she hired the high-profile Las Vegas legal team of David Chesnoff and Richard Schonfeld, known in part for their high-profile criminal defense work representing wealthy and famous clients who get into trouble in Las Vegas, such as Paris Hilton and Bruno Mars. Chesnoff was part of the legal team of the real estate heir Robert Durst during his 2021 murder trial. (He was convicted of murder.)

Some close friends of Tony's thought that Pham's filings were heartless, particularly given the timing. She wanted access to items from a warehouse of Tony's, including Burning Man supplies, furniture, two golf carts, artwork, and bicycles. Many of the belongings had sentimental value. But some of Tony's friends questioned why Pham would take legal action, forcing Tony's family to respond so soon after the tragedy.

In court filings, Pham emphasized her closeness to Tony over Andy and the Hsieh family, contrasting her intimacy to the icier relationship between Tony and his father and brother, as she described it. In court filings, her attorneys pointed out that Andy Hsieh had moved to Park City with his brother, but "that is not an indication of a familial bond as he was offered a $1,000,000 annual salary in exchange for said move."

Tony's family shot back, describing Tony's physical and mental decline over the months before he died and the way the estrangement of close friends and family had left him vulnerable in the end. Pham and her boyfriend, Roberto Grande, were among those who had exploited him, the family claimed. During that time, Tony's health had become so poor that a health care provider had said he wouldn't have longer than six months to live without an intervention.

In court, the Hsieh family noted that it had been obvious to Pham and her boyfriend that Tony was "physically and mentally unwell, and that he was in no condition to consider, let alone approve, significant investments or contracts for investments. Witnesses who saw Tony at this time describe him as having lost a tremendous amount of weight. Witnesses describe a belief that Tony's death was imminent." Pham and Grande have denied the family's claims about them in court.

Meanwhile, others from Tony's past also came forward claiming the estate owed them money. An artist named Toshie McSwain filed a claim for $40,000 for a prototype for a sculpture of a brain that was to have been built and installed on a ceiling. Mark Evensvold, the restaurant manager from Las Vegas who had agreed to manage Tony's in-house bars in Park City, filed a claim for $12.5 million, citing his sticky-note contract. Tony Lee, the old family friend convinced by Andy Hsieh to leave Fort Worth for Park City to work for Tony in the last months of his life, filed a nearly $6.9 million lawsuit after he was notified that he would no longer be paid by the Hsiehs. In court filings, Lee argued that Andy Hsieh had picked out Lee and other people around Tony as "scapegoats," while Andy Hsieh actually conducted much of the acts that he has accused others of. That included, according to Mr. Lee's filings, that Andy Hsieh plied his brother with alcohol despite knowing he suffered from cirrhosis, "arranged for the purchase of thousands of canisters of nitrous oxide at an alarming rate," and asked Lee to "divert millions of dollars from Tony Hsieh's holdings to Andy himself." Suzie Baleson, through her company, filed a nearly $8.8 million claim, saying she was owed for services on Tony's projects including a "magic castle" in Park City that involved performers and live streaming. By December 2021, the Hsieh family had come up with a preliminary estimate for the remaining value of Tony's fortune: about $500 million.

Tony's entourage in Park City scattered, many of them continuing their lives as if nothing had happened. Justin Weniger went back to Las Vegas to help plan the Life Is Beautiful music festival in September 2021, in which he and Baleson organized a group meditation session at the start of the event, led by Deepak Chopra, in honor of Tony. Otherwise, there were few public tributes of Tony at the biggest public celebration in downtown Las Vegas since his passing. Rachael Brown stayed in her New London, Connecticut home where Tony had tragically been trapped in the shed. Don Calder moved back to Los Angeles to operate a T-shirt company. Anthony Hebert's whereabouts are unknown. Daniel Park continues to tour and play music. Elizabeth Pezzello and Brett Gorman got married in Park City but moved back to Naples, Florida, to open a business called Vitamin Bar Naples, which delivers vitamins to customers intravenously. An

Instagram post from March 2021 shows the couple smiling in matching white T-shirts, holding a sign for their new business.

Tony did not leave a will and also appeared not to have used other planning techniques often employed by the wealthy to shelter their heirs from having to pay steep federal estate taxes, such as moving assets into trusts. The Hsiehs told a judge that they would need to raise cash to pay a looming tax bill, possibly by liquidating the estate's stocks or obtaining a loan. They also filed notices in court saying that dozens of Tony's properties in Las Vegas could be put up for sale, including undeveloped lots and more thriving downtown assets such as Container Park.

The move set off a controversy in Las Vegas, even though the Hsiehs vowed they weren't looking to dismantle Tony's legacy there. "Tony Hsieh's Family to Sell Off Much of Las Vegas Real Estate Empire," a headline in the *Las Vegas Review-Journal* read in February 2021.

But some people in downtown Las Vegas welcomed the idea of new owners bringing more diverse ideas to the city's future who would be like a "Tony Hsieh 2.0," said Las Vegas councilwoman Olivia Diaz. "His fingerprints will always be on that part of town," she remarked.

On a beautiful evening in May 2021, a crowd of people surrounded Tony's praying mantis sculpture in front of Container Park, clapping and cheering as the insect blasted fire from its antennae. Inside the development, kids happily tore through the tree house playground as their parents sipped wine at nearby tables; a guitarist tuned his instrument, gearing up to play a concert at one end of the park. Tourists and locals filled the walkways, restaurants, and nearby candy shop. It was exactly as Tony had hoped.

At a nearby restaurant, someone had scribbled in big letters across several windows: WE LOVE TONY.

In *Delivering Happiness*, Tony described a magic trick he had once taught himself: how to take a coin and make it seem as though it could dissolve into a piece of rubber. He had always been fond of magic tricks, basking in the amazement of his audience when pulling off a seemingly impossible feat.

In the end, he brought joy to people around him while performing his most challenging sleight of hand: throughout his life, he kept up the appearances of eternal hope and infallible optimism, even as he suffered privately from mental health and substance abuse issues.

When we began reporting on Tony in the fall of 2020, we kept hearing a similar description of Tony's life story from the people we spoke to, many of whom said they had seen and interacted with Tony regularly over many years. The story line was a simple one: there had been nothing wrong with Tony until the fall of 2019, when he had begun taking ketamine.

Many months of research into his life revealed how Tony, who had poured his life into experiences for other people, ultimately felt alone. He had severe social anxiety. He drank alcohol to diminish it, turning it into another quirk of his personality and part of his giving to others through parties and Zappos events. He struggled with facial blindness, and so he learned to recognize friends' voices and relied on a select few to guide him. He wondered if he had some form of autism but was never diagnosed.

It's not surprising that few people really knew this other side of Tony and the many issues with which he struggled. Tony was many things to many people: the party organizer; the audacious entrepreneur; the humble boss; the investor in other people's dreams; the quirky neighbor in an Airstream trailer park, living with his pet alpaca. His audience was eager to believe in that picture. When the Hsieh family filed court documents as part of his estate battle in 2021, it was the first time anyone had publicly acknowledged that Tony had drunk as a coping mechanism, even though his heavy daily drinking had been well known by his friends and colleagues. "Tony's mind moved at an incredible speed, and Tony described using alcohol as a social lubricant to alleviate his social anxiety and to allow him to better communicate and make deeper connections to the people around him," the Hsieh family's attorneys wrote.

But the gulf between how people viewed Tony and his private struggles exposes a much greater societal problem: the taboo surrounding mental health problems and addiction. Both issues are still discussed in whispers, willfully ignored, unacknowledged even when they are in plain view. Without a dialogue surrounding addiction and mental illness, those who are suffering must do so alone, hiding their problems and putting on happy faces. They use drugs and alcohol to mask their pain and anxiety. Tony embodied that lonely struggle. After the tennis player Naomi Osaka withdrew from the French Open in the spring of 2021 to focus on her mental health, she wrote in an essay for *Time* that she had been struck by the outpouring of messages she had received. "It has become apparent to me that literally everyone either suffers from issues related to their mental health or knows someone who does," she wrote.

People who are suffering don't make it easy for others to help them, and Tony was the epitome of that problem. He was skilled at explaining away concerns and shied away from confrontation and criticism. He continued to perform at a high level. Even when his good friend Jewel brought a mental health program to Zappos, he still managed to avoid the conversation. He normalized first his heavy drinking and later his drug use, his coping mechanisms to deal with the people around him. He handed friends books and showed them TED Talks to explain himself. Even if anyone had thought to question his drinking, it was an even farther leap to wonder why he needed so much alcohol: What was the underlying issue? As the therapists at Cirque Lodge say, drug or alcohol abuse is always covering up another issue. Tony didn't invite that kind of examination from even his closest friends, and certainly his adoring fans, particularly later in his life, wouldn't have examined any problems. His character, full of so many contradictions—awkward but exceedingly fun, unfailingly generous but lacking empathy—was so unusual anyway that it was even easier to explain away any inconsistencies. As Ali Bevilacqua, Tony's ex-girlfriend, put it, "People give a lot of excuses in a room for people who are geniuses and eccentrics."

Tech founders such as Tony are even more susceptible to this sort of toxic idolization complex because Silicon Valley doesn't just accept strangeness from its titans, it expects and celebrates it. But some of the same traits—mania, magnetism, and almost singular focus—that can catapult leaders to stardom can ultimately spell their downfall.

In recent years, countless tech CEOs have been exalted only to suffer a steep downfall, Travis Kalanick at Uber, Elizabeth Holmes at Theranos, and Adam Neumann at WeWork among them. In each of these cases, the executives were later revealed to have presided over ruthless cultures or to have behaved recklessly, if not potentially criminally. Tony, who led with a sense of purpose, doesn't fit into this narrative, but he was put onto a pedestal in a similar way, only to come crashing down later. His death exposes the pitfalls of putting so much blind faith in our leaders, no matter how inspiring they may be, and the vast disparity between the public persona and private life of celebrity, a status Tony had achieved by the end of his life.

Additionally, the tech community has embraced biohacking, experimenting with ways to push one's body beyond human limits, to operate like a machine, by using ice baths, fasting, changing sleep patterns, microdosing LSD. It can quickly spiral out of control, as Tony's last years illustrated. The idea of solving one's own health problems without therapy or traditional medication can mask deeper struggles.

Tony ignored his own self-care even as he worked so hard to spread happiness to those around him. We may never know exactly where that desire came from or how it originated. Did his strict childhood make him crave anything lighthearted and fun? Was he an extreme people pleaser, unable to stop himself from giving? Was he so scared of what he might find inside himself that he refused to look inward? We have asked ourselves, and others, these very questions over these many months.

Tony—whether trotting through the office in his T-shirt and black Asics sneakers or going out with friends with a mohawk and sequined jacket—always valued each person's inherent "weirdness" and individuality. In many ways, his values, his fast-paced curiosity, and his appetite for risk kept him open to the world—to other people, new ideas, and a hopeful future.

If we had a similar culture around mental health, one of acceptance and openness, maybe Tony could have found healing. If admitting one's pain wasn't stigmatized, if we acknowledged our common internal struggles, maybe the people around Tony could have recognized the warning signs. Maybe Tony could have put down the magic tricks and stepped off the stage.

In August 2021, I (Kirsten Grind) called the customer service line at Zappos for the very first time. I had bought a pair of Cobian flip-flops earlier in the summer to wear when I took my dog swimming at the beach near my house in the San Francisco Bay Area. But after only a few weeks with my new shoes, one of the flip-flops disappeared. I knew the culprit immediately: my dog, a two-year-old chocolate lab named Charlie. He will eat and chew on anything.

Out of curiosity, I called Zappos' customer service line to see if they could do anything and see what kind of service I might receive.

The first automated prompt asked me if I would like to press five to hear a joke before proceeding. Of course I did! "What do ghosts eat for supper?" "Spookghetti!"

A cheery customer service representative came on the line immediately after and introduced herself as Hallie. I explained to her what had happened: my dog had literally eaten my flip-flop. Hallie started laughing. "Oh, no, little pup, I'm so sorry," she sympathized.

It took us many minutes to find my account, as I had listed it under an old email address, and Hallie stood by patiently until I finally found my confirmation email. "We will figure it out!" she exclaimed at one point.

Once we had accessed my order, Hallie told me she would investigate what Zappos could do. "While we're looking, how's your day going?" she asked as though she were speaking to a friend.

I told her it was fine, that the weather in the Bay Area was unfortunately cooler than I would have liked for summer, 65 degrees and cloudy. "I'm working in Las Vegas," Hallie told me, where "it's very hot." The day had flown by, though, "talking to some great customers," she continued. "It's been a pretty good day if I do say so myself."

Later she told me she was working at home in her pajamas and slippers. "It's so great, I love it," she added.

After almost no time at all and no holding, she told me that Zappos would send me a new pair of $31 flip-flops for free. When she checked on the delivery date, about a week from when we were speaking, she said, "Let me see if I can get that quicker."

In return, she asked if I could please send my extra flip-flop—the one Charlie hadn't eaten—to Soles4Souls, an organization that Zappos partners with to donate shoes and clothing. She sent an email to me with the link, signed with her name, and told me that Zappos would pay for the shipping.

"What's your dog's name?" she asked before I hung up, and soon we were talking about her own pet, who had unfortunately passed away in 2020 after a decade together. Now it was my turn to sympathize.

"Have a great night with Charlie," she said to end the call. "Give him lots of kisses for me!"

A year had passed since Tony had stepped down from Zappos and more than two decades since he had redefined the meaning of customer service. Zappos was still fulfilling his mission. The call was almost textbook what Tony would have asked from his customer loyalty team and echoed dozens of stories Katherine Sayre and I had read and heard about Zappos' customer service as we reported this book. Hallie's Personal Service Level, the metric Tony employed to judge personal connection, was off the charts. Even the joke of the day, which Tony had launched at Zappos years earlier, having often called 976-JOKE during his childhood, was still in place. Tony liked to say that Zappos wasn't a shoe company—it was a service company that sold shoes. That was clearly still true.

But among Tony's close friends and even at Zappos, there has been a realization that the search for happiness shouldn't just be that—a relentless quest to cultivate joy all around you. The path starts inward. It is built on confronting our human struggles with the help of trusted people who are on journeys that parallel ours.

Zappos' management is still trying to maintain the happy workplace that Tony had established, although it has paused holacracy and market-based dynamics as it has focused more heavily on what it has always done: selling shoes. In the summer of 2021, with temperatures soaring in Las Vegas, the company launched a program to deliver air conditioners to workers whose units had failed. Most Zappos employees were still working from home because of the pandemic, so it was particularly important that they be able to do their jobs comfortably. It was a small gesture but exactly the sort of thing Tony would have done to help his workforce be happy.

Some aspects of workplace culture are changing at Zappos, though. Following Tony's death, executives realized that employees need to focus on their own needs first before those of others, something Tony was never able to do for himself. The company is therefore encouraging its employees to think about health and wellness. It is focused more now on what some executives are calling "the whole human," much like Jewel's prior work there: encouraging things such as taking mental health days and limiting work hours. Parties and happy hours have died down anyway because of the pandemic.

In December 2021, Zappos employees were again facing a management transition, when Kedar Deshpande said he would step down after only a year at the helm of Zappos to take the CEO role at Groupon. In an internal email to Zappos employees he wrote, "One of the things Tony instilled in me and strived to instill in every employee, was the importance of Delivering WOW—not only while at Zappos, but anywhere our futures may lead us." Deshpande said he would carry on the tradition.

Tony ended his own book with a wish. He hoped to bring the reader happiness, to have it passed on to others, even one day to get the entire world moving in that direction. "I don't have all the answers," he wrote. "But hopefully I've succeeded in getting you to start asking yourself the right questions."

APPENDIX

MENTAL HEALTH RESOURCES

If you or someone you know is in immediate danger, calling 911 might be necessary; callers should notify operators that it is a psychiatric emergency and ask for police officers trained in crisis prevention and psychiatric emergencies, according to the **National Alliance on Mental Illness**.

National Suicide Prevention Lifeline is free, confidential, and available twenty-four hours a day, seven days a week. It connects people to a nearby crisis center, which can provide counseling and referrals to mental health care. Call 1-800-273-TALK (8255) or 1-888-628-9454 en español.

Crisis Text Line connects with a trained crisis counselor twenty-four hours a day, seven days a week. Text 741741 in the United States and Canada.

The Substance Abuse and Mental Health Services Administration offers an information line to connect to local treatment: 1-800-662-HELP (4357).

The National Institute of Mental Health also recommends speaking with a primary care practitioner about mental health to discuss concerns and get referrals for further treatment.

The National Alliance on Mental Illness is a nonprofit mental health organization that includes more than six hundred local groups and forty-eight state organizations working in communities, supporting people with mental health concerns and their friends and families. More information, including a live chat with a specialist, can be found at www.nami.org or by calling the helpline at 1-800-950-NAMI (6264).

ACKNOWLEDGMENTS

Writing a book is a monumental challenge, and it would have been impossible in this case without the help of Tony Hsieh's many friends and loved ones. We talked to dozens of them over the course of this reporting, but a handful of his close friends went above and beyond, spending hours and hours with us to make sure we clearly understood Tony's thinking and his actions over the years, especially because we didn't have the ability to ask him ourselves. Some of them spoke despite the threat of legal action and other circumstances that put them at personal risk. You know who you are, and we can't thank you enough for all your help, and patience, over many months.

This book originated out of our investigative reporting for the *Wall Street Journal* about the circumstances surrounding Tony Hsieh's death, and would not have been possible without that foundation. We'd like to thank our trusted editors, Brad Reagan and Liz Rappaport, for their extensive work on those stories, and for initially understanding the importance of Tony's life and death. We have a masterful enterprise editing team at the *WSJ* led by Matthew Rose and Tammy Audi, and we were lucky enough to work with Sam Enriquez and Dan Kelly, who helped polish our narratives in two of our longer stories, as well as Ethan Smith in Exchange. Other editors to thank: Jamie Heller, for her exuberance and unwavering support; Jason Dean, one of the hardest-working editors we know; and our executive editor, Matt Murray, a strong supporter of this kind of work. Some of our *WSJ* colleagues helped us along the way, including Bob Hagerty, who worked with us on our first story after Tony died, and Kate King, who was on the ground in Connecticut. Others who gave us great advice, or listened to various quandaries related to book reporting, include Erich Schwartzel, Greg Zuckerman, Jennifer Levitz, Colin Barr, Eliot Brown, and Tripp Mickle.

We could not have found a better home for this book than Simon & Schuster and in our editor, Stephanie Frerich. Stephanie's enthusiasm for Tony's story and clear vision for the narrative helped us immensely, as did her deft edits and questions, which always improved our writing significantly, and helped us sharpen our framing throughout the story. Her editorial assistant, Emily Simonson, has been hugely helpful throughout, explaining details large and small. Our copyediting manager, Jessica Chin, and our lawyer, Jeff Miller, also provided much-needed assistance. Thank you also to Michael Nagin, cover designer; Erika Genova, interior designer; and Alicia Brancato, production manager.

This book might not have happened at all without the keen eyes of our agent, Todd Shuster at Aevitas Creative. He and another editor, Daniella Cohen, were hugely helpful in initially shaping the format of the book, and pushing us to figure out the best way to lay out Tony's story. Allison Warren at Aevitas was fast and proactive about selling movie and documentary rights, and we look forward to Tony's story being shared again in new ways.

From Kirsten: There is no way I could have taken on a project like this while raising two small children without the full support of a heroic partner like my husband, Steve Grind. He patiently took care of the kids on weekends and nights for months as we wrote and reported this book, all while starting a new job. He listened to me talk about Tony and his story nonstop and had great advice on how to handle different aspects of the book. Thank you endlessly, Steve. The last time I wrote a book I didn't have kids, and my two sons, Ellis and Wesley, had to sacrifice a lot of mom time over the months we put this together. They were very patient, and also excited about the prospect of their mom writing a book, even though it wouldn't have pictures. Our pandemic dog, Charlie, actually appears in this book, and was a trusted—if not somewhat annoying—companion during the long days when everyone was back at work and school except me. I have some really good friends who are amazing journalists and who helped enormously through this process, in particular Jessica Silver-Greenberg, who continually goes above and beyond to support me in anything I take on, and will take a panicked phone call day or night despite her own small children. My former editor at the *WSJ*, now at the *New York Times*, David Enrich, was a wise counsel on this project, especially early on. Sue Craig listened to me time and again rattle on about various aspects of this story and always has sage advice. Other longtime friends whom I love dearly and always help me, even from afar: Kimmy Torch, Kelly Kennedy, and Karen Johnson. Even though we were separated by the pandemic, my *WSJ* row mates and fellow Alcatraz swimmers Georgia Wells and Bob McMillan in San Francisco still managed to offer counsel and support, even when I bailed on our last swim—sorry again! Last but certainly not least, my parents, Pat Orsini and Klaus Meinhard, are always so supportive of me in whatever I take on, and are always so proud of my career accomplishments. My sisters, Sonja Revilla and Iman Rosario, are always there to encourage me, even when we can't all be together.

From Katherine: Thank you to my parents, Barbara and Jon Lindenmayer and Alan and Terri Sayre, for your love and encouragement. A special thanks to Terri for helping me get started on my best professional adventures. Mom, you taught me empathy, a gift in life and in journalism. I am grateful for a family of past editors and reporting colleagues whom I've learned much from, in particular my investigative pals Manuel Torres, Jonathan Bullington, and Rich Webster. To everyone from the former NOLA newsroom, all of your endeavors continue to inspire me. You have all given me a life lesson in resiliency. I'm in awe of the amazing fact-checking skills of Mandy Tust and Sara Sneath, who spent many hours backing me up on this book. My family of friends, in New Orleans and beyond, whom I have missed dearly in recent years, have been there for me across the miles through the writing process. Chelsea Brasted's steady faith in me, and her joyful spirit, were invaluable. Sara Brownlee is a true best friend—thank you for always listening, even when it felt like Groundhog Day. Thanks most of all to my husband, Mike Joe, the best dog-dad to Sandy and Ziggy, whose love and support, in so many ways, have carried me all the way.

NOTES

Many people spoke to us on background only, not for attribution, because of confidentiality agreements, ongoing litigation, or other reasons preventing them from speaking on the record. Other sources of information are noted below.

Prologue: "A Freak Accident"

2   *As a kid, he pretended*: Greg Smith, "Curcio Takes the Reins at New London Fire Department," *The Day*, September 12, 2018, https://www.theday.com/article /20180912/NWS01/180919805.

2   *at an official ceremony*: Ibid.

3   *"He's barricaded"*: Lee Hawkins, "Before Tony Hsieh's Death, Firefighters Rushed to Burning Home with Trapped Man," *Wall Street Journal*, November 29, 2020, https://www.wsj.com/articles/before-tony-hsiehs-death-firefighters -rushed-to-burning-home-with-trapped-man-11606691000.

3   *Curcio moved on*: Interviews with Chief Thomas Curcio, May 2021 and September 2021.

4   *Soon Curcio's phone lit up*: Ibid.

7   *Naomi Osaka*: Naomi Osaka, "Naomi Osaka: 'It's O.K. Not to Be O.K.,'" *Time*, July 8, 2021, https://time.com/6077128/naomi-osaka-essay-tokyo-olympics/.

7   *Simone Biles*: Alice Park, "How the Tokyo Olympics Changed the Conversation About Mental Health," *Time*, August 8, 2021, https://time.com/6088078/mental -health-olympics-simone-biles/.

Chapter 1: "A Very Optimistic, Innocent Time"

14   *Cirque Lodge charges most patients*: Interviews with Cirque Lodge staff, May 2021 and September 2021.

14   *about $64,000 a month*: Ibid.

14   *Big-name former clients*: Claudia Wallace, "Rehab for the Rich and Famous," *Fortune*, October 20, 2009, https://archive.fortune.com/2009/10/16/news /companies/cirque_lodge.fortune/index.htm.

15   *Called the Laundry Room*: "Legend of the Laundry Room," The Laundry Room, https://www.laundryroomlv.com.

16   *"A fake protest"*: Reyhan Harmanci, "Interested in the Jejune Institute? It's Too Late," *New York Times*, April 21, 2011, https://www.nytimes.com/2011/04/2 2/us/22bcculture.html.

17   *would also have just ended*: "2020 Sundance Film Festival Schedule," Sundance Institute, https://www.sundance.org/blogs/news/2020-sundance-features-announced.

18   *Beck and Losee early on*: Interview with Dave Beck, May 2020.

19   *Oracle's business is not exciting*: "1970s: Defying Conventional Wisdom," Oracle, May 2007, https://www.oracle.com/us/corporate/profit/p27anniv-timeline-151918.pdf.

19   *was bringing in*: Reuters, "Company Reports; Oracle Corp. (ORCL,NMM)," *New York Times*, June 23, 1995, https://www.nytimes.com/1995/06/23/business /company-reports-oracle-corp-orclnnm.html.

19   *The $40,000 salary*: Tony Hsieh, *Delivering Happiness: A Path to Profits, Passion, and Purpose* (New York: Grand Central Publishing, 2010), 30.

19   *His parents, Richard and Judy*: Hsieh, *Delivering Happiness*, 8.

20   *he wanted to build something*: Ibid., 10.

20   *no one was tracking*: Ibid., 31.

20   *Richard Hsieh told him*: Ibid., 37.

20   *only about 3 percent*: "Americans Going Online . . . Explosive Growth, Uncertain Destinations," Pew Research Center, October 16, 1995, https://www.pew research.org/politics/1995/10/16/americans-going-online-explosive-growth -uncertain-destinations/.

20   *Oracle became one*: "1970s: Defying Conventional Wisdom," Oracle.

21   *Demand for the stock*: Adam Lashinsky, "Remembering Netscape: The Birth of the Web," CNN Money, July 25, 2005, https://money.cnn.com/magazines /fortune/fortune_archive/2005/07/25/8266639/.

21   *the first one had launched*: Ryan Singel, "Oct. 27, 1994: Web Gives Birth to Banner Ads," *Wired*, October 27, 2010, https://www.wired.com/2010/10/1027hotwired -banner-ads/.

22   *When an important*: Julia Angwin, "Internet World Is a Stage / Startups Hope to Catch Eyes at the Largest Web-Users Convention," SFGATE, March 12, 1997, https://www.sfgate.com/business/article/Internet-World-Is-a-Stage-Startups -hope-to-2849478.php.

23   *A San Francisco Focus*: Author and title unknown, *San Francisco Focus*, August 1997.

26   *Named for*: "Yahoo History—Complete History of the Yahoo Search Engine," History Computer, July 15, 2021, https://history-computer.com/software /yahoo-history-complete-history-of-the-yahoo-search-engine/.

26   *Yang wanted to buy*: Hsieh, *Delivering Happiness*, 42.

27   *Sometimes parties took place*: David Garber, "Meet the Renegade DJ Crew Who Helped Bring Rave Culture to the West Coast," Vice, October 18, 2016, https:// www.vice.com/en/article/4x88gq/wicked-san-fransisco-anniversary-feature.

28   *The warehouse was massive*: Hsieh, *Delivering Happiness*, 78.

28   *"As someone who is"*: Ibid., 79.

29   *Hundreds of people*: Julia Angwin, "Where Wuppies Gather / DrinkExchange Draws Hundreds Every Month," SFGATE, September 6, 1997, https://www.sfgate.com/business/article/Where-Wuppies-Gather-DrinkExchange-draws-2808693.php.

29   *One clunky online invitation*: "NOTE: DrinkExchange on October 30!!!," Drink-Exchange, October 11, 1999, https://web.archive.org/web/19991011095757/http://www.drinkexchange.com:80/sanfran/.

29   *a financial crisis in Russia*: "IPOs Roar Back to Life," CNN Money, December 1, 1998, https://money.cnn.com/1998/12/01/investing/ipo/.

29   *sparked in part*: Peter Delevett, "Partovi Twins Quietly Emerge as Top Silicon Valley Angel Investors," *Mercury News*, March 7, 2014, https://www.mercurynews.com/2014/03/07/partovi-twins-quietly-emerge-as-top-silicon-valley-angel-investors/.

30   *paid $265 million*: Hsieh, *Delivering Happiness*, 49.

30   *"Against the backdrop"*: Paulette Thomas, "Rewriting the Rules," *Wall Street Journal*, May 22, 2000, https://www.wsj.com/articles/SB958491110748477546.

30   *eBay, the online auction site*: Aaron Lucchetti, "eBay IPO, Priced at $18, Breaks a Long Dry Spell," *Wall Street Journal*, September 24, 1998, https://www.wsj.com/articles/SB906553299573701000.

30   *He would have earned*: Hsieh, *Delivering Happiness*, 49.

Chapter 2: Treasure Mountain

31   *Park City nearly disappeared*: Tina Stahlke Lewis, "How Park City Survived the Ghost Town Years of the 1950s," *Park City Magazine*, December 8, 2018, https://www.parkcitymag.com/arts-and-culture/2018/12/how-park-city-survived-the-ghost-town-years-of-the-1950s.

31   *that become biking routes*: "Open Space & Trails," Park City, https://www.parkcity.org/about-us/bus-bike-walk/open-space-trails.

31   *like those of other*: "Mining Towns in the Western United States," Western Mining History, https://westernmininghistory.com/map/.

31   *The town was home*: Alison Butz, "Park City's History," Historic Park City Utah, October 13, 2010, https://historicparkcityutah.com/news/park-citys-history.

31   *survived big fires*: Jami Balls, "History of Park City," History to Go, https://historytogo.utah.gov/history-park-city/.

31   *catastrophic mine collapses*: Tom Clyde, "Tom Clyde: The Second Daly West Mine Disaster," *Park Record*, May 15, 2015, https://www.parkrecord.com/opinion/letters/tom-clyde-the-second-daly-west-mine-disaster/.

32   *were boarded up*: Lewis, "How Park City Survived the Ghost Town Years of the 1950s."

32   *appeared in a guidebook*: Ibid.

32   *1,150 people still lived there*: "Park City History Timeline," Park City Museum, https://parkcityhistory.org/park-city-historic-timeline/.

32   *set on a new course*: "Dying Mining Town to Become Ski Resort," *New York Times*, April 15, 1963, http://timesmachine.nytimes.com/timesmachine/1963 /04/15/102285644.html?pageNumber=98.

32   *Treasure Mountain ski resort*: Shontai M. Pohl, "The Way We Were: Treasure Mountain Inn," *Park Record*, June 9, 2015, https://www.parkrecord.com/news /park-city/the-way-we-were-treasure-mountain-inn/.

32   *about 8,400 people*: "Park City city, Utah," United States Census Bureau, https://data.census.gov/cedsci/profile?g=1600000US4958070.

32   *More than 100,000 people*: Bubba Brown, "Sundance 2019 Dipped Slightly but Still Brought In $182.5 Million and More than 120K Attendees," *Park Record*, May 31, 2019, https://www.parkrecord.com/news/sundance-2019-dipped -slightly-but-still-brought-in-182-5-million-and-more-than-120k-attendees/.

32   *walk the press line*: Tiffini Porter, "Park City's Beloved George S. and Dolores Doré Eccles Center Celebrates 20 Years," *Park City Magazine*, December 15, 2017, https://www.parkcitymag.com/arts-and-culture/2017/12/stage-of-many-players.

32   *current booming industry*: Jeff Dempsey, "Park City Area Real Estate Had a Banner Year in 2020," *Park Record*, February 14, 2021, https://www.parkrecord .com/news/park-city-area-real-estate-had-a-banner-year-in-2020/.

33   *reported the first known*: Bubba Brown, "First Known Instance of Coronavirus Community Spread in Summit County Discovered (Updated)," *Park Record*, March 14, 2020, https://www.parkrecord.com/news/officials-announce-first -instance-of-coronavirus-community-spread-in-summit-county/.

33   *In the following days*: "Declarations/Announcements," Park City, https://www .parkcity.org/government/covid-19/declarations-announcements.

33   *foresaw an economic crisis*: Leia Larsen and Tony Semerad, "With Sales Taxes Down Sharply Due to COVID-19, Utah Cities Face Painful Budget Choices," *Salt Lake Tribune*, June 8, 2020, https://www.sltrib.com/news/2020/06/08/ with-sales-taxes-down/.

33   *arts and culture district*: Sean Higgins, "Park City Council to Revisit Arts and Culture District Funding This Week," KPCW, February 24, 2021, https://www .kpcw.org/post/park-city-council-revisit-arts-and-culture-district-funding-week.

33   *thrown into question*: Jay Hamburger, "Park City Funding for Arts District Questioned amid Coronavirus Pandemic," *Park Record*, December 23, 2020, https://www.parkrecord.com/news/park-city/park-city-funding-for-arts-district -questioned-amid-coronavirus-pandemic/.

36   *1000 Van Ness Avenue*: Cindy, "The Don Lee Building," Art and Architecture, June 20, 2013, https://www.artandarchitecture-sf.com/the-don-lee-building.html.

36   *originally designed*: "National Register #01001179: Don Lee Building," NoeHill in San Francisco, https://noehill.com/sf/landmarks/nat2001001179.asp.

36   *Developers were converting*: Tony Hsieh, *Delivering Happiness: A Path to Profits, Passion, and Purpose* (New York: Grand Central Publishing, 2010), 55–56.

36   *the group eventually owned*: Ibid., 56.

37   *OpenTable*: "OpenTable Dines Out on $10 Million," OpenTable, January 8, 2000, https://press.opentable.com/news-releases/news-release-details/opentable-dines-out-10-million/.

37   *a native of England*: Nathan Mollat, "Dragons FC Soccer Swoops into Burlingame," *San Mateo Daily Journal*, December 9, 2014.

37   *unable to find*: "Who We Are," Zappos, https://www.zappos.com/about/who-we-are.

37   *Tony would later recount*: Tony Hsieh, "How I Did It: Zappos's CEO on Going to Extremes for Customers," *Harvard Business Review*, July–August 2010, https://hbr.org/2010/07/how-i-did-it-zapposs-ceo-on-going-to-extremes-for-customers.

37   *offered up some statistics*: Jay Yarow, "The Zappos Founder Just Told Us All Kinds of Crazy Stories—Here's the Surprisingly Candid Interview," Insider, November 28, 2011, https://www.businessinsider.com/nick-swinmurn-zappos-rnkd-2011-11.

37   *wearing board shorts*: Katie Abel, "A Friendship for the Ages: Fred Mossler + the OG Zappos Crew Share Untold Tales About the Incredible Tony Hsieh," *Footwear News*, December 21, 2020, https://footwearnews.com/2020/business/retail/tony-hsieh-zappos-friends-legacy-1203085996/.

37   *Tony urged Swinmurn*: Hsieh, *Delivering Happiness*, 58.

37   *found Fred Mossler*: Abel, "A Friendship for the Ages."

37   *spent eight years*: Hsieh, *Delivering Happiness*, 60.

37   *once Venture Frogs agreed*: "Zappos.com, World's Largest Shoe Store, Receives $1.1 Million in Financing," PR Newswire, January 19, 2000.

37   *he quit*: Hsieh, *Delivering Happiness*, 61.

38   *"Owning the loft"*: Ibid., 77.

39   *"wasn't just dumb luck"*: Ibid., 89.

39   *Tony emailed Zappos staff*: Ibid., 94.

39   *a round of layoffs*: Ibid., 95.

39   *faster shipping methods*: "20 Years, 20 Milestones: How Zappos Grew Out of Just Shoes," Zappos, June 5, 2019, https://www.zappos.com/about/stories/zappos-20th-birthday.

39   *live there rent-free*: Hsieh, *Delivering Happiness*, 97.

39   *before selling the loft*: Ibid., 115.

39   *posted $70 million*: Hsieh, "How I Did It: Zappos's CEO on Going to Extremes for Customers."

40   *Zappos would give them*: "20 Years, 20 Milestones: How Zappos Grew Out of Just Shoes."

40   *Amazon would launch*: Jason Del Rey, "The Making of Amazon Prime, the Internet's Most Successful and Devastating Membership Program," Vox, May 3, 2019, https://www.vox.com/recode/2019/5/3/18511544/amazon-prime-oral-history-jeff-bezos-one-day-shipping.

40   *it had become difficult*: Hsieh, "How I Did It."

42   *New hires were offered*: Katie Canales, "Tony Hsieh, the Late Former CEO of Zappos, Famously Pioneered the Concept of Paying New, Unhappy Employees

$2,000 to Quit in Order to Maintain a Happy, Productive Workforce," Insider, November 30, 2020, https://www.businessinsider.com/zappos-tony-hsieh-paid-new-workers-to-quit-the-offer-2020-11.

42 *toy cars racing*: Rice Sport Management, "Tony Hsieh, CEO of Zappos, Featured on 20/20," YouTube, https://www.youtube.com/watch?v=Lfp9LHFIXfI.

43 *"We really want"*: CBS Sunday Morning, "From 2010: Zappos CEO Tony Hsieh," YouTube, November 28, 2020, https://www.youtube.com/watch?v=wSHG3EU1EZ4.

43 *$635 million*: Sarah Lacy, "What Everyone Made from the Zappos Sale," TechCrunch, July 27, 2009, https://social.techcrunch.com/2009/07/27/what-everyone-made-from-the-zappos-sale/.

43 *"an e-commerce powerhouse"*: Tony Hsieh, "Why I Sold Zappos," *Inc.*, June 1, 2010, https://www.inc.com/magazine/20100601/why-i-sold-zappos.html.

43 *Some early investors*: Hsieh, *Delivering Happiness*, 210.

43 *"Tony's social experiments"*: Hsieh, "Why I Sold Zappos."

43 *"The board wanted me"*: Ibid.

44 *relied on revolving credit*: Ibid.

44 *had unsuccessfully approached Zappos*: Hsieh, *Delivering Happiness*, 212.

44 *launched its own competitor*: Alistair Barr, "Amazon to Close Fashion Website endless.com," Reuters, September 18, 2012, https://www.reuters.com/article/uk-amazon-endless-idUKBRE88H1DF20120918.

44 *an encounter he described*: Hsieh, "Why I Sold Zappos."

44 *In the video*: 07272009july, "Video from Jeff Bezos about Amazon and Zappos," YouTube, July 22, 2009, https://www.youtube.com/watch?v=-hxX_Q5CnaA.

45 *"In 20 years"*: Matt Rosoff, "Tony Hsieh: Don't Rule Out a Zappos Airline," Insider, September 28, 2011, https://www.businessinsider.com/in-20-years-there-could-be-a-zappos-airline-2011-9.

46 *he had invented*: The Employees of Zappos.com as told to Mark Dagostino, *The Power of WOW: How to Electrify Your Work and Your Life by Putting Service First* (Dallas, TX: BenBella Books, 2019), 94.

46 *His wife had taken*: Yitzi Weiner, "Why Zappos Has a Chief Fungineer," Authority Magazine, January 31, 2019, https://medium.com/authority-magazine/why-zappos-has-a-chief-fungineer-e1bfa283d011.

46 *statistics showed*: Motoko Rich, "Why Is This Man Smiling?," *New York Times*, April 8, 2011, https://www.nytimes.com/2011/04/10/fashion/10HSEIH.html.

46 *So Williams made*: Michael Gaskell, "Tyler Williams—Zappos! Core Values," YouTube, January 24, 2011, https://www.youtube.com/watch?v=6uevQ0LYMBo.

46 *Called "Porta Parties"*: "Meet Porta Party, the World's Most Reimagined Outhouse," Zappos, https://www.zappos.com/portaparty.

47 *Tony asked him*: The Employees of Zappos.com and Dagostino, *The Power of WOW*, 95.

47 *the people who succeed*: Jeff Olson, *The Slight Edge: Turning Simple Disciplines into Massive Success & Happiness* (Lake Dallas, TX: Success Books, 2013).

48   *The book outlines*: Steven Kotler and Jamie Wheal, *Stealing Fire* (New York: Dey Street Books, 2017).

48   *called* biohacking: Sigal Samuel, "How Biohackers Are Trying to Upgrade Their Brains, Their Bodies—and Human Nature," Vox, November 15, 2019, https://www.vox.com/future-perfect/2019/6/25/18682583/biohacking-transhumanism-human-augmentation-genetic-engineering-crispr.

48   *One biohacker described*: Ibid.

48   *Biohacking started gaining popularity*: Roc Morin, "The Man Who Would Make Food Obsolete," *Atlantic*, April 28, 2014, https://www.theatlantic.com/health/archive/2014/04/the-man-who-would-make-eating-obsolete/361058/.

48   *described it as tasting "rancid"*: Keith A. Spencer, "What Soylent Tells Us about Silicon Valley," Salon, May 28, 2017, https://www.salon.com/2017/05/28/what-soylent-tells-us-about-silicon-valley/.

48   *raised over $70 million*: Craig Giammona, "Soylent Rolls Out Its Drinks to More 7-Eleven Stores, Touting Them as Fast Food," *Hartford Courant*, February 5, 2018, https://www.courant.com/la-fi-tn-soylent-20180205-story.html.

48   *"the most joyless"*: Farhad Manjoo, "The Soylent Revolution Will Not Be Pleasurable," *New York Times*, May 28, 2014, https://www.nytimes.com/2014/05/29/technology/personaltech/the-soylent-revolution-will-not-be-pleasurable.html.

49   *"calmer, thinner, extroverted:"* Stefanie Marsh, "Extreme Biohacking: The Tech Guru Who Spent $250,000 Trying to Live for Ever," *Guardian*, September 21, 2018, http://www.theguardian.com/science/2018/sep/21/extreme-biohacking-tech-guru-who-spent-250000-trying-to-live-for-ever-serge-faguet.

49   *He detailed his procedure*: Serge Faguet, "I'm 32 and Spent $200k on Biohacking. Became Calmer, Thinner, Extroverted, Healthier & Happier," Hacker Noon, September 24, 2017, https://hackernoon.com/im-32-and-spent-200k-on-biohacking-became-calmer-thinner-extroverted-healthier-happier-2a2e846ae113.

49   *a drug frequently used*: "Lithium for Bipolar Disorder," WebMD, https://www.webmd.com/bipolar-disorder/guide/bipolar-disorder-lithium.

49   *"the embodiment of"*: Marsh, "Extreme Biohacking."

49   *own annual conference*: "8th Annual Biohacking Conference," Upgrade Labs, https://biohackingconference.com/.

49   *the antithesis of an executive*: Kirsten Grind and Georgia Wells, "Twitter's Jack Dorsey: A Hands-Off CEO in a Time of Turmoil," *Wall Street Journal*, October 27, 2020, https://www.wsj.com/articles/twitters-jack-dorsey-a-hands-off-ceo-in-a-time-of-turmoil-11603822774.

49   *Dorsey's practice involves*: Molly Longman, "Twitter's CEO Only Eats One Meal per Day," Refinery29, January 22, 2020, https://www.refinery29.com/en-us/2020/01/9265628/twitter-jack-dorsey-intermittent-fasting-one-meal-per-day.

49   *He starts his day*: Julia Naftulin, "Jack Dorsey Drinks a Concoction Called 'Salt Juice' Every Morning, but There's No Proof It Does Anything Beneficial for

Most People," Insider, May 6, 2019, https://www.businessinsider.com/why -jack-dorsey-drinks-salt-juice-every-morning-2019-5.

49   *He takes ice baths*: Grind and Wells, "Twitter's Jack Dorsey."

49   *its benefits are mixed*: Allison Torres Burtka, "Do Ice Baths Work? Why Most People Can Skip the Cold Post-workout Soak, According to Athletic Trainers," Insider, April 15, 2021, https://www.insider.com/ice-bath.

49   *Another time he went*: Kirsten Grind, James R. Hagerty, and Katherine Sayre, "The Death of Zappos's Tony Hsieh: A Spiral of Alcohol, Drugs and Extreme Behavior," *Wall Street Journal*, December 6, 2020, https://www.wsj.com/articles/the-death-of -zappos-tony-hsieh-a-spiral-of-alcohol-drugs-and-extreme-behavior-11607264719.

50   *The author Michael Pollan discovered*: Michael Pollan, *How to Change Your Mind: What the New Science of Psychedelics Teaches Us About Consciousness, Dying, Addiction, Depression, and Transcendence* (New York: Penguin, 2018).

50   *"What was missing"*: Ibid., 7.

51   *drowned in a flotation tank*: Amber Tong, "'Biohacker' Traywick Accidentally Drowned, Official Confirms," Endpoints News, July 2, 2018, https://endpts .com/biohacker-traywick-accidentally-drowned-bloomberg/.

51   *A relative told*: Jonah Engel Bromwich, "Death of a Biohacker," *New York Times*, May 19, 2018, https://www.nytimes.com/2018/05/19/style/biohacker -death-aaron-traywick.html.

51   *Months before his death*: Facebook Live video, News2Share, https://www.face book.com/watch/live/?ref=watch_permalink&v=1668713259903223.

52   *Summit Series founders had organized*: Paul Lewis, "Welcome to Powder Mountain—a Utopian Club for the Millennial Elite," *Guardian*, March 16, 2018, http://www.theguardian.com/technology/2018/mar/16/powder-mountain -ski-resort-summit-elite-club-rich-millennials.

52   *owners in financial distress*: Leigh Kamping-Carder, "In Utah, These Entrepreneurs Are Creating Their Own Version of Eden," *Wall Street Journal*, September 19, 2019, https://www.wsj.com/articles/in-utah-these-entrepreneurs-are-creating -their-own-version-of-eden-11568905597.

52   *"The folks that are here"*: Ibid.

Chapter 3: Collisions

53   *The festival started*: "Welcome to the Burning Man Timeline," Burning Man, https://burningman.org/timeline/.

53   *a startup called Google*: "Doodles," Google, https://www.google.com/doodles/about.

54   *"If you haven't been"*: Nellie Bowles, "At HBO's 'Silicon Valley' Premiere, Elon Musk Has Some Notes," Vox, April 3, 2014, https://www.vox. com/2014/4/3/11625260/at-hbos-silicon-valley-premiere-elon-musk-is-pissed.

54   *a term coined by*: Jillian D'Onfro, "How Zappos CEO's Obsession with Raving Helped Him Create a Billion-Dollar Company," Insider, October 31, 2014, https://www .businessinsider.com/heres-why-zappos-ceo-tony-hsieh-was-obsessed-with-raving-2014-10.

54   *"When you experience it"*: David Hochman, "Playboy Interview: Tony Hsieh," April 16, 2014, https://web.archive.org/web/20150829011059/https://www .playboy.com/playground/view/playboy-interview-tony-hsieh-zappos?page=4.

54   *"ignited a light"*: "Tony Hsieh's Legacy Reminds Us All of the Importance of Community," Burning Man Project, December 10, 2020, https://journal.burning man.org/2020/12/news/global-news/tony-hsieh-legacy/.

55   *"Gluing a few tchotchkes"*: "Art Cars on the Playa," Burning Man, https://burning man.org/culture/history/art-history/perspectives-on-playa-art/art-cars-on-the-playa/.

58   *"What Happens Here"*: "What Happens Here, Stays Here," Las Vegas Convention and Visitors Authority, https://www.lvcva.com/destination-marketing/advertising -campaigns/what-happens-here-stays-here/.

58   *fascinated by poker*: "What Poker Taught Tony Hsieh About Business," Delivering Happiness, https://blog.deliveringhappiness.com/blog/what-poker-taught- tony-hsieh-about-business.

58   *later taking weekend trips*: Hsieh, *Delivering Happiness*, 68.

58   *"I realized that once"*: Ibid., 69.

59   *"Most tourists never see"*: Timothy Pratt, "What Happens in Brooklyn Moves to Vegas," *New York Times Magazine*, October 19, 2012, https://www.nytimes .com/2012/10/21/magazine/what-happens-in-brooklyn-moves-to-vegas.html.

59   *The 2008 financial crisis*: Caitlyn Belcher, "How We Stack Up: Financial Experts Weigh in on Las Vegas' Recovery," *Las Vegas Review-Journal*, March 26, 2016, https://www.reviewjournal.com/news/special-features/neon-rebirth/how- we-stack-up-financial-experts-weigh-in-on-las-vegas-recovery/.

60   *"human collaboration is the central"*: Edward L. Glaeser, *Triumph of the City: How Urban Spaces Make Us Human* (London: Pan Books, 2012), 15.

61   *Bob Coffin likened the project*: Dave Toplikar, "Las Vegas City Council Approves Final Deal Bringing Zappos Downtown," *Las Vegas Sun*, February 1, 2012, https://lasvegas sun.com/news/2012/feb/01/las-vegas-city-council-approves-final-deal-bringin/.

62   *before dawn on a train*: "Howard Hughes," Online Nevada Encyclopedia, https:// www.onlinenevada.org/articles/howard-hughes.

62   *checked into a penthouse suite*: Mary Manning, "Howard Hughes: A Revolutionary Recluse," *Las Vegas Sun*, May 15, 2008, https://lasvegassun.com/news/2008/ may/15/how-vegas-went-mob-corporate/.

62   *"the largest single property owner"*: Stefan Al, *The Strip: Las Vegas and the Architecture of the American Dream* (Cambridge, MA: MIT Press, 2017), 151.

62   *Hughes bought six casinos*: "The History of Gaming in Nevada, 1864–1931," Nevada Resort Association, https://www.nevadaresorts.org/about/history/.

62   *having never ventured out*: Tim O'Reiley, "Howard Hughes Changed Vegas," *Las Vegas Review-Journal*, December 28, 2013, https://www.reviewjournal.com/ uncategorized/howard-hughes-changed-vegas/.

62   *Tony convinced dozens*: Aimee Groth, "Five Years in, Tony Hsieh's Downtown Project Is Hardly Any Closer to Being a Real City," Quartz, January 4, 2017,

https://qz.com/875086/five-years-in-tony-hsiehs-downtown-project-is-hardly-any-closer-to-being-a-real-city/.

62   *ten thousand new residents*: Pratt, "What Happens in Brooklyn Moves to Vegas."

62   *it had a headline-grabbing goal*: Ibid.

62   *Tony came up with*: Erica Breunlin, "Zappos CEO Seeks 'Return on Community,'" BizTimes, April 22, 2013, https://biztimes.com/zappos-ceo-seeks-return-on-community/.

62   *Downtown Project would create*: Figures provided by DTP companies.

62   *Tony bought the Gold Spike*: Benjamin Spillman, "Downtown Project Buys Gold Spike, Casino to Close on Sunday," *Las Vegas Review-Journal*, April 12, 2013, https://www.reviewjournal.com/business/casinos-gaming/downtown-project-buys-gold-spike-casino-to-close-on-sunday/.

63   *The number of strollers*: Kindra Cooper, "Zappos CEO Tony Hsieh on the Evolution of a Billion-Dollar, Mission-Driven Brand," CCW Digital, July 3, 2019, https://www.customercontactweekdigital.com/customer-experience/articles/tony-hsieh-ccw-vegas-downtown-project.

63   *Before he met Tony*: Kirsten Grind and Katherine Sayre, "Zappos CEO Tony Hsieh Bankrolled His Followers. In Return, They Enabled His Risky Lifestyle," *Wall Street Journal*, March 26, 2021, https://www.wsj.com/articles/tony-hsieh-zappos-death-entourage-11616761915.

64   *Plants filled one*: Sarah Feldberg, "At Home with Tony Hsieh: Post-its, Llamas and an Indoor Jungle," *Las Vegas Weekly*, October 2, 2014, https://lasvegasweekly.com/news/2014/oct/02/home-tony-hsieh-post-its-llamas-and-indoor-jungle/#/0.

64   *Energy drinks*: Aimee Groth, "Zappos CEO Tony Hsieh's Incredible Apartment in Las Vegas," Insider, October 2, 2012, https://www.businessinsider.com/zappos-ceo-tony-hsieh-apartment-las-vegas-2012-9.

64   *He rented fifty*: Leigh Gallagher, "Tony Hsieh's New $350 Million Startup," *Fortune*, January 23, 2012, https://fortune.com/2012/01/23/tony-hsiehs-new-350-million-startup/.

64   *had proven herself indispensable*: Court records filed by attorneys representing Mimi Pham in Las Vegas say that Pham was Tony's assistant, "right hand person," and friend for seventeen years before his death, including their sharing an address on their driver's licenses, his using Pham's number as his main phone number, and having utilities in her name. See *Baby Monster LLC v. PCVI LLC, Richard Hsieh and Andrew Hsieh*, Complaint and Demand for Jury Trial, A-21-828090-C, Eighth District Court of Nevada.

64   *With an investment*: Nolan Lister, "Film Studio to Spotlight Downtown," *Las Vegas Review-Journal*, May 24, 2013, https://www.reviewjournal.com/local/local-las-vegas/downtown/film-studio-to-spotlight-downtown/.

64   *quit her job*: "From International Accountant to Wellth Expert with Suzie Baleson," Blair Badenhop, March 4, 2018, https://blairbadenhop.com/podcast/international-accountant-to-wellth-expert-with-suzie-baleson/.

65   *"Tony collects people"*: Sara Corbett, "How Zappos' CEO Turned Las Vegas into a Startup Fantasyland," *Wired*, January 21, 2014, https://www.wired .com/2014/01/zappos-tony-hsieh-las-vegas/.

65   *whom she described*: Deepak Chopra said in a statement that Suzie Baleson had been a friend for close to a decade. "We have a friendship and have worked together," he said.

65   *"One can only imagine"*: "From International Accountant to Wellth Expert with Suzie Baleson."

65   *Even her account*: Ibid.

66   *In a photo*: michael_atmore, "Village People," Instagram, October 14, 2016, https://www.instagram.com/p/BLi6ubHjz7_/.

66   *"produce fitness and wellness-focused events"*: Wellth Collective, https://wellth collective.com/.

67   *Airbnb itself*: Kirsten Grind, Jean Eaglesham, and Preetika Rana, "Airbnb's Coronavirus Crisis: Burning Cash, Angry Hosts and an Uncertain Future," *Wall Street Journal*, April 8, 2020, https://www.wsj.com/articles/airbnbs-corona virus-crisis-burning-cash-angry-hosts-and-an-uncertain-future-11586365860.

67   *Airbnb went public*: Noor Zainab Hussain and Joshua Franklin, "Airbnb Valuation Surges Past $100 Billion in Biggest U.S. IPO of 2020," Reuters, December 10, 2020, https://www.reuters.com/article/airbnb-ipo-idUSKBN28K261.

67   *canceled the event*: Jay Hamburger, "Tour of Utah, a Big Summertime Event in Park City, Canceled amid Spread of Coronavirus," *Park Record*, April 7, 2020, https://www.parkrecord.com/news/tour-of-utah-a-big-summertime-event-in -park-city-canceled-amid-spread-of-coronavirus/.

67   *Next came the shutdown*: Jay Hamburger, "Park City Approves Return of Silly Market After 2020 Coronavirus Cancellation," *Park Record*, May 1, 2021, https://www.parkrecord.com/news/park-city/park-city-approves-return-of-silly -market-after-2020-coronavirus-cancellation/.

68   *could be in "limbo"*: Jay Hamburger, "Park City Summer Tourism Seen in 'Limbo' Caused by Coronavirus," *Park Record*, April 3, 2020, https://www.parkrecord .com/news/park-city-summer-tourism-seen-in-limbo-caused-by-corona virus/.

68   *bringing back sales tax revenues*: Jay Hamburger, "Park City Economy Roared as Coronavirus Raged, City Hall Numbers Show," *Park Record*, September 7, 2021, https://www.parkrecord.com/news/park-city/park-city-economy-roared -as-coronavirus-raged-city-hall-numbers-show/.

68   *began helping Tony with*: People familiar with Justin Weniger and Suzie Baleson said that they had not been running the 10X project.

68   *an annual music festival*: Justin Weniger said that Life Is Beautiful is "a community revitalization project aimed at shifting the focus from the problems of our community to the possibility of our community."

68   *never quite earning*: Justin Weniger said that he had separated from some of the

people in Tony's inner circle "for a variety of reasons" but that he and Tony had always been "very, very close."

68   *a possible sale*: Penske Media Corporation, the owner of *Rolling Stone* magazine, did not return a request for comment.

68   *Weniger was eager*: Justin Weniger said he had had "zero interest" in Tony's Park City business plans.

69   *"Utah friends, anyone"*: Shaun Kimball, Facebook, July 24, 2020, https://www .facebook.com/shaundiego/posts/10156931155041626.

Chapter 4: Delivering Happiness

71   *"backup brain"*: Tony Hsieh, *Delivering Happiness: A Path to Profits, Passion, and Purpose* (New York: Grand Central Publishing, 2010), xv.

71   *In just eight days*: Motoko Rich, "Why Is This Man Smiling?," *New York Times*, April 9, 2011, https://www.nytimes.com/2011/04/10/fashion/10HSEIH.html.

71   *at Tony's party loft*: Hsieh, *Delivering Happiness*, 106.

71   *they worked on the book*: Katie Abel, "Reading Tony Hsieh," *Footwear News*, June 1, 2010, https://footwearnews.com/2010/business/news/reading-tony-hsieh-76614/.

71   *"We tried coffee"*: Ibid.

72   *Zappos had reached $1 billion*: Jeremy Twitchell, "From Upstart to $1 Billion Behemoth, Zappos Marks 10 Years," *Las Vegas Sun*, June 16, 2009, https:// lasvegassun.com/news/2009/jun/16/upstart-1-billion-behemoth-zappos-marks -10-year-an/.

72   *"So, in terms of this book"*: Jack Covert, "Review: 'Delivering' Happiness," *Inc.*, July 1, 2010, https://www.inc.com/articles/2010/07/book-review-delivering -happiness.html.

72   *"It is hard not to like"*: Paul B. Carroll, "Getting a Foothold Online," *Wall Street Journal*, June 7, 2010, https://www.wsj.com/articles/SB100014240527487040 02104575290742364322212.

72   *"We only hire happy people"*: Frances X. Frei, Robin J. Ely, and Laura Winig, "Zappos.Com 2009: Clothing, Customer Service, and Company Culture," Harvard Business School Case Study no. 6100015, June 27, 2011.

72   *Zappos was named*: "100 Best Companies to Work For: Zappos.com," *Fortune*, 2015, https://fortune.com/best-companies/2015/zappos-com/.

72   *within five to seven years*: Hsieh, *Delivering Happiness*, 197.

72   *averaged 160 hours*: According to Zappos.

73   *The starting pay*: According to Zappos.

73   *had hired only 250 people*: Tony Hsieh, "How I Did It: Zappos's CEO on Going to Extremes for Customers," *Harvard Business Review*, July–August 2010, https:// hbr.org/2010/07/how-i-did-it-zapposs-ceo-on-going-to-extremes-for-customers.

73   *"Job interviews took place"*: Noah Askin, Gianpiero Petriglieri, and Joanna Lockard, "Tony Hsieh at Zappos: Structure, Culture and Change," INSEAD, August 26, 2016, 7.

73   *The application forms included*: Frances X. Frei, Robin J. Ely, and Laura Winig, "Zappos.Com 2009: Clothing, Customer Service, and Company Culture," *Harvard Business School* 9-610–015 (June 27, 2011).

73   *his staff listed dog day care*: Stephen J. Dubner, "PLAYBACK (2015): Could the Next Brooklyn Be . . . Las Vegas?! (Ep. 205)," produced by Greg Rosalsky, Freakonomics, December 6, 2020, https://freakonomics.com/podcast/playback -tony-hsieh/.

74   *if you can do your laundry*: nodesireusername, "Google's HQ—Googleplex, CA," YouTube, March 25, 2010,https://www.youtube.com/watch?v=8sOtjBDPQdU.

74   *Zappos encouraged managers*: Kai Ryssdal, "Zappos CEO on Corporate Culture and 'Happiness,'" Marketplace, August 19, 2010, https://www.marketplace .org/2010/08/19/zappos-ceo-corporate-culture-and-happiness/.

74   *"A lot of companies talk"*: David Gelles, "At Zappos, Pushing Shoes and a Vision," *New York Times*, July 17, 2015, https://www.nytimes.com/2015/07/19/business/ at-zappos-selling-shoes-and-a-vision.html.

75   *another of the reasons*: 07272009july, "Video from Jeff Bezos about Amazon and Zappos," YouTube, July 22, 2009, https://www.youtube.com/watch?v=-hxX_Q5CnaA.

75   *A customer in Florida*: Jennie Bell, "Zappos Employees Reveal What Customers Really Call Them About," *Footwear News*, May 6, 2019, https://footwearnews .com/2019/business/retail/zappos-customer-service-stories-calls-1202778070/.

77   *"Party with your peers"*: Derek Noel, "Driving Company Culture with a Little Bit of Luck," Zappos, March 24, 2016, https://www.zappos.com/about/stories /driving-company-culture-with-a-little-bit-of-luck.

78   *The next year*: Julianna Young, "Come One, Come All: Annual Vendor Party Runs Away with the 'Untamed Circus,'" Zappos, August 25, 2016, https://www .zappos.com/about/stories/untamed-circus.

78   *Drai's Beachclub and Nightclub*: Drai's Beachclub and Nightclub, https://drais group.com/las-vegas/.

78   *"So if I am around"*: Rich, "Why Is This Man Smiling?"

79   *"Is this a cult?"*: "Tony Hsieh," *The Colbert Report*, Comedy Central, aired August 1, 2011, https://www.cc.com/video/mqbxt0/the-colbert-report-tony-hsieh.

80   *"Ideally psychology:"* Martin Seligman, "The American Psychological Association 1998 Annual Report President's Address," *American Psychologist* 54, no. 8 (August 1999): 537–68. https://doi.org/10.1037/0003-066X.54.8.537.

80   *"pop positive thinking"*: Barbara Ehrenreich, *Bright-Sided: How the Relentless Promotion of Positive Thinking Has Undermined America* (New York: Metropolitan Books, 2009), 168.

80   *Eastern philosophies*: Daniel Horowitz, *Happier? The History of a Cultural Movement That Aspired to Transform America* (New York, NY: Oxford University Press, 2018), 104.

80   *Cultural movement*: Ibid, 7.

80   *Positive psychologists tried*: Ibid., 148.

80   *embraced methods echoing*: Ibid.

80   *including publishing books*: Ibid., 149.

80   *it was about happiness leading*: Ibid., 158.

81   *"Happy, or positive, people"*: Ibid., 159.

81   *The book argues*: Jonathan Haidt, *The Happiness Hypothesis: Finding Modern Truth in Ancient Wisdom* (New York: Basic Books, 2006), 272–73.

81   *"comes from between"*: Ibid.

81   *achieving a longtime goal*: Hsieh, *Delivering Happiness*, 231.

81   *winning the lottery*: Some research has connected winning the lottery with increased overall life satisfaction. See, e.g., Erik Lindqvist, Robert Östling, and David Cesarini, "Long-Run Effects of Lottery Wealth on Psychological Well-Being," Working Paper, National Bureau of Economic Research, May 2018, https://doi.org/10.3386/w24667.

81   *"The question for you to ask"*: Hsieh, *Delivering Happiness*, 231.

81   *Lim, with the help of Tony*: Jenn Lim, "How to Achieve (and Keep) a Great Company Culture," *Inc.*, October 21, 2015, https://www.inc.com/jenn-lim/how-to-achieve-and-keep-a-great-work-culture.html.

81   *spun off* Delivering Happiness: Sindy, "Keeping 2011 SXSW Happy," Delivering Happiness, https://blog.deliveringhappiness.com/blog/keeping-2011-sxsw-happy.

82   *The consulting team would grow*: "Meet the Team," Delivering Happiness, https://www.deliveringhappiness.com/meet-the-team.

82   *Jolly Good Fellow*: Steve Lohr, "Hey, Who's He? With Gwyneth? The Google Guy," *New York Times*, September 1, 2007, https://www.nytimes.com/2007/09/01/technology/01google.html.

82   *He developed a mindfulness course*: "About," Search Inside Yourself Leadership Institute, https://siyli.org/about/.

82   *"Imagine two human beings"*: Carolyn Gregoire, "Google's 'Jolly Good Fellow' on the Power of Emotional Intelligence," HuffPost, September 29, 2013, https://www.huffpost.com/entry/googles-jolly-good-fellow_n_3975944.

82   *McDonald's named its mascot clown*: Stefano Hatfield, "Lovin' Every Minute? Not Likely," *Guardian*, September 3, 2003, http://www.theguardian.com/media/2003/sep/03/comment.

82   *"the latest, creepiest job"*: Josh Kovensky, "Chief Happiness Officer Is the Latest, Creepiest Job in Corporate America," *New Republic*, July 22, 2014, https://newrepublic.com/article/118804/happiness-officers-are-spreading-across-america-why-its-bad.

84   *can have the paradoxical effect*: Iris B. Mauss et al., "Can Seeking Happiness Make People Unhappy? Paradoxical Effects of Valuing Happiness," *Emotion* 11, no. 4 (August 2011): 807–15, https://doi.org/10.1037/a0022010.

84   *In one experiment*: Ibid.

85   *In a separate study*: Iris B. Mauss et al., "The Pursuit of Happiness Can Be Lonely," *Emotion* 12, no. 5 (October 2012): 908–12, https://doi.org/10.1037/a0025299.

85   *Daniel Horowitz, a historian*: Horowitz, *Happier? The History of a Cultural Movement That Aspired to Transform America.*

85   Ibid., 274.

85   *"hedonic treadmill"*: Jennifer Senior, "Happiness Won't Save You: Philip Brickman Was an Expert in the Psychology of Happiness, but He Couldn't Make His Own Pain Go Away," *New York Times*, November 24, 2020, https://www.ny times.com/2020/11/24/opinion/happiness-depression-suicide-psychology .html.

85   *Brickman committed suicide*: "Professor's Death Is Termed Suicide," *Detroit Free Press*, May 16, 1982.

86   *"The best way off"*: C. B. Wortman and D. Coates, "Obituary: Philip Brickman (1943–1982)," *American Psychologist* 40, no. 9 (1985), 1051–52, https://doi .org/10.1037/h0092212.

86   *Some research has linked*: Brett Q. Ford, Iris B. Mauss, and June Gruber, "Valuing Happiness Is Associated with Bipolar Disorder," *Emotion* 15, no. 2 (April 2015): 211–22, https://doi.org/10.1037/emo0000048.

86   *and depression*: Brett Q. Ford et al., "Desperately Seeking Happiness: Valuing Happiness Is Associated with Symptoms and Diagnosis of Depression," *Journal of Social and Clinical Psychology* 33, no. 10 (December 2014): 890–905, https://doi.org/10.1521/jscp.2014.33.10.890.

86   *high levels of positive emotions*: June Gruber, Iris B. Mauss, and Maya Tamir, "A Dark Side of Happiness? How, When, and Why Happiness Is Not Always Good," *Perspectives on Psychological Science* 6, no. 3 (May 2011): 222–23, https://doi.org/10.1177/1745691611406927.

86   *said he had become convinced*: Amir Mandel, "Why Nobel Prize Winner Daniel Kahneman Gave Up on Happiness," *Haaretz*, October 7, 2018, https://www .haaretz.com/israel-news/.premium.MAGAZINE-why-nobel-prize-winner-daniel -kahneman-gave-up-on-happiness-1.6528513.

86   *He suffered from*: A court filing by the Hsieh family in Las Vegas in August 2021 said, "Despite his professional successes, Tony struggled with significant social anxiety." *Baby Monster LLC vs. PCVI LLC, Richard Hsieh and Andrew Hsieh*, A-21-828090-C, Eighth Judicial District Court Nevada, August 23, 2021, PCVI LLC's Answer to Second Amended Complaint, Counterclaim, Third Party Complaint and Demand for Jury Trial (n.d.).

86   *a developmental disability associated*: "Autism Spectrum Disorder (ASD)," Centers for Disease Control and Prevention, March 25, 2020, https://www. cdc.gov/ncbddd/autism/facts.html.

87   *Oliver Sacks wrote devastatingly*: Oliver Sacks, "Face-Blind," *New Yorker*, August 23, 2010, http://www.newyorker.com/magazine/2010/08/30/face-blind.

88   *He took Adderall*: A Las Vegas court filing filed by the Hsieh family in August 2021 described the medications Tony had taken. *Baby Monster LLC vs. PCVI LLC, Richard Hsieh and Andrew Hsieh*, A-21-828090-C, Eighth Judicial District Court

Nevada, August 23, 2021, PCVI LLC's Answer to Second Amended Complaint, Counterclaim, Third Party Complaint and Demand for Jury Trial (n.d.).

88   *a medication generally associated*: "Adderall—Uses, Side Effects, and More," WebMD, https://www.webmd.com/drugs/2/drug-63163/adderall-oral/details.

88   *It should not*: "Dangers of Mixing Adderall and Alcohol," Healthline, February 4, 2019, https://www.healthline.com/health/adhd/adderall-and-alcohol.

89   *a cross-country road trip*: "Delivering Happiness Bus Tour—Tour Map," Delivering Happiness Bus, September 24, 2010, https://web.archive.org/web/20100924043821/http://deliveringhappinessbus.com/tour.

89   *Starting in Las Vegas*: "Delivering Happiness Bus Tour—City Stops and Dates," Delivering Happiness Bus, September 24, 2010, https://web.archive.org/web/20100924005133/http://www.deliveringhappinessbus.com/stops.

89   *sack races in Colorado*: "Happy Wrap" (video), Delivering Happiness Bus, https://blog.deliveringhappiness.com/blog/happy-wrap.

89   *a happy hour*: Jeff Slobotski, "Behind the Scenes of the Delivering Happiness Bus Tour," *Silicon Prairie News*, September 7, 2010, https://siliconprairienews.com/2010/09/behind-the-scenes-of-the-delivering-happiness-bus-tour/.

89   *hula-hooping in Rhode Island*: "Happy Wrap."

89   *caught up with the actor*: Amy, "Delivering Happiness with Ashton Kutcher," Delivering Happiness, https://blog.deliveringhappiness.com/blog/delivering-happiness-with-ashton-kutcher.

89   *in a later interview*: DeliveringHappiness, "Delivering Happiness with Ashton Kutcher and Demi Moore—Part One," YouTube, https://www.youtube.com/watch?v=z-K0r5821Kw.

90   *Zappos employees rode*: DeliveringHappiness, "Delivering Happiness in Times Square," YouTube, September 9, 2010, https://www.youtube.com/watch?v=UFQL3Yj8QZk.

Chapter 5: The Ghost in the Machine

94   *Sold for about $7 million*: "2636 Aspen Springs Dr, Park City, UT 84060," Zillow, https://www.zillow.com/homedetails/2636-Aspen-Springs-Dr-Park-City-UT-84060/68846639_zpid/.

94   *was listed for $14.9 million*: Ibid.

94   *He offered to pay*: Kirsten Grind, James R. Hagerty, and Katherine Sayre, "The Death of Zappos's Tony Hsieh: A Spiral of Alcohol, Drugs and Extreme Behavior," *Wall Street Journal*, December 7, 2020, https://www.wsj.com/articles/the-death-of-zappos-tony-hsieh-a-spiral-of-alcohol-drugs-and-extreme-behavior-11607264719.

94   *"explained to me"*: Ibid.

94   *lived in the $4 million*: "1422 Empire Ave, Park City, UT 84060," Zillow, https://www.zillow.com/homedetails/1422-Empire-Ave-Park-City-UT-84060/89095788_zpid/.

95   *trails that can reach:* "Open Space & Trails," Park City, https://www.parkcity
      .org/about-us/bus-bike-walk/open-space-trails.

95   *On those long walks:* Patrick McKeown, *The Oxygen Advantage: Simple, Scien-
      tifically Proven Breathing Techniques to Help You Become Healthier, Slimmer,
      Faster, and Fitter* (New York: William Morrow, 2016).

97   *SpaceX had launched two astronauts:* Andy Pasztor, "Elon Musk's SpaceX
      Launches NASA Astronauts into Orbit," *Wall Street Journal,* May 30, 2020,
      https://www.wsj.com/articles/elon-musks-spacex-tries-again-to-launch-nasa-as
      tronauts-into-orbit-11590831001.

98   *He began repeating:* Adrienne Burke, "Why Zappos CEO Hsieh Wants to Ena-
      ble More Collisions in Vegas," *Forbes,* November 15, 2013, https://www.forbes
      .com/sites/techonomy/2013/11/15/why-zappos-ceo-hsieh-wants-to-enable
      -more-collisions-in-vegas/.

98   *"Cities have stood":* Wharton School, "Tony Hsieh | 2016 Wharton People
      Analytics Conference," YouTube, June 15, 2016, https://www.youtube.com/
      watch?v=81uYlpLzuJY.

98   *Tony's thinking seemed inspired:* "Video: Watch Zappos CEO Tony Hsieh's Talk
      on Urban Renewal in Santa Fe," Santa Fe Institute, September 30, 2014,
      https://www.santafe.edu/news-center/news/hsieh-talk-announce.

98   *Geoffrey West:* Luis M. A. Bettencourt et al., "Growth, Innovation, Scaling, and
      the Pace of Life in Cities," *Proceedings of the National Academy of Sciences of
      the United States of America* 104, no. 17 (April 24, 2007): 7301–06, https://doi
      .org/10.1073/pnas.0610172104.

98   *His and others' work:* Luis Bettencourt and Geoffrey West, "A Unified Theory of
      Urban Living," *Nature,* October 21, 2010, https://www.nature.com/articles/467912a.

98   *as a city doubled in size:* Jonah Lehrer, "A Physicist Solves the City," *New
      York Times,* December 17, 2010, https://www.nytimes.com/2010/12/19/maga
      zine/19Urban_West-t.html.

98   *a 15 percent rise:* Ibid.

98   *crime, traffic congestion:* Bettencourt and West, "A Unified Theory of Urban
      Living."

98   *more than three-quarters:* Zack Guzman, "Zappos CEO Tony Hsieh on Getting
      Rid of Managers: What I Wish I'd Done Differently," CNBC, September 13,
      2016, https://www.cnbc.com/2016/09/13/zappos-ceo-tony-hsieh-the-thing-i
      -regret-about-getting-rid-of-managers.html.

99   *"I think of my role":* The Employees of Zappos.com as told to Mark Dagostino,
      *The Power of WOW: How to Electrify Your Work, Your Community, and Your Life
      by Putting Service First* (Dallas, TX: BenBella Books, 2019), 131.

99   *about two hundred corporate leaders:* Conscious Capitalism, "A Look at the 2019
      CEO Summit," https://www.consciouscapitalism.org/story/2019-ceo-summit.

99   *Conscious Capitalism offered an answer:* Rachel Emma Silverman, "At 'Con-
      scious Capitalism' Gathering, CEOs Say Business Isn't Bad," *Wall Street Jour-*

nal, October 25, 2016, https://www.wsj.com/articles/at-conscious-capital ism-gathering-ceos-say-business-isnt-bad-1477408088.

99   *as having a rebellious streak*: HolacracyOne, "Brian Robertson's Personal Journey with Holacracy®—at Zappos' All Hands," YouTube, April 1, 2014, https://www .youtube.com/watch?v=vstsmA_cc7o.

100   *after he had nearly crashed*: TEDx Talks, "Holacracy: A Radical New Approach to Management | Brian Robertson | TEDxGrandRapids," YouTube, July 2, 2015, https://www.youtube.com/watch?v=tJxfJGo-vkI.

100   *with only twenty hours*: TEDx Talks, "Why Not Ditch Bosses and Distribute Power: Brian Robertson at TEDxDrexelU," YouTube, June 17, 2012, https:// www.youtube.com/watch?v=hR-8AOccyj4.

100   *"How do I build"*: TEDx Talks, "Holacracy: A Radical New Approach to Management."

100   *"Research shows"*: Brian J. Robertson, *Holacracy: The New Management System for a Rapidly Changing World* (New York: Henry Holt, 2015), 15.

100   *Holacracy is a form*: Holacracy, https://www.holacracy.org.

100   *"where all members"*: Davi Gabriel da Silva, "Holacracy: Quick Beginner's Guide," Target Teal, March 1, 2017, https://targetteal.com/en/blog/holacracy -quick-beginners-guide/.

101   *Problems are called "tensions"*: Chris Cowan, "Holacracy® Basics: Understanding Tensions," Holacracy, May 25, 2018, https://blog.holacracy.org/holacracy -basics-understanding-tensions-98fc3c032acf.

101   *Each circle holds governance meetings*: "Governance Meetings," Holacracy, https://www.holacracy.org/governance-meetings.

101   The Ghost in the Machine: Steve Denning, "Making Sense of Zappos and Holacracy," *Forbes*, January 15, 2014, https://www.forbes.com/sites/stevedenning /2014/01/15/making-sense-of-zappos-and-holacracy/.

101   *things that are simultaneously independent*: Kurt C. Stange, "A Science of Connectedness," *Annals of Family Medicine* 7, no. 5 (September 2009): 387–95, https://doi.org/10.1370/afm.990.

101   *known as a holarchy*: Denning, "Making Sense of Zappos and Holacracy."

101   *"It captured the spirit"*: Brian Robertson, "History of Holacracy®," Holacracy, July 28, 2014, https://blog.holacracy.org/history-of-holacracy-c7a8489f8eca.

101   *He announced the change*: Aimee Groth, "Zappos Is Going Holacratic: No Job Titles, No Managers, No Hierarchy," Quartz, December 30, 2013, https://qz.com/161210/ zappos-is-going-holacratic-no-job-titles-no-managers-no-hierarchy/.

101   *The event also included*: Ibid.

101   *a 4,500-word email*: Tony Hsieh, "CEO Letter: A Teal Organization," Zappos, https://www.zappos.com/about/stories/a-teal-organization.

102   *Laloux created an overview*: Frederic Laloux, "Reinventing Organizations," Excerpt and Summaries, Change Factory, March 2014, https://www.rein ventingorganizations.com/uploads/2/1/9/8/21988088/140305_laloux_reinvent ing_organizations.pdf.

102 *wisdom of emotions*: Ibid.

103 *"Like all the bold steps"*: Hsieh, "CEO Letter."

103 *In early May 2015*: Rachel Emma Silverman, "At Zappos, Some Employees Find Offer to Leave Too Good to Refuse," *Wall Street Journal*, May 7, 2015, https://www.wsj.com/articles/at-zappos-some-employees-find-offer-to-leave -too-good-to-refuse-1431047917.

103 *That number increased*: Guzman, "Zappos CEO Tony Hsieh on Getting Rid of Managers."

103 *Tony felt frustrated*: Gregory Ferenstein, "The Zappos Exodus Wasn't About Holacracy, Says Tony Hsieh," *Fast Company*, January 19, 2016, https://www.fastcom pany.com/3055657/the-zappos-exodus-wasnt-about-holacracy-says-tony-hsieh.

103 *founded more than four hundred*: According to a spokeswoman for Virgin.

103 *"The most extraordinary people"*: VirginLimitedEdition, "Richard Branson's Story of Necker Island," YouTube, April 28, 2014, https://www.youtube.com/ watch?v=STCqSXCbbcw.

103 *He and Tony had crossed paths*: Richard Branson, "Tony Hsieh Remembered," Virgin, November 30, 2020, https://virgin.com/branson-family/richard-branson -blog/tony-hsieh-remembered.

104 *"I love you," Tony thought*: Inspiringchildren, "Tony Hsieh & Jewel Conversation @Zappos All Hands," YouTube, February 15, 2021, https://www.youtube.com/ watch?v=KJ_8e5BNBwA.

104 *Jewel Kilcher had relied*: Jewel, *Never Broken: Songs Are Only Half the Story* (New York: Blue Rider Press, 2015).

104 *after Tony invited her*: Inspiringchildren, "Tony Hsieh & Jewel Conversation @Zappos All Hands."

105 *Jewel had herself struggled*: Jewel, "My Life's Work Has Not Been About Music. It Has Been About Solving for Pain," *Vogue*, May 27, 2021, https://www.vogue .com/article/jewel-mental-health.

106 *"an urban version of Burning Man"*: Noah Kulwin, "Tony Hsieh Wants Us to Forget the Zappos Drama and Behold the 'Rainforest,'" Vox, May 18, 2016, https://www.vox.com/2016/5/18/11698856/zappos-tony-hsieh-holacracy-video -code-commerce.

106 *"world's largest living room"*: Alan Snel, "Different Sites in Downtown Las Vegas Both Feature Airstream Trailers," *Las Vegas Review-Journal*, December 3, 2015, https://www.reviewjournal.com/business/different-sites-in-downtown-las -vegas-both-feature-airstream-trailers/.

106 *Five cats lived there*: The Employees of Zappos.com as told to Mark Dagostino, *The Power of WOW: How to Electrify Your Work, Your Community, and Your Life by Putting Service First* (Dallas, TX: BenBella Books, 2019), 94.

106 *he had spontaneously adopted*: Ibid., p. 97.

106 *Sarah Jessica Parker posed*: Ibid.

106 *Tony was suffering from*: A filing by the Hsieh family in August 2021 in a Las Vegas court confirms that Tony suffered from "significant social anxiety."

107   *When Tyler Williams was asked*: Yitzi Weiner, "Why Zappos Has a Chief Fung-
      ineer," Authority Magazine, January 31, 2019, https://medium.com/authority
      -magazine/why-zappos-has-a-chief-fungineer-e1bfa283d011.

109   *have limited access to care*: Azza Altiraifi and Nicole Rapfogel, "Mental Health
      Care Was Severely Inequitable, Then Came the Coronavirus Crisis," Center for
      American Progress, September 10, 2020, https://www.americanprogress.org/
      issues/disability/reports/2020/09/10/490221/mental-health-care-severely-ineq
      uitable-came-coronavirus-crisis/.

109   *as violent, unpredictable*: Julio Arboleda-Flórez and Heather Stuart, "From
      Sin to Science: Fighting the Stigmatization of Mental Illnesses," *Cana-
      dian Journal of Psychiatry* 57, no. 8 (August 2012): 457–63, https://doi
      .org/10.1177/070674371205700803.

109   *Oprah Winfrey and Prince Harry launched*: Mary Louise Kelly, Elena Bur-
      nett, and Courtney Dorning, "Oprah and Prince Harry on Mental Health,
      Therapy and Their New TV Series," NPR, May 21, 2021, https://www.npr
      .org/2021/05/21/999229547/-this-is-a-service-to-the-world-oprah-and-prince
      -harry-on-new-mental-health-seri.

109   *"You see everything"*: Kanye West on *My Next Guest Needs No Introduction with
      David Letterman*, Netflix, aired May 31, 2019.

110   *around 17 million at the time*: Michael Sheetz, "Elon Musk Asked His Twitter
      Followers for Tesla Feedback—Here's What They Said," CNBC, December 26,
      2017, https://www.cnbc.com/2017/12/26/elon-musk-asked-his-twitter-followers
      -for-tesla-feedback--heres-what-they-said.html.

110   *"The reality is great highs"*: Elon Musk, Twitter, July 30, 2017, https://twitter
      .com/elonmusk/status/891710778205626368.

110   *while hosting* Saturday Night Live: Rebecca Elliott and John Jurgensen, "Elon
      Musk on 'SNL' Says He Has Asperger's, Jokes About Dogecoin," *Wall Street
      Journal*, May 9, 2021, https://www.wsj.com/articles/elon-musks-quips-about
      -his-aspergers-to-kick-off-snl-host-gig-11620534790.

111   *a study that continued*: Michael A. Freeman et al., "The Prevalence and Co-
      Occurrence of Psychiatric Conditions Among Entrepreneurs and Their Fam-
      ilies," *Small Business Economics* 53, no. 2 (August 2019): 323–42, https://doi
      .org/10.1007/s11187-018-0059-8.

111   *"Are entrepreneurs touched"*: Michael A. Freeman, Sheri L. Johnson, Paige J.
      Staudenmaier, and Mackenzie R. Zisser, "Are Entrepreneurs 'Touched with
      Fire?'" Pre-Publication Manuscript, April 17, 2015, https://www.michaelafree
      manmd.com/Research_files/Are%20Entrepreneurs%20Touched%20with%20
      Fire%20(pre-pub%20n)%204-17-15.pdf.

111   *one in five people experiences*: "You Are Not Alone," National Alliance on Mental
      Illness, 2020, https://www.nami.org/NAMI/media/NAMI-Media/Infographics/
      NAMI_YouAreNotAlone_2020_FINAL.pdf.

111   *committed suicide*: "RSS Creator Aaron Swartz Dead at 26," *Harvard Magazine*,

January 14, 2013, https://www.harvardmagazine.com/2013/01/rss-creator-aaron
-swartz-dead-at-26.

111   *"I feel ashamed"*: Aaron Swartz, "Sick," Raw Thought, November 27, 2007, http://www.aaronsw.com/weblog/verysick.

113   *He told people*: According to a Las Vegas court filing by the Hsieh family in August 2021.

114   *Though the parade*: "Kalispell, Bigfork Fourth of July Parades Canceled," *Daily Inter Lake*, June 2, 2020, https://dailyinterlake.com/news/2020/jun/02/kalispell-bigfork-fourth-of-july-parades-6/.

Chapter 6: A Creative Solution

118   *Tony had enticed*: Aimee Groth, "Five Years In, Tony Hsieh's Downtown Project Is Hardly Any Closer to Being a Real City," Quartz, January 5, 2017, https://qz.com/875086/five-years-in-tony-hsiehs-downtown-project-is-hardly-any-closer-to-being-a-real-city/.

118   *commitment to spend $350 million*: "$350M Investment," DTP Companies, https://dtplv.com/breakdown/.

118   *One of the first to move*: Jennifer Robison, "With Boom Over, Las Vegas Enters Era of Normal," *Las Vegas Review-Journal*, April 28, 2012, https://www.reviewjournal.com/local/local-las-vegas/with-boom-over-las-vegas-enters-era-of-normal/.

118   *The Vegas Tech Fund*: Alyson Shontell, "A Grave Financial Error Sank a Startup and Contributed to Its Founder's Suicide," Insider, April 24, 2013, https://www.businessinsider.com/jody-sherman-ecomom-and-a-grave-financial-error-2013-4.

118   *For Ecomom, that included*: "Ecomom and David Arquette Help Fight Hunger in the U.S.," Ecomom, May 30, 2012, https://www.prnewswire.com/news-releases/ecomom-and-david-arquette-help-fight-hunger-in-the-us-155701935.html.

118   *Sherman died*: Andrea Chang, "After Jody Sherman Death, Tech Community Seeks Dialogue on Suicide," *Los Angeles Times*, February 1, 2013, https://www.latimes.com/business/la-xpm-2013-feb-01-la-fi-tn-jody-sherman-death-20130201-story.html.

118   *the company had burned*: Shontell, "A Grave Financial Error Sank a Startup and Contributed to Its Founder's Suicide."

118   *shut Ecomom down*: Sarah Lacy, "Ecomom Is Liquidating and Shutting Down; Investors Are Stunned," Pando, February 14, 2013, https://pando.com/2013/02/14/ecomom-is-liquidating-and-shutting-down-investors-are-stunned/.

118   *a public mental health discussion*: Chang, "After Jody Sherman Death, Tech Community Seeks Dialogue on Suicide."

118   *the pressures*: Patrick Clark, "After Suicide of Jody Sherman, a Call to Talk About the Emotional Strain of Life at Startups," Observer, January 31, 2013, https://observer.com/2013/01/after-suicide-of-jody-sherman-a-call-to-talk-about-the-emotional-strain-of-life-at-startups/.

118 *died by suicide*: One of the suicides was listed as an apparent suicide. See Nellie Bowles, "The Downtown Project Suicides: Can the Pursuit of Happiness Kill You?," Vox, October 1, 2014, https://www.vox.com/2014/10/1/11631452/the-downtown-project-suicides-can-the-pursuit-of-happiness-kill-you.

119 *"a jarring moment"*: Bowles, "The Downtown Project Suicides: Can the Pursuit of Happiness Kill You?"

119 *had launched a manufacturing company*: Ingrid Lunden, "Tony Hsieh, Vegas Tech Fund Put $10M into Factorli, a Factory for US Hardware Startups," Tech-Crunch, May 21, 2014, https://social.techcrunch.com/2014/05/21/tony-hsieh-vegas-tech-fund-put-10m-into-factorli-a-factory-for-us-hardware-startups/.

119 *Her company was even mentioned*: "Remarks by the President at the White House Maker Faire," The White House, June 18, 2014, https://obamawhitehouse.archives.gov/the-press-office/2014/06/18/remarks-president-white-house-maker-faire.

119 *"I just trusted Tony"*: Nellie Bowles, "Factorli, an Early Casualty of the Las Vegas Downtown Project," Vox, September 30, 2014, https://www.vox.com/2014/9/30/11631412/factorli-an-early-casualty-of-the-las-vegas-downtown-project.

119 *Factorli shut down*: Alan Snel, "Downtown Tech Manufacturer Factorli Closes," *Las Vegas Review-Journal*, August 12, 2014, https://www.reviewjournal.com/business/downtown-tech-manufacturer-factorli-closes/.

119 *and other businesses there were closing*: Bowles, "Factorli, an Early Casualty of the Las Vegas Downtown Project."

119 *had decided to move away*: Joe Schoenmann, "Joe Downtown: Is Romotive's Departure a Sign of the Future?," *Las Vegas Weekly*, March 20, 2013, https://lasvegasweekly.com/column/joe-downtown/2013/mar/20/joe-downtown-vegas techfunds-romotive-silicon-valle/.

119 *Tony had picked up detractors*: Leah Meisterlin, "Antipublic Urbanism: Las Vegas and the Downtown Project," *Avery Review*, http://averyreview.com/issues/3/antipublic-urbanism.

119 *without consideration*: Joe Schoenmann, "Joe Downtown: Gentrification or Positive Progress? The Great Downtown Debate," *Las Vegas Sun*, June 20, 2013, https://lasvegassun.com/news/2013/jun/20/joe-downtown-not-everyone-embracing-downtown-proje/.

121 *Downtown Project stopped using*: Joe Schoenmann, "Joe Downtown: Hsieh Says Downtown Project Not a Charity, Can't Solve Every Community Problem," *Las Vegas Sun*, February 7, 2014, https://vegasinc.lasvegassun.com/business/2014/feb/07/joe-downtown-hsieh-says-downtown-project-not-chari/.

121 *There are a lot*: "Downtown Project: Collisions, Co-Learning, Connectness," Evernote, February 7, 2014, https://www.evernote.com/shard/s16/sh/66aed622-6730-4009-86b0-2d2ffe7ea26f/0fca9f01d630275220b4caea45a4bb41.

121 *and instead turn to*: Ibid.

121 *Downtown Project laid off*: Alan Snel, "Downtown Project Lays Off 30 Workers; Hsieh Role Unchanged," *Las Vegas Review-Journal*, September 30, 2014, https://

www.reviewjournal.com/business/downtown-project-lays-off-30-workers -hsieh-role-unchanged/.

121 called a *"bloodletting"*: Las Vegas Weekly Staff, "'Bloodletting' at Downtown Project with Massive Layoffs," *Las Vegas Weekly*, September 30, 2014, https:// lasvegasweekly.com/as-we-see-it/2014/sep/30/breaking-bloodletting-down town-project-layoffs/.

121 *"a collage of decadence"*: Las Vegas Weekly Staff, "An Open Letter to Tony Hsieh from Former DTPer David Gould," *Las Vegas Weekly*, September 29, 2014, https://lasvegasweekly.com/as-we-see-it/2014/sep/30/david-gould-letter-resig nation-tony-hsieh-DTP/.

121 *Vox noted that*: Bowles, "The Downtown Project Suicides: Can the Pursuit of Happiness Kill You?"

122 *"I'm not on the board"*: Snel, "Downtown Tech Manufacturer Factorli Closes."

122 *"Suicides happen anywhere"*: Bowles, "The Downtown Project Suicides: Can the Pursuit of Happiness Kill You?"

122 *skipping out on shifts*: The Employees of Zappos.com as told to Mark Dagostino, *The Power of WOW: How to Electrify Your Work, Your Community, and Your Life by Putting Service First* (Dallas, TX: BenBella Books, 2019). Zappos said that for a short time in 2015, the challenge had been "having enough team members available during certain windows to fill them," not workers' skipping shifts.

122 *not enough resources*: Bethany Tomasian, "Q&A with John Bunch: Holacracy Helps Zappos Swing from Job Ladder to Job Jungle Gym," Workforce.com, March 29, 2019, https://workforce.com/news/qa-with-john-bunch-holacracy -helps-zappos-swing-from-job-ladder-to-job-jungle-gym.

123 *meetings in each "circle"*: Virginia Heffernan, "Meet Is Murder," *New York Times Magazine*, February 25, 2016, https://www.nytimes.com/2016/02/28/magazine/ meet-is-murder.html.

123 *had given it up*: Andy Doyle, "Management and Organization at Medium," Medium, March 4, 2016, https://blog.medium.com/management-and-organi zation-at-medium-2228cc9d93e9.

123 *which the company blamed*: Ibid.

125 *"If every circle"*: Aimee Groth, "Zappos Has Quietly Backed Away from Hol-acracy," Yahoo! Quartz, January 29, 2020, https://www.yahoo.com/now/zap pos-quietly-backed-away-holacracy-090102533.html.

126 *Amazon's famously aggressive*: Jodi Kantor and David Streitfeld, "Inside Amazon: Wrestling Big Ideas in a Bruising Workplace," *New York Times*, August 15, 2015, https://www.nytimes.com/2015/08/16/technology/inside-amazon-wrestling -big-ideas-in-a-bruising-workplace.html.

126 *he dashed one off*: Ben Bergman, "Former Amazon Consumer CEO Jeff Wilke on Why He Left, Unionization and 'Nomadland,'" GeekWire, May 3, 2021, https://dot.la/jeff-wilke-2652855402.html.

127 *"You're tired"*: Patti Greco, "What Zappos CEO Tony Hsieh Does All Day,"

WeWork, September 17, 2019, https://www.wework.com/ideas/professional-de
velopment/management-leadership/what-does-zappos-ceo-tony-hsieh-do-all-day.

127   *at least seven hours of sleep:* "Sleep and Sleep Disorders: Data and Statistics,"
       Centers for Disease Control and Prevention, May 2, 2017, https://www.cdc
       .gov/sleep/data_statistics.html.

127   *Tony had long before:* Zappos said that the company has a drug-and alcohol-use
       policy that prohibits illegal drug use in the workplace and requires that alcohol
       consumption in company offices or at work-related events be done responsibly.

127   *He had even built:* The Employees of Zappos.com and Dagostino, *The Power of
       WOW,* 49.

128   *At Cirque Lodge:* During the author Kirsten Grind's visit to Cirque Lodge in
       May 2021, Cirque provided several therapists for her to speak with about the
       facility and drug and alcohol addiction in general.

130   *its website asks:* "Understanding Alcohol Use Disorder," National Institute on
       Alcohol Abuse and Alcoholism, April 2021, https://www.niaaa.nih.gov/sites/
       default/files/publications/Alcohol_Use_Disorder_0.pdf.

132   *"Psychedelics are really":* Rick Doblin, "The Future of Psychedelic-Assisted
       Psychotherapy," TED2019, April 2019, https://www.ted.com/talks/rick_doblin
       _the_future_of_psychedelic_assisted_psychotherapy.

136   *rather than arrest him:* Weniger said, "Clearly, neither Suzie or I could have any
       influence in directing law enforcement or medical personnel." He said that he
       and Baleson had worked with police "to build a profile of who Tony was and
       how he was thinking and what the best potential tactic in approaching him
       might be."

136   *Instead, the house was cleaned:* Some parties involved dispute that the house was
       cleaned.

Chapter 7: The Family Business

137   *read a December 1987 headline:* Cinda Becker, "Local Boy Has Got What It
       Takes!," *San Rafael News,* December 1, 1987.

137   *Tony had launched:* Tony Hsieh, *Delivering Happiness: A Path to Profits, Passion,
       and Purpose* (New York: Grand Central Publishing, 2010), 13.

137   *Tony mailed them back:* Ibid., 13.

137   *Customers found him:* Ibid.

137   *What caught the local reporter's:* Becker, "Local Boy Has Got What It Takes!"

138   *enrolled in a US university:* The University of Illinois Urbana-Champaign con-
       firmed that Chuan-Kang Hsieh, known as Richard, enrolled in 1969, and
       Shiao-Ling Lee Hsieh, known as Judy, enrolled in 1968. The registrations did
       not include their names Richard and Judy.

138   *that banned or severely limited:* D'Vera Cohn, "How U.S. Immigration Laws
       and Rules Have Changed Through History," Pew Research Center, September

30, 2015, https://www.pewresearch.org/fact-tank/2015/09/30/how-u-s-immigra
tion-laws-and-rules-have-changed-through-history/.

138 *In the early 1960s*: Abby Budiman and Neil G. Ruiz, "Key Facts About Asian
Americans, a Diverse and Growing Population," Pew Research Center, April
29, 2021, https://www.pewresearch.org/fact-tank/2021/04/29/key-facts-about
-asian-americans/.

138 *signed into law*: "Signing of the Immigration and Nationality Act, October 3,
1965," LBJ Presidential Library, https://www.lbjlibrary.org/object/text/sign
ing-immigration-and-nationality-act-10-03-1965.

138 *It set a cap*: "Overturning Exclusion, Limiting Immigration," United States House of
Representatives, https://history.house.gov/Exhibitions-and-Publications/APA/Histor
ical-Essays/Exclusion-to-Inclusion/Overturning-Exclusion-Limiting-Immigration/.

138 *The new system had preferences*: Ibid.

138 *students from Taiwan*: Kevin O'Neil, "Brain Drain and Gain: The Case of
Taiwan," Migration Policy Institute, September 1, 2003, https://www.migration
policy.org/article/brain-drain-and-gain-case-taiwan.

138 *a nine-thousand-person demonstration*: "Student Life at Illinois: 1960–1969,"
Student Life and Culture Archives, University of Illinois, https://archives
.library.illinois.edu/slc/research-education/timeline/1960-1969/.

138 *Taiwanese students created*: Salvatore De Sando, "Illini Everywhere: Taiwanese
Illini, Since 1922," Student Life and Culture Archives, University of Illinois,
February 28, 2018, https://archives.library.illinois.edu/slc/taiwanese-illini/.

138 *a doctoral degree in chemical engineering*: The University of Illinois Urbana-
Champaign confirmed that Chuan-Kang Hsieh had earned a master's of science
in chemical engineering in June 1971 and a doctor of philosophy in chemical
engineering in June 1973. He had been known as Richard, though the university did not have the name Richard on file.

138 *a master's degree in social work*: The University of Illinois Urbana-Champaign
confirmed that Shiao-Ling Lee Hsieh had earned a master's in social work in
1971. She had been known as Judy, but the university did not have the name
Judy registered.

138 *She would later earn*: "Qualifications," Dr. Judy Hsieh, http://www.drjudyhsieh
.com/qualifications.html.

139 *"your typical Asian American parents"*: Hsieh, *Delivering Happiness*, 7.

139 *being called "doctor"*: Ibid., 9.

139 *learning to play musical instruments*: ABC News, "The Mastermind of 'Delivering Happiness,'" YouTube, August 3, 2012, https://www.youtube.com/watch?
v=p4OBZFVwuls.

139 *The Hsiehs socialized*: Hsieh, *Delivering Happiness*, 8.

139 *"That was just part"*: Ibid.

139 *studied piano, violin*: Ibid., 9.

140 *played tape recordings*: "From 2010: Zappos CEO Tony Hsieh," *Sunday Morning*,

CBS, https://www.cbs.com/shows/cbs-sunday-morning/video/FKDsNLkN8DgpY
6XUIa_yrCgegIpzFdod/from-2010-zappos-ceo-tony-hsieh/.

140   *"I always fantasized"*: Hsieh, *Delivering Happiness*, 10.

140   *Today, Branson charges*: "Admissions FAQ," The Branson School, https://www
.branson.org/admissions/admissions/faq.

140   *studied Japanese, Spanish, French*: Hsieh, *Delivering Happiness*, 18.

140   *he also joined*: Ibid., 18–19.

140   *He got another paying gig*: Ibid., 20.

140   *using the computer lab's dial-up system*: Ibid., 16.

140   *an earthworm farm*: SBN Staff, "Zappos' Tony Hsieh on the Role of Fun in a Company's Success," Smart Business Network, April 1, 2015, https://www.sbnonline
.com/article/zappos-tony-hsieh-on-the-role-of-fun-in-a-companys-success/.

140   *the Delivering Happiness bus visited*: Amy, "On a Worm Farm . . . Where It All
Began," Delivering Happiness, https://blog.deliveringhappiness.com/blog/on-a
-worm-farm-where-it-all-began.

140   *a magic tricks kit*: James R. Hagerty, "Former Zappos CEO Tony Hsieh Dies
at 46 from Injuries Connected to House Fire," *Wall Street Journal*, November 28, 2020, https://www.wsj.com/articles/former-zappos-ceo-tony-hsieh
-dies-at-46-11606572300.

141   *received hundreds of mail orders*: Hsieh, *Delivering Happiness*, 14.

141   *He missed his last dance*: Motoko Rich, "Why Is This Man Smiling?," *New York
Times*, April 9, 2011, https://www.nytimes.com/2011/04/10/fashion/10HSEIH
.html.

141   *In his senior yearbook*: The Branson School, http://gencat.eloquent-systems
.com/branson_permalink.html?key=382.

141   *When the* New York Times *asked*: Rich, "Why Is This Man Smiling?"

141   *Asian Americans are less likely*: Michael S. Spencer et al., "Discrimination and
Mental Health–Related Service Use in a National Study of Asian Americans,"
American Journal of Public Health 100, no. 12 (December 2010): 2410–17,
https://doi.org/10.2105/AJPH.2009.176321.

141   *high cultural expectations*: Koko Nishi, "Mental Health Among Asian-
Americans," American Psychological Association, 2012, https://www.apa.org
/pi/oema/resources/ethnicity-health/asian-american/article-mental-health.

141   *the myth of the "model minority"*: Connie Hanzhang Jin, "6 Charts That Dismantle the Trope of Asian Americans as a Model Minority," NPR, May 25,
2021, https://www.npr.org/2021/05/25/999874296/6-charts-that-dismantle-the
-trope-of-asian-americans-as-a-model-minority.

142   *Tony stood onstage*: Aimee Groth, *The Kingdom of Happiness: Inside Tony Hsieh's
Zapponian Utopia* (New York: Touchstone, 2017), 213.

142   *managed a pan-Asian restaurant*: GraceAnn Walden, "Venture Frogs Leaps on
the Scene," SFGATE, April 12, 2000, https://www.sfgate.com/insidescoop/arti
cle/Venture-Frogs-Leaps-on-the-Scene-2764663.php.

142   *with Silicon Valley references*: "Venture Frogs Restaurant," Venture Frogs, https://web.archive.org/web/20010211030141/http://www.vfrogs.com/restaurant/press_release.html.

143   *"I'm not opposed"*: Alex Williams, "Dating Profiles of High-Tech, High-Worth Bachelors," *New York Times*, June 7, 2012, https://www.nytimes.com/slideshow/2012/06/07/fashion/20120607-BACHELOR-ETTES/s/20120607-BACHELOR-slide-Z2XQ.html.

143   *Willow Smith*: "Willow Smith Opens Up About Being Polyamorous," BBC News, April 29, 2021, https://www.bbc.com/news/newsbeat-56852099.

143   *"I think it's pretty hard"*: David Hockman, "*Playboy* Interview: Tony Hsieh," *Playboy*, April 16, 2014, https://web.archive.org/web/20150829011059/https://www.playboy.com/playground/view/playboy-interview-tony-hsieh-zappos?page=4.

144   *The last time*: Nick Swinmurn, "RIP Tony," Medium, November 28, 2020, https://nickswinmurn.medium.com/rip-tony-6e99695ae3de.

144   *Tony seemed confused*: Ibid.

147   *Tony agreed to pay Andy*: Attorneys for Mimi Pham have stated this $1 million agreement in court records. See *Baby Monster LLC v. PCVI LLC, Richard Hsieh, and Andrew Hsieh*, No. A-21-828090-C.

147   *He'd gotten bachelor's and master's*: Andrew Hsieh, LinkedIn, https://www.linkedin.com/in/andrewhsi3h/.

147   *Andy Hsieh tried*: Jessica Guynn, "Facebook IPO Fuels Bay Area Spending Boom," *Los Angeles Times*, May 17, 2012, https://www.latimes.com/archives/la-xpm-2012-may-17-la-fi-facebook-boom-20120517-story.html.

148   *So in 2013*: Kristy Totten, "Lux Delux Now Delivering Meals by Bicycle," *Las Vegas Review-Journal*, December 3, 2013, https://www.reviewjournal.com/business/lux-delux-now-delivering-meals-by-bicycle/.

Chapter 8: Utopia

149   *"The wiser course"*: "A Human Approach to World Peace," His Holiness the 14th Dalai Lama of Tibet, https://www.dalailama.com/messages/world-peace/a-human-approach-to-world-peace.

150   *He dispatched*: According to schedules viewed by the authors.

152   *"The employee's sphere"*: Pravir Malik, "Forbes Articles on Light," Medium, November 13, 2020, https://pravirmalik.medium.com/forbes-articles-on-light-ef3e8f469fc8.

152   *Frankl wrote*: "Statue of Responsibility," Statue of Responsibility Foundation, 2021, https://www.statueofresponsibility.com/.

154   *Daniel Park Elmhorst*: "I Tried Out for America's Got Talent!," Daniel Park Music, January 15, 2012, http://www.danielparkmusic.com/news/2012/01/15/americas-got-talent.

154   *Victoria Recaño*: "Victoria Recaño," *Inside Edition*, https://www.insideedition.com/bios/victoria-recano.

154   *she had cofounded and designed*: Janice Lopez, application to the Weber County Ogden Valley Planning Commission, June 25, 2019, http://www.webercounty utah.gov/agenda_files/G4%20%20OVPC%20Packet%20to%20County%20 Commission.pdf.

154   *Rachael Brown*: Michael Boley, "Meet The Women Who've Changed Zappos History," Zappos, March 5, 2019, https://www.zappos.com/about/stories/womens -history-zappos.

155   *A cellist, Brown had trained*: John Katsilometes, "Vegas Musician Owns House at Center of Tony Hsieh Incident," *Las Vegas Review-Journal*, November 29, 2020. https://www.reviewjournal.com/entertainment/entertainment-columns/ kats/vegas-musician-owns-house-at-center-of-tony-hsieh-incident-2195958/.

155   *Tony's "soul mate"*: Rick Lessard, "OCME Says Smoke Inhalation from New London Fire Killed Zappos Founder," FOX61, November 30, 2020, https:// www.fox61.com/article/news/local/man-dies-as-a-result-of-new-london -fire/520-28ae7356-d2f5-4cf4-992e-c93f67818536.

155   *the house she had purchased*: Some people interviewed by the authors said Tony had purchased the house for Brown and transferred the title to her.

155   *Brown's $1.3 million house*: Taylor Hartz, "What Happened Nov. 18 at 500 Pequot Avenue?," *The Day*, October 10, 2021, https://www.theday.com/article /20201205/NWS01/201209647.

155   *her parents still live nearby*: Property records of Rachael's parents, Lynn and Jean Brown.

155   *a real-life Schitt's Creek*: Kirsten Grind, "Schitt's Creek, but in Real Life: Owner Tries Selling California Desert Town," *Wall Street Journal*, May 27, 2021, https://www.wsj.com/articles/schitts-creek-but-in-real-life-owner-tries-selling -california-desert-town-11622126653.

156   *which wanted to build*: Derek Hawkins, "Cannabis Company Aims to Turn California Ghost Town into an Oasis for Weed Lovers," *Washington Post*, August 8, 2017, https://www.washingtonpost.com/news/morning-mix/wp/2017/08/08/can nabis-company-aims-to-turn-california-ghost-town-into-an-oasis-for-weed-lovers/.

156   *He wanted to get involved*: "Don Knight—Cannabis Connoisseur and Entrepreneur," Pfeiffer Law, September 26, 2018, https://www.pfeifferlaw.com/enter tainment-law-blog/don-knight-cannabis-connoisseur-and-entrepreneur.

157   *estimated years earlier*: Peter Holley, "Why This CEO Is Worth Almost $1 Billion but Lives in a Trailer Park," *Washington Post*, July 21, 2015, https://www .washingtonpost.com/news/the-switch/wp/2015/07/21/why-a-ceo-worth-840-million -lives-in-a-trailer-park-with-his-pet-alpaca/.

157   *$30,000 per month*: The family of Tony Hsieh claimed in court filings that Pham's compensation had increased to that amount in 2020 after she had previously been paid a $9,000 monthly fee. See *Baby Monster LLC v. PCVI LLC, Richard Hsieh and Andrew Hsieh*, A-21-828090-C, Eighth Judicial District Court Nevada, August 23, 2021, PCVI LLC's Answer to Second Amended Complaint, Counterclaim, Third Party Complaint and Demand for Jury Trial, n.d.

158   *when Tony wanted to retrofit*: Pham filed a claim against Tony Hsieh's estate through one of her companies, Baby Monster LLC, related to the bus retrofitting contract. See *In the Matter of the Estate of Anthony Hsieh, Creditor's Claim, Baby Monster LLC*, March 3, 2021, Case No. P-20-105105-E, Eighth Judicial District Court, Clark County, Nevada.

158   *her business*: "What We Do," Wellth Collective, 2017, https://wellthcollective .com/get-wellthy/.

158   *who called herself*: Emails obtained from city officials in Park City describe Suzie Baleson as Tony Hsieh's business manager, and she said the same to others in Park City; a spokesperson for Baleson disputes that she held that role.

158   *now referred to himself*: Weniger disputed in fact-checking that he had referred to himself as Tony's bodyguard.

158   *As an organizer*: Justin Weniger 3rd, LinkedIn, https://www.linkedin.com/in/ justin-weniger-16472a10/.

158   *a former competitive swimmer*: "USMS Individual Meet Results for Elizabeth M Pezzello (11 Swims)," U.S. Masters Swimming, https://www.usms.org/comp/ meets/indresults.php?SwimmerID=071YZ.

158   *Miss New York USA contestant*: Elizabeth Pezzello, Instagram, https://www .instagram.com/leeza_piza/?hl=en.

158   *she had briefly worked*: Elizabeth Pezzello, LinkedIn, https://www.linkedin.com/ in/elizabeth-pezzello-5ba07aa7/.

158   *an investment manager*: Brett Gorman, LinkedIn, https://www.linkedin.com/in/ brett-gorman-9a9a443b/.

159   *For that job and several others*: Kirsten Grind and Katherine Sayre, "Zappos CEO Tony Hsieh Bankrolled His Followers. In Return, They Enabled His Risky Lifestyle," *Wall Street Journal*, March 26, 2021, https://www.wsj.com/articles/tony -hsieh-zappos-death-entourage-11616761915.

159   *The glossy newsletter*: We reviewed newsletters produced by Gorman.

159   *Tony's brother Andy*: Grind and Sayre, "Zappos CEO Tony Hsieh Bankrolled His Followers."

Chapter 9: Good and Evil Reconciled

163   *Into this pervading genius*: Quoted in Adam Green, *"Oh Excellent Air Bag": Under the Influence of Nitrous Oxide, 1799–1920* (Cambridge, UK: PDR Press, 2016), 89.

163   *The sound of running water*: The video "The Nitrous Oxygen Advantage" was viewed by the authors.

164   *uses her soothing, trained voice*: Much of Victora Recaño's script was copied directly from Dmitri Tymoczko, "The Nitrous Oxide Philosopher," *Atlantic*, May 1996, https://www.theatlantic.com/magazine/archive/1996/05/the-nitrous -oxide-philosopher/376581/.

165   *discovered two centuries ago*: Mark A. Gillman, "Mini-review: A Brief History of Nitrous Oxide (N2O) Use in Neuropsychiatry," *Current Drug Research Reviews*

11, no. 1 (February 26, 2019): 12–20, https://doi.org/10.2174/1874473711666181008163107.

165 *sometimes leads to hallucinations*: Matthew Mo Kin Kwok, Jane de Lemos, and Mazen Sharaf, "Drug-Induced Psychosis and Neurological Effects Following Nitrous Oxide Misuse: A Case Report," *British Columbia Medical Journal* 61, no. 10 (December 2019): 385–87, https://bcmj.org/articles/drug-induced-psychosis-and-neurological-effects-following-nitrous-oxide-misuse-case-report.

165 *it fades away*: James P. Zacny et al., "Time Course of Effects of Brief Inhalations of Nitrous Oxide in Normal Volunteers," *Addiction* 89, no. 7 (July 1994): 831–39, https://doi.org/10.1111/j.1360-0443.1994.tb00986.x.

165 *alleviate the symptoms*: Jim Dryden, "Laughing Gas Relieves Symptoms in People with Treatment-Resistant Depression," Washington University School of Medicine in St. Louis, June 9, 2021, https://medicine.wustl.edu/news/laughing-gas-relieves-symptoms-in-people-with-treatment-resistant-depression/.

165 *and labor pain*: Shawn Collins et al., "Nitrous Oxide for the Management of Labor Analgesia," *AANA Journal* 86, no. 1 (February 2018): 72–80, https://www.aana.com/docs/default-source/aana-journal-web-documents-1/journal-course-6-nitrous-oxide-for-the-management-of-labor-anesthesia-february-2018.pdf?sfvrsn=442d42b1_6.

165 *One pure hit can cause*: Jan van Amsterdam, Ton Nabben, and Wim van den Brink, "Recreational Nitrous Oxide Use: Prevalence and Risks," *Regulatory Toxicology and Pharmacology* 73, no. 3 (December 2015): 790–96, https://doi.org/10.1016/j.yrtph.2015.10.017.

165 *can make a person disassociate*: "Nitrous Oxide," Alcohol and Drug Foundation, https://adf.org.au/drug-facts/nitrous-oxide/.

165 *William James*: Jane S. Moon, Catherine M. Kuza, and Manisha S. Desai, "William James, Nitrous Oxide, and the Anaesthetic Revelation," *Journal of Anesthesia History* 4, no. 1 (January 2018): 1–6, https://doi.org/10.1016/j.janh.2017.10.012.

165 *who went on to become*: "William James," Department of Psychology, Harvard University, https://psychology.fas.harvard.edu/people/william-james.

165 *"Nevertheless, the sense"*: William James, *The Varieties of Religious Experience* (Digireads.com Publishing, 2011), 213.

165 *he first used the term*: "Stream of Consciousness," Encyclopaedia Britannica, https://www.britannica.com/art/stream-of-consciousness.

166 *while high on nitrous oxide*: Tymoczko, "The Nitrous Oxide Philosopher."

166 *"What's a mistake"*: Quoted in Adam Green, *"Oh Excellent Air Bag": Under the Influence of Nitrous Oxide, 1799–1920*.

166 *profoundly influenced James's thinking*: Tymoczko, "The Nitrous Oxide Philosopher."

166 *who suffered from bouts*: Peter Gibbon, "The Thinker Who Believed in Doing," *Humanities* 39, no. 1 (Winter 2018), https://www.neh.gov/humanities/2018/winter/feature/the-thinker-who-believed-in-doing-0.

166 *wondered whether nitrous oxide*: Moon et al., "William James, Nitrous Oxide, and the Anaesthetic Revelation."

166 *after being introduced*: Tymoczko, "The Nitrous Oxide Philosopher."

166 Rolling Stone *profiled*: Robin Green, "Nitrous Oxide: After Acid, Wha'? Researches Chemical and Philosophical, Chiefly Concerning Nitrous Oxide and Its Respiration," *Rolling Stone*, July 3, 1975, https://www.rollingstone.com/culture/culture-news/nitrous-oxide-234197/.

166 *Bhagwan Shree Rajneesh*: William E. Schmidt, "U.S. Indicts Oregon Guru and Says He Tried to Flee Country," *New York Times*, October 29, 1985, https://www.nytimes.com/1985/10/29/us/us-indicts-oregon-guru-and-says-he-tried-to-flee-country.html.

166 *Rajneeshpuram*: Hugh Urban "Rajneeshpuram Was More than a Utopia in the Desert. It Was a Mirror of the Time," *Humanities* 39, no. 2 (Spring 2018), https://www.neh.gov/humanities/2018/spring/feature/rajneeshpuram-was-more-utopia-desert-it-was-mirror.

166 *had a special dental room*: Swami Devageet, *Osho: The First Buddha in the Dental Chair: Amusing Anecdotes by His Personal Dentist* (Boulder, CO: Sammasati Publishing, 2013).

166 *"His dentist, a follower"*: Ibid.

166 *wrote down the meandering thoughts*: Rusty King, "Minisode 3: Noah's Ark," *Building Utopia: Bhagwan Shree Rajneesh*, January 20, 2019, https://podcasts.google.com/feed/aHR0cHM6Ly9idWlsZGluZ3V0b3BpYXBvZGNhc3QubGlic3luLmNvbS9yc3M?sa=X&ved=0CAMQ4aUDahcKEwiQ4uWmxZjzAhUAAAAAHQAAAAQAQ&hl=en; Devageet, *Osho the First Buddha in the Dental Chair*.

166 *He called the dental chamber*: Devageet, *Osho the First Buddha in the Dental Chair*.

166 *published as three books*: King, "Minisode 3: Noah's Ark."

166 *"It must be absolutely unprecedented"*: King, "Minisode 3: Noah's Ark."

167 *in 1984, his followers committed*: Scott Keyes, "A Strange but True Tale of Voter Fraud and Bioterrorism," *Atlantic*, June 10, 2014, https://www.theatlantic.com/politics/archive/2014/06/a-strange-but-true-tale-of-voter-fraud-and-bioterrorism/372445/.

167 *poisoning more than 750 people*: Ibid.

167 *The FBI learned*: "Rajneeshee Bioterror Attack," Homeland Security Digital Library, https://www.hsdl.org/c/tl/rajneeshee-bioterror-attack/.

167 *law enforcement scrambled*: "Information Bulletin—Raves," National Drug Intelligence Center, Department of Justice, April 2001, https://www.justice.gov/archive/ndic/pubs/656/656t.htm#History.

167 *three people died*: Michael Connelly, "Deaths of 3 Men, Source of Gas Tanks Investigated," *Los Angeles Times*, March 10, 1992, https://www.latimes.com/archives/la-xpm-1992-03-10-me-3490-story.html.

167 *Fliers for raves*: Ibid.

167 *in 1998 a video game developer*: "Video Game: Sony PlayStation N2O: Nitrous Oxide," Google Arts & Culture, https://artsandculture.google.com/asset/video-game-sony-playstation-n2o-nitrous-oxide/LAFuj8dleUwHMg.

167 *with promotions that declared*: Michael Colton, "To Some Critics, N2O's Not a Gas; Ads for Video Game Featuring Nitrous Oxide Evoke Drug Culture," *Washington Post*, June 18, 1998, https://www.washingtonpost.com/wp-srv/style/features/nitro.htm.

167 *Figures wearing gas masks*: Vysethedetermined2, "N2O: Nitrous Oxide Game Sample—Playstation," YouTube, December 18, 2009, https://www.youtube.com/watch?v=Ohp3Ix_KWww.

167 *One online nitrous oxide supplier*: "Burning Man Festival Customer Information," CreamRight, https://web.archive.org/web/20160226213245/http://www.creamright.com/category/burning-man-discounts.html.

167 *"Whipped cream and Burning Man?"*: Ibid.

167 *The use of laughing gas*: Ezra Marcus, "Nitrous Nation," *New York Times*, February 1, 2021, https://www.nytimes.com/2021/01/30/style/nitrous-oxide-whippets-tony-hsieh.html.

167 *particularly between 2014 and 2019*: Mathias B. Forrester, "Nitrous Oxide Misuse Reported to Two United States Data Systems During 2000–2019," *Journal of Addictive Diseases* 39, no. 1 (December 1, 2020): 46–53, https://doi.org/10.1080/10550887.2020.1813361.

168 *according to the annual Global Drug Survey*: A. R. Winstock et al., "Global Drug Survey 2020 Psychedelics Key Findings Report," Global Drug Survey, 2021, https://www.globaldrugsurvey.com/wp-content/uploads/2021/03/GDS2020-Psychedelics-report.pdf.

168 *Nitrous oxide use ranked*: Adam Winstock, "Global Drug Survey 2020 Key Findings Report, Executive Summary," Global Drug Survey, 2021, https://www.globaldrugsurvey.com/wp-content/uploads/2021/01/GDS2020-Executive-Summary.pdf.

168 *experts say*: Marcus, "Nitrous Nation,."

168 *Drug overdose deaths surged*: "Drug Overdose Deaths in the U.S. Up 30% in 2020," Centers for Disease Control and Prevention, July 14, 2021, https://www.cdc.gov/nchs/pressroom/nchs_press_releases/2021/20210714.htm.

168 *Nitrous oxide robs the body*: John Williamson, Saif Huda, and Dinesh Damodaran, "Nitrous Oxide Myelopathy with Functional Vitamin B_{12} Deficiency," *BMJ Case Reports* 12, no. 2 (February 2019): e227439, https://doi.org/10.1136/bcr-2018-227439.

168 *spinal degeneration*: Stephen Keddie et al., "No Laughing Matter: Subacute Degeneration of the Spinal Cord Due to Nitrous Oxide Inhalation," *Journal of Neurology* 265, no. 5 (May 2018): 1089–95, https://doi.org/10.1007/s00415-018-8801-3.

168 *weakness, numbness*: Alexander G. Thompson et al., "Whippits, Nitrous Oxide and the Dangers of Legal Highs," *Practical Neurology* 15, no. 3 (June 2015): 207–09, https://doi.org/10.1136/practneurol-2014-001071.

168 *loss of bodily control*: "Nitrous Oxide," Alcohol and Drug Foundation, October 6, 2021, https://adf.org.au/drug-facts/nitrous-oxide/.

168   *can cause asphyxiation*: Charles L. Winek, Wagdy W. Wahba, and Leon Rozin, "Accidental Death by Nitrous Oxide Inhalation," *Forensic Science International* 73, no. 2 (May 1995): 139–41, https://doi.org/10.1016/0379-0738(95)01729-3.

168   *lead to accidental injuries*: Forrester, "Nitrous Oxide Misuse Reported to Two United States Data Systems During 2000–2019."

169   *Mimi Pham jokingly called*: This is a claim made by Tony Hsieh's family in court filings. See *Baby Monster LLC v. PCVI LLC, Richard Hsieh, and Andrew Hsieh*, PCVI LLC's Answer to Second Amended Complaint, Counterclaim, Third Party Complaints and Demand for Jury Trial, Eighth Judicial District Court Nevada, No. A-21-828090-C, August 23, 2021. Attorneys for Pham have denied this in a court filing.

169   *sells whipped cream cartridges*: Whip-It!, https://whipit.com/.

169   *through Amazon*: A spokeswoman for Amazon said, "Nitrous oxide is commonly used to create whipped cream and other foods, and is sold by many major retailers. Unfortunately, like many products, it can be misused. Our detail pages clearly notify customers that the products are intended only for food preparation and our Conditions of Use limit shopping on Amazon to customers 18 and older." See also "Whip-It!," Amazon.com, https://www.amazon.com/stores/page /A4F0C69E-1F26-45AD-A0B3-48EE90619E5F.

169   *A case of 600 cartridges*: "Whip-It! Elite 100 Pack, Case of 600: Industrial & Scientific," Amazon.com, https://www.amazon.com/Whip-Elite-100-Pack-Case /dp/B092MSP6W8?ref_=ast_sto_dp.

169   *the company was ordered*: "Nitrous Oxide Distributor to Pay Civil Penalty for Failure to Verify Age and Provide Health Warnings," Office of the District Attorney County of San Diego, October 21, 2020, https://www.sdcda.org/content /office/newsroom/tempDownloads/45cf8e42-ed1a-4677-b3a7-10220f515b33_ Nitrous%20Oxide%20Whip%20it%20News%20Release%2010-21-2020.pdf.

169   *had identified United Brands*: Ken Stone, "Nitrous Oxide Seller Whip-It! to Pay $50K for Not Warning Minors, SD DA Says," *Times of San Diego*, October 21, 2020, https://timesofsandiego.com/business/2020/10/21/nitrous-oxide-seller -whip-it-to-pay-50k-for-not-warning-minors-sd-da-says/.

169   *under its authority*: "Authorities Charge Four Individuals and Shut Down Businesses Across SoCal That Allegedly Sold Nitrous Oxide as Recreational Drug," United States Attorney's Office, Central District of California, March 22, 2013, https://www.justice.gov/usao-cdca/pr/authorities-charge-four-individuals -and-shut-down-businesses-across-socal-allegedly.

169   *Utah law*: Section 76-10-107.5, Utah Code, https://le.utah.gov/xcode/Title76/ Chapter10/76-10-S107.5.html.

170   *"is exceptionally skilled"*: "Welcome," RMA, https://www.drhallerman.com.

171   *She is herself*: Ruby Warrington, "Elisa Hallerman Offers the Newest Trend in Recovery: The Personalized Rehab Manager," *Observer*, July 31, 2014, https:// observer.com/2014/07/elisa-hallerman-offers-the-newest-trend-in-recovery -the-personalized-rehab-manager/.

171 *"If we were to reframe"*: "Welcome," RMA.

171 *He was suspended*: Ellen Gamerman, "As Britney Spears's Father Is Suspended from Conservatorship, Supporters Target Larger Reform," *Wall Street Journal*, September 30, 2021, https://www.wsj.com/articles/as-britney-spearss-father-is-suspended-from-conservatorship-supporters-target-larger-reform-11633020435.

171 *is typically a last resort*: Spencer Bokat-Lindell, "Britney Spears and the Last Resort of Mental Health Care," *New York Times*, June 29, 2021, https://www.nytimes.com/2021/06/29/opinion/britney-spears-conservatorship.html.

171 *In early August*: This account of the intervention attempt is based on interviews with many of the parties involved or people who knew about the intervention, public records from the Summit County Sheriff's Office, and video and police reports viewed by the authors. The Park City Police Department declined to release records related to the intervention.

173 *The police found Tony*: The sale of the house had not been finalized at the time police arrived. A limited liability company associated with Tony Hsieh, 2635 Aspen Springs LLC, purchased the house at 2635 Aspen Springs Drive in a sale that was recorded in Summit County, Utah, records on October 21, 2020. The seller signed the sale agreement on October 15, 2020, according to county records. It's not clear what arrangement was made for Tony to move in prior to the sale closing.

Chapter 10: Save Your Soul

177 *Showers and sinks ran*: Kirsten Grind and Katherine Sayre, "Zappos CEO Tony Hsieh Bankrolled His Followers. In Return, They Enabled His Risky Lifestyle," *Wall Street Journal*, March 26, 2021, https://www.wsj.com/articles/tony-hsieh-zappos-death-entourage-11616761915.

177 *the algorithm for world peace*: Ibid.

178 *Jewel had observed*: David Konow, "Jewel Reveals How She Learned to Combat Anxiety, PTSD," The Fix, April 4, 2017, https://www.thefix.com/jewel-reveals-how-she-learned-combat-anxiety-ptsd.

178 *she later wrote*: Jewel, *Never Broken: Songs Are Only Half the Story* (New York: Blue Rider Press, 2016).

178 *"I saw that no one"*: Ibid., 25.

179 *Baleson said she ran*: This process was confirmed by a series of sticky notes in a photo viewed by the authors.

179 *"But from the first notes"*: Teri Orr, "Teri Orr: One Shoe, Two Shoes—Red Shoe, No Shoes," *Park Record*, December 11, 2020, https://www.parkrecord.com/opinion/teri-orr-one-shoe-two-shoes-red-shoe-no-shoes/.

181 *He didn't say anything*: Justin Weniger said it wouldn't have been his place to talk about the intervention to Jewel and others.

182 *sat with Tony*: This interaction between Mark Evensvold and Tony is based on a court reporter's transcript of the meeting, filed as part of Evensvold's claim against

Tony's estate. See *In the Matter of the Estate of Anthony Hsieh*, Creditor's Claim, Mark Evensvold, Eighth Judicial District Nevada, P-20-105105-E, June 1, 2021.

182 *Evensvold would take:* Mark Evensvold's legal claim asks for 20 percent of Tony's share in Nacho Daddy; the transcript of their meeting says Evensvold agreed to take 20 percent and leave Tony with 5 percent.

182 *On August 24, 2020:* Bailey Schulz and Richard N. Velotta, "Zappos CEO Tony Hsieh, Champion of Downtown Las Vegas, Retires," *Las Vegas Review-Journal*, August 24, 2020, https://www.reviewjournal.com/business/zappos-ceo-tony -hsieh-champion-of-downtown-las-vegas-retires-2102935/.

183 *The short Review-Journal story:* Ibid.

183 *A longer follow-up story:* Eli Segall, "Ex–Zappos Chief Tony Hsieh on Home-buying Spree in Utah," *Las Vegas Review-Journal*, August 28, 2020, https://www .reviewjournal.com/business/ex-zappos-chief-tony-hsieh-on-homebuying -spree-in-utah-2107177/.

184 *"traveling salesman problem":* Erica Klarreich, "Computer Scientists Find New Shortcuts for Infamous Traveling Salesman Problem," *Wired*, https://www .wired.com/2013/01/traveling-salesman-problem/.

184 *Some computer scientists:* Ibid.

184 *the company held a tribute:* It's unclear if Tony himself made an appearance during the tribute.

185 *a minimum of twelve weeks' pay:* Details from Zappos.

186 *Zappos' senior leaders:* Zappos said that senior leadership had been told in advance, and it was not true that select employees had been receiving calls.

186 *took the offer hard:* Zappos disagreed with the description of employees' reaction to the offer.

186 *trying to get rid of:* Zappos said that that had not been the intent of the buyout offer.

187 *In 2017, Park City:* Lee Davidson, "Park City Is Now the Nation's 2nd Wealth-iest Small Urban Area, with Average Incomes $27,000 More than in Salt Lake City," *Salt Lake Tribune*, December 6, 2017, https://www.sltrib.com/news/pol itics/2017/12/07/park-city-is-now-the-nations-2nd-wealthiest-small-urban-ar ea-with-average-incomes-27000-more-than-in-salt-lake-city/.

187 *told the police department:* The Park City Police Department released some records and video related to incidents at Tony's properties in Park City through a Government Records Access and Management Act (GRAMA) request but declined to release all of them.

187 *One night in early September:* Park City Police Department reports.

188 *The Park City Fire District:* Katija Collins, "Park City Bans the Use of Fireworks and Open Fires," FOX13, July 22, 2020, https://www.fox13now.com/news/ local-news/park-city-bans-the-use-of-fireworks-and-open-fires.

188 *she didn't have a license:* In a statement, Puoy Premsrirut said that Utah counsel had also been engaged to "address any issues, citations, or if matters escalated."

188   *When Andy Hsieh came out*: Park City Police Department reports.

188   *This time*: Park City Police Department video of the incident.

190   *After one of the incidents*: Ibid.

190   *they didn't go inside*: According to the records and video released by the Park City Police Department.

191   *which could catch fire*: Carter Williams, "Most of Utah Is Now in an 'Extreme' Drought," KSL.com, September 18, 2020, https://www.ksl.com/article/50018 933/most-of-utah-is-now-in-an-extreme-drought.

191   *"This is not a Burning Man community"*: Interview with Police Chief Wade Carpenter, September 2021.

192   *an ecstasy drug bust*: San Mateo County, California, court records show that Mimi Pham was arrested after her boyfriend sold MDMA pills to an undercover police officer in Redwood City on January 16, 2001. According to court records, she was a passenger in the car, while her boyfriend, the driver, made the transaction. She later pleaded guilty to possession of a controlled substance. She was sentenced to four months, to be served in a work furlough program, and was credited for three days already served, according to a judge's order. In 2016, the conviction was dismissed under California expungement law, according to court records. See *The State of California v. Jennifer Michelle Pham*, Superior Court for the County of San Mateo, Docket Number SC48966.

192   *Just one night after*: Park City Police Department reports.

192   *the police showed up*: Park City Police Department video.

192   *the police forwarded*: Park City Police Department email records.

193   *Tony Lee*: Tony Lee's account of events in the summer and fall of 2020 were laid out in a lawsuit filed by his company, Pelagic LLC, after Tony's death. See *Pelagic LLC v. PCVI LLC, Richard Hsieh and Andrew Hsieh*, First Amended Complaint, Eighth Judicial District Court Nevada, A-21-833547-C.

194   *competed to convince*: Ibid.

194   *He stored dozens of boxes*: Photos of the Ranch viewed by the authors and interviews with people familiar with the nitrous supply.

194   *nitrous oxide*: Mr. Lee later said in court filings that Andy Hsieh arranged for the purchase of nitrous oxide for his brother. "Plaintiff/Counter-Defendant's Motion to Dismiss PCVI LLC's Counterclaim," *Pelagic LLC vs. PCVI LLC, Richard Hsieh and Andrew Hsieh*, Eighth Judicial District Court of Nevada, October 11, 2021.

194   *stacked neatly on the shelves*: Photos of the Ranch viewed by the authors.

194   *urges readers to journey*: Michael A. Singer, *The Untethered Soul: The Journey Beyond Yourself* (New York: New Harbinger Publications, 2007).

194   *according to her website*: "About Alana," Alana Fairchild, https://alanafairchild .com/about-alana/.

197   *Jewel's team sent*: Justin Weniger confirmed that Jewel had sent him the letter but said he didn't know who at the Ranch had posted it.

Chapter 11: The Cult of Tony Hsieh

203   *"a high number of calls"*: Sawyer D'Argonne, "Summit County Sheriff's Office to Launch Second Mental Health Response Team," *Summit Daily*, September 1, 2020, https://www.summitdaily.com/news/summit-county-sheriffs-office-to -launch-second-mental-health-response-team/.

203   *A similar pilot program*: "NYC's Non-Police Mental Health Pilot Increasing Rate of Those Getting Aid, Data Show," NBC New York, July 22, 2021, https:// www.nbcnewyork.com/investigations/nycs-non-police-mental-health-pilot-in creasing-rate-of-those-getting-aid-data-show/3165520/.

204   *the officer had called*: In an interview, Police Chief Wade Carpenter said that the officer had found Suzie Baleson to be listed as involved in a prior incident.

204   *according to Park City police*: Summit County Sheriff's Office records confirm parts of Dr. Guadagnoli's account, stating in dispatch summary that the officer was told by someone close to Tony that everything was fine and "he is on a busi-ness call right now." Park City Police Department declined to release the police report of the incident.

205   *Suzie Baleson was getting*: In a statement to the *Wall Street Journal* in the spring of 2021, Suzie Baleson said, "The allegations about me are shameful and without a scintilla of truth." She also said in the statement that "it has been unbearable to witness the exchange of gossip, innuendo and outright lies after Tony's untimely passing."

206   *had told him about the 10X plan*: Mayor Andy Beerman said he knew little about the 10X program, but he did hear from several restaurant owners that Tony and his entourage were patronizing and supporting local restaurants.

206   *he had planned to summit*: Jane Gendron, "From the Crag to City Hall: One-on-One with Mayor Andy Beerman," *Park City Magazine*, June 18, 2018, https:// www.parkcitymag.com/news-and-profiles/2018/06/from-the-crag-to-city-hall.

206   *operated the Treasure Mountain Inn*: Sean Higgins, "Park City Mayor Andy Beerman Says He Intends to Run for Second Term," KPCW, April 30, 2021, https://www .kpcw.org/post/park-city-mayor-andy-beerman-says-he-intends-run-second-term.

206   *subsidized artists to paint*: Jay Hamburger, "Artists Paint Giant Black Lives Mat-ter Mural on Main Street (Updated)," Park Record, July 7, 2020, https://www .parkrecord.com/news/artists-paint-giant-black-lives-matter-mural-on-main-street/.

206   *Soon after, vandals*: Jay Hamburger, "Black Lives Matter Mural Vandalized, Trig-gering Discourse and Vow to Repair Damage (Updated)," Park Record, July 10, 2020, https://www.parkrecord.com/news/black-lives-matter-mural-on-main -street-apparently-vandalized/.

206   *but he demurred*: Mayor Beerman said, "I was not interested in parties or social invites and declined several invites."

207   *was working with the mayor*: Mayor Beerman said that the wellness initiative had been "discussed, never pursued."

207   *Mayor Beerman invited Baleson*: Mayor Beerman said that Baleson had
      expressed an interest in becoming more involved in politics and he had invited
      her along with a hundred other people to the fundraiser.

208   *Their other ideas included*: According to photos of sticky notes viewed by the
      authors.

209   *Some members of the group*: In the fall of 2021, nearly a year after Tony's death,
      some friends and employees still believed that his drug abuse and mental health
      issues had been "overblown."

209   *Tony used a rating system*: Kirsten Grind and Katherine Sayre, "Zappos CEO
      Tony Hsieh Bankrolled His Followers. In Return, They Enabled His Risky Life-
      style," *Wall Street Journal*, March 26, 2021, https://www.wsj.com/articles/tony
      -hsieh-zappos-death-entourage-11616761915.

211   *"disloyalty penalty"*: Attorneys for Richard and Andy Hsieh recount this "dis-
      loyalty penalty" in a court filing. Attorneys for Pham have generally denied the
      Hsiehs' claims in court. See *Baby Monster LLC v. PCVI LLC, Richard Hsieh and
      Andrew Hsieh*, PCVI LLC's Answer to Second Amended Complaint, Counter-
      claim, Third Party Complaint and Demand for Jury Trial, Eighth Judicial Dis-
      trict Court Nevada, A-21-828090-C, August 23, 2021.

211   *He ended up paying*: Attorneys for Richard and Andy Hsieh recounted that "dis-
      loyalty penalty" in a court filing. Attorneys for Pham have generally denied the
      Hsiehs' claims in court. See ibid.

211   *He asked for a meeting*: The events around the Bryn Mooser meeting are recounted
      in a court filing by attorneys for Richard and Andy Hsieh, who are being sued by
      Mimi Pham. See *Mr. Taken LLC v. Pickled Entertainment v. Jennifer "Mimi" Pham,
      Roberto Grande and Baby Monster LLC*, A-21-829006-B, Eighth Judicial District
      Court, Nevada, Pickled Entertainment's Answer, Affirmative Defenses, Counter-
      claims, Third Party Claims and Demand for Jury Trial, May 25, 2021, 20.

211   *Mooser's previous producing work*: "Bryn Mooser," IMDb, http://www.imdb.com/
      name/nm1666274/.

211   *Tony agreed to spend*: *Mr. Taken LLC v. Pickled Entertainment v. Jennifer "Mimi"
      Pham, Roberto Grande and Baby Monster LLC*, A-21-829006-B, Eighth Judicial
      District Court, Nevada, Pickled Entertainment's Answer, Affirmative Defenses,
      Counterclaims, Third Party Claims and Demand for Jury Trial, May 25, 2021.

212   *Tony extended his trust in Pham*: According to attorneys for Richard and Andy
      Hsieh. See ibid.

212   *Pham and Grande would later file*: Mimi Pham, Roberto Grande, and their com-
      pany, Mr. Taken, filed a lawsuit in 2021 against Richard and Andy Hsieh as the
      administrators of Tony's estate who held control of Tony's businesses after his
      death. See *Mr. Taken LLC v. Pickled Entertainment v. Jennifer "Mimi" Pham,
      Roberto Grande and Baby Monster LLC*, A-21-829006-B, Eighth Judicial Dis-
      trict Court, Nevada.

212   *in turn increasing*: The financial terms of the deal are described in court filings

by Richard and Andy Hsieh. See *Mr. Taken LLC v. Pickled Entertainment v. Jennifer "Mimi" Pham, Roberto Grande and Baby Monster LLC*, A-21-829006-B, Eighth Judicial District Court, Nevada, Pickled Entertainment's Answer, Affirmative Defenses, Counterclaims, Third Party Claims and Demand for Jury Trial, May 25, 2021.

212   *"Tony is one"*: Peter White, "Non-Fiction Studio XTR Secures $17.5M Investment from Ex–Zappos CEO Tony Hsieh to Bolster Doc Plans," Deadline, October 7, 2020, https://deadline.com/2020/10/xtr-17-5m-investment-former-zappos-ceo-tony-hsieh-1234592707/.

212   *while Pham and Grande provided*: According to attorneys for Richard and Andy Hsieh. See *Mr. Taken LLC v. Pickled Entertainment v. Jennifer "Mimi" Pham, Roberto Grande and Baby Monster LLC*, A-21-829006-B, Eighth Judicial District Court, Nevada, Pickled Entertainment's Answer, Affirmative Defenses, Counterclaims, Third Party Claims and Demand for Jury Trial, May 25, 2021, 25.

212   *Tony bought the eleven-story*: Eli Segall and Subrina Hudson, "Zappos' New Landlord Is a Familiar Face," *Las Vegas Review-Journal*, October 22, 2020, https://www.reviewjournal.com/business/zappos-new-landlord-is-a-familiar-face-2158031/.

212   *They had bought the building*: According to the deed of sale recorded in Clark County, Nevada, on April 3, 2012.

213   *"Tony is one infectious guy"*: Caitlin McGarry, "Nevadan at Work: Developer Has No Doubt Downtown Will Thrive," *Las Vegas Review-Journal*, August 26, 2012, https://www.reviewjournal.com/business/casinos-gaming/nevadan-at-work-developer-has-no-doubt-downtown-will-thrive/.

213   *The property had been listed*: Eli Segall, "Zappos Office Building for Sale in Downtown Las Vegas," *Las Vegas Review-Journal*, April 2, 2019, https://www.reviewjournal.com/business/zappos-office-building-for-sale-in-downtown-las-vegas-1631589/.

213   *Tony paid nearly four times*: Dave Toplikar, "Las Vegas City Council Approves Final Deal Bringing Zappos Downtown," *Las Vegas Sun*, February 1, 2012, https://lasvegassun.com/news/2012/feb/01/las-vegas-city-council-approves-final-deal-bringin/.

213   *it's unclear why*: In 2012, Zappos said it was undertaking a $40 million renovation of the building. Benjamin Spillman, "Zappos Renovating Old City Hall for Future Use," *Las Vegas Review-Journal*, April 14, 2012, https://www.reviewjournal.com/local/local-las-vegas/zappos-renovating-old-city-hall-for-future-use/.

213   *Tony's group planned*: According to photos of sticky notes viewed by the authors.

Chapter 12: The Shed

215   *The Shed*: The details of the shed fire and the hours leading up to it are based in large part on dozens of incident reports, videos, and photos released by the New London Police and Fire Departments in 2021 as part of their investigation

into the November 18, 2020 fire, as well as the report itself. The authors also talked through each detail with members of the New London Fire and Police Departments who were on the scene and who contributed to the later report on the fire's causes. Other sources are noted in the narrative or in the endnotes.

215   *"I have always felt"*: Maria Popova, "A Lifeline for the Hour of Despair: James Baldwin on 4AM, the Fulcrum of Love, and Life as a Moral Obligation to the Universe," Literary Affairs, https://literaryaffairs.net/a-lifeline-for-the-hour-of-despair/.

217   *the moon a thin sliver*: "Waxing Crescent on 17 November 2020 Tuesday," Lunaf.com, https://lunaf.com/lunar-calendar/2020/11/17/#:~:text=Waxing%20Crescent%20is%20the%20lunar%20phase%20on%2017%20November%202020%2C%20Tuesday%20.

218   *Pierce had invested heavily*: Neil Strauss, "Brock Pierce: The Hippie King of Cryptocurrency," *Rolling Stone*, July 26, 2018, https://www.rollingstone.com/culture/culture-features/brock-pierce-hippie-king-of-cryptocurrency-700213/.

218   *took a more whimsical view*: Ibid.

219   *Tony heard what Pierce*: Interview with Brock Pierce, March 2021.

221   *not approved by*: Jake Harper, "Addiction Clinics Market Unproven Infusion Treatments to Desperate Patients," NPR, August 22, 2019, https://www.npr.org/sections/health-shots/2019/08/22/741115178/addiction-clinics-market-unproven-infusion-treatments-to-desperate-patients.

221   *The treatment is supposed*: "NAD Therapy," Addiction Center, https://www.addictioncenter.com/treatment/nad-therapy/.

221   *had been reviewing*: Tony Lee's account of events in the summer and fall of 2020 was laid out in a lawsuit filed by his company, Pelagic LLC, after Tony's Hsieh's death. See *Pelagic LLC v. PCVI LLC, Richard Hsieh and Andrew Hsieh*, First Amended Complaint, Eighth Judicial District Court Nevada, A-21-833547-C.

221   *known locally as "Mr. Bitcoin"*: Strauss, "Brock Pierce."

222   *took Blizzy to a nearby vet*: Schedules of Tony Hsieh's employees in Park City and elsewhere viewed by the authors.

222   *"When are you able to travel?"*: Text message viewed by the authors.

223   *"Tony is in trouble"*: Kirsten Grind, James R. Hagerty, and Katherine Sayre, "The Death of Zappos's Tony Hsieh: A Spiral of Alcohol, Drugs and Extreme Behavior," *Wall Street Journal*, December 6, 2020, https://www.wsj.com/articles/the-death-of-zappos-tony-hsieh-a-spiral-of-alcohol-drugs-and-extreme-behavior-11607264719.

225   *The door clicked*: The New London Fire Department as part of its investigation reviewed security camera footage around the property and wrote about it in their later report.

225   *"barricaded"*: Lee Hawkins, "Before Tony Hsieh's Death, Firefighters Rushed to Burning Home with Trapped Man," *Wall Street Journal*, November 29, 2020, https://www.wsj.com/articles/before-tony-hsiehs-death-firefighters-rushed-to-burning-home-with-trapped-man-11606691000.

226   *She called 911*: Recording of 911 call released by New London Police and Fire
       Departments.

229   *The smoke, soot, and fire*: A report from the New London Police Department
       states, "Investigator Pellamargio reported the deceased had brain edema from
       the actual fire from the hot gases, soot, and was placed on a vent. The deceased
       was extubated at the request of the family."

229   *in which the brain swells*: Beth Roybal, "Brain Swelling," WebMD, https://www
       .webmd.com/brain/brain-swelling-brain-edema-intracranial-pressure.

229   *On the ninth day*: A New London Police Department report states that the
       "deceased was extubated at the request of the family." Sources have told
       the authors that the decision would have been made by Richard and Judy
       Hsieh.

229   *Tony was gone*: It's unclear how much time elapsed between Tony's being taken
       off the ventilator and the time he died.

Epilogue

231   *a transition that can take*: "Death and the Afterlife: How Buddhist Funerals
       Reflect Beliefs about the Afterlife," BBC, https://www.bbc.co.uk/bitesize/
       guides/zyhmk2p/revision/4.

232   *"The world has lost"*: Matthew S. Schwartz, "Tony Hsieh, Former Zap-
       pos CEO, Dies at 46," NPR, November 28, 2020, https://www.npr.org
       /2020/11/28/939697651/tony-hsieh-former-zappos-ceo-dies-at-46.

232   *"The world lost you"*: Jeff Bezos, "The world lost you way too soon @downtown-
       tony. Your curiosity, vision, and relentless focus on customers leave an indelible
       mark. You will be missed by so many, Tony. Rest In Peace," Instagram, Novem-
       ber 28, 2020, https://www.instagram.com/p/CIJYUQhHzLq/.

232   *"I treasure every conversation"*: Bill Clinton, Twitter, November 30, 2020, https://
       twitter.com/billclinton/status/1333578663380520961?lang=en.

232   *offered her praise of Tony*: Ivanka Trump, Twitter, November 28, 2020, https://
       twitter.com/ivankatrump/status/1332719265900879872.

233   *"I'll never meet Tony"*: Alfred Lin, "My Final Letter to Tony Hsieh," *Forbes*, Dec-
       ember 1, 2020, https://www.forbes.com/sites/alexkonrad/2020/12/01/my-final
       -letter-to-tony-hsieh-by-alfred-lin/?sh=107d8d44239b.

233   *"As you watch the world turn"*: Ibid.

233   *"It was never about"*: Katie Abel, "A Friendship for the Ages: Fred Mossler +
       the OG Zappos Crew Share Untold Tales About the Incredible Tony Hsieh,"
       Footwear News, December 21, 2020, https://footwearnews.com/2020/business/
       retail/tony-hsieh-zappos-friends-legacy-1203085996/.

233   *"He was a complex puzzle"*: Nick Swinmurn, "RIP Tony," Medium, November
       28, 2020, https://nickswinmurn.medium.com/rip-tony-6e99695ae3de.

234   *Zappos also unfurled*: Mick Akers, "Zappos Remembers Longtime CEO Tony
       Hsieh with Massive Building Wraps," *Las Vegas Review-Journal*, January 5,

2021, https://www.reviewjournal.com/local/local-las-vegas/downtown/zappos
-remembers-longtime-ceo-tony-hsieh-with-massive-building-wraps-2242847/.

234 *A petition appeared online*: "Honor Tony Hsieh's Legacy with a Memorial Art Installation in Las Vegas!," Change.org, https://www.change.org/p/honor-tony
-hsieh-s-legacy-with-a-memorial-art-installation-in-las-vegas.

234 *his memory shouldn't be confined*: Caroline Bleakley, "Mayor Goodman Said Hsieh Talked of Plans to Bring a 747 to Downtown Las Vegas," KLAS, December 2, 2020, https://www.8newsnow.com/news/local-news/mayor-goodman
-said-hsieh-talked-of-plans-to-bring-a-747-to-downtown-las-vegas/.

234 *"A street is so perpendicular"*: Morty, "M&C Talk to Mayor Carolyn Goodman on the Passing of Tony Hsieh," 96.3 KKLZ, December 1, 2020, https://963kklz
.com/2020/12/01/mc-talk-to-mayor-carolyn-goodman-on-the-passing-of-tony
-hsieh/.

235 *Jewel turned on the camera*: Jewel, "Elegy for Tony Hsieh," Instagram, December 1, 2020, https://www.instagram.com/tv/CIQ_i8bnZIu/?hl=en.

235 *The world didn't yet know*: Jewel's letter to Tony in Park City was first reported by *Forbes* in early December 2020 and the details of her intervention attempt by the *Wall Street Journal* in March 2021.

240 *told us in*: Kirsten Grind and Katherine Sayre, "Sorting Out Tony Hsieh's Estate, from LLCs to Thousands of Sticky Notes," *Wall Street Journal*, December 11, 2020, https://www.wsj.com/articles/sorting-out-tony-hsiehs-estate-from-llcs-to
-thousands-of-sticky-notes-11607715492.

241 *Tony had earned $32 million*: Tony Hsieh, *Delivering Happiness: A Path to Profits, Passion, and Purpose* (New York: Grand Central Publishing, 2010), 49.

241 *$1.2 billion all-stock deal*: "Amazon Closes Zappos Deal, Ends Up Paying $1.2 Billion," TechCrunch, November 2, 2009, https://social.techcrunch.
com/2009/11/02/amazon-closes-zappos-deal-ends-up-paying-1-2-billion/.

241 *with some journalists using*: Peter Holley, "Why This CEO Is Worth Almost $1 Billion but Lives in a Trailer Park," *Washington Post*, July 21, 2015, https://
www.washingtonpost.com/news/the-switch/wp/2015/07/21/why-a-ceo-worth
-840-million-lives-in-a-trailer-park-with-his-pet-alpaca/.

241 *Within days of his death*: *In the Matter of the Estate of Anthony Hsieh,* Eighth Judicial District Court Nevada, P-20-105105-E, Order Granting Application for Appointment of Special Administrator, for Issuance of Letters of Special Administration with General Powers, December 4, 2020.

241 *"require immediate attention"*: Ibid., 1.

242 *agreed to pay Andy $1 million*: Attorneys for Mimi Pham have stated this $1 million agreement in court records. See *Baby Monster LLC v. PCVI LLC, Richard Hsieh, and Andrew Hsieh*, Complaint and Demand for Jury Trial, Eighth Judicial District Court Nevada, No. A-21-828090-C, January 20, 2021.

242 *Mimi Pham sued Richard and Andy Hsieh*: Ibid.

242 *owed more than $90 million*: Mimi Pham and her associated companies, Rove and

Whim LLC, Baby Monster LLC, and Mr. Taken LLC, filed claims against Tony Hsieh's estate in 2021 for more than $90 million. See *In the Matter of the Estate of Anthony Hsieh*, Eighth Judicial District Court Nevada, P-20-105105-E.

242 *an estimated $75 million*: In the Matter of the Estate of Anthony Hsieh, Eighth Judicial District Court Nevada, P-20-105105-E, Creditor's Claim, Mr. Taken LLC, March 3, 2021.

242 *another $7.5 million*: Ibid.

243 *They were part*: Charles V. Bagli, "Robert Durst Found Guilty of Murder After Decades of Suspicion," *New York Times*, September 17, 2021, https://www.nytimes.com/2021/09/17/us/robert-durst-murder-trial.html.

243 *"She wanted access"*: In the Matter of the Estate of Anthony Hsieh, Eighth Judicial District Court Nevada, P-20-105105-E, Creditor's Claim, Jennifer Pham, March 3, 2021.

243 *"that is not an indication"*: Mr. Taken v. Pickled Entertainment LLC., Eighth Judicial District Court Nevada, Verified Complaint for Injunctive Relief and Damages, and Plaintiff's Demand for Jury Trial," A-21-829006-C, February 5, 2021.

243 *Tony's family shot back*: Mr. Taken v. Pickled Entertainment LLC and Pickled Investments LLC v. Third-party Defendants Jennifer "Mimi" Pham, Roberto Grande and Baby Monster LLC, Eighth Judicial District Court Nevada, Pickled Entertainment's Answer, Counterclaims and Third Party Claims, A-21-829006-C, May 25, 2021.

243 *"he wouldn't have longer"*: Ibid.

243 *physically and mentally*: Baby Monster LLC vs. PCVI LLC, Richard Hsieh and Andrew Hsieh, A-21-828090-C, Eighth Judicial District Court Nevada, August 23, 2021, PCVI LLC's Answer to Second Amended Complaint, Counterclaim, Third Party Complaint and Demand for Jury Trial (n.d.).

243 *Toshie McSwain*: In the Matter of the Estate of Anthony Hsieh, Eighth Judicial District Court Nevada, Creditor's Claim, TMLabs dba wigcraft.vegas, P-20-105105-E, June 22, 2021.

244 *Mark Evensvold*: In the Matter of the Estate of Anthony Hsieh, Eighth Judicial District Court Nevada, Creditor's Claim, Mark Evensvold, P-20-105105-E, June 1, 2021.

244 *Tony Lee*: In the Matter of the Estate of Anthony Hsieh, Eighth Judicial District Court Nevada, Creditor's Claim, Pelagic LLC, P-20-105105-E, June 22, 2021.

244 *In court filings*: Pelagic LLC v. PCVI LLC, Richard Hsieh and Andrew Hsieh, Plaintiff/Counter-Defendant's Motion to Dismiss PCVI LLC's Counterclaim, Eighth Judicial District Court Nevada, A-21-833547-C.

244 *Suzie Baleson, through her company*: In the matter of the Estate of Anthony Hsieh, Eighth Judicial District Court Nevada, Creditor's Claim, The Wellth Collective LLC, P-20-105105-E, November, 11, 2021.

244 *Daniel Park continues*: Daniel Park, "Night 1 at @descendonbend," Instagram, September 10, 2021, www.instagram.com/p/CTpdlFCpmnv.

244   *An Instagram post*: Vitamin Bar Naples, "The Vitamin Bar Naples is proud to serve," Instagram, March 11, 2021, www.instagram.com/p/CMR6eDggqbN.

245   *The Hsiehs told a judge*: In the Matter of the Estate of Anthony Hsieh, Eighth Judicial District Court Nevada, Ex Parte Petition to Transfer the Estate Accounts, All Personal Accounts, and Wholly Owned Entity Accounts of Anthony Hsieh Held at Morgan Stanley and Other Financial Institutions to Different Financial Institutions of the Co–Special Administrators' Choice, Authorizing Liquidation of Stocks and Securities and/or Obtaining Loans to Pay Federal Estate Tax, P-20-105105-E, July 29, 2021.

245   *including undeveloped lots*: Eli Segall, "Tony Hsieh's Family to Sell Off Much of Las Vegas Real Estate Empire," *Las Vegas Review-Journal*, February 17, 2021, https://www.reviewjournal.com/business/tony-hsiehs-family-to-sell-off-much-of-las-vegas-real-estate-empire-2283365/.

245   *"Tony Hsieh's Family"*: Ibid.

245   *"Tony Hsieh 2.0"*: Eli Segall and Shea Johnson, "Downtown Sell Off: Family of Tony Hsieh Looks to Unload His Vast Holdings," *Las Vegas Review-Journal*, March 13, 2021, https://www.reviewjournal.com/local/local-las-vegas/downtown/tony-hsieh-property-sell-off-could-energize-downtown-las-vegas-2300617/.

246   *Tony's mind moved*: Baby Monster LLC vs. PCVI LLC, Richard Hsieh and Andrew Hsieh, A-21-828090-C, Eighth Judicial District Court Nevada, August 23, 2021, PCVI LLC's Answer to Second Amended Complaint, Counterclaim, Third Party Complaint and Demand for Jury Trial (n.d.).

247   *"It has become apparent to me"*: Naomi Osaka, "Naomi Osaka: 'It's O.K. Not to Be O.K.,'" *Time*, July 8, 2021, https://time.com/6077128/naomi-osaka-essay-tokyo-olympics/.

250   *Even the joke of the day*: The Employees of Zappos.com as told to Mark Dagostino, *The Power of WOW: How to Electrify Your Work, Your Community, and Your Life by Putting Service First* (Dallas, TX: BenBella Books, 2019), 48.

251   *"I don't have all the answers"*: Hsieh, *Delivering Happiness*, 240.

ABOUT THE AUTHORS

Kirsten Grind is an enterprise reporter for the *Wall Street Journal*, where she has worked since 2012. She has received more than a dozen national awards for her work, including a Pulitzer Prize finalist citation for her coverage of the financial crisis, and a Loeb Award for her coverage of the downfall of a famous bond fund manager. Her first book, *The Lost Bank*, about the collapse of Washington Mutual during the financial crisis, was named the best investigative book of 2012 by the Investigative Reporters & Editors association. She lives in the San Francisco Bay Area.

Katherine Sayre is a reporter with the *Wall Street Journal*, where she has worked since 2019. As the gambling reporter, she writes about the Las Vegas Strip, the rise of betting on sports in the US, and the global casino industry. Before joining the *Journal*, she was a lead reporter for the *Times-Picayune*'s investigative team in New Orleans, Louisiana. Her reporting on failures in the state's mental health care system won a national prize from the Association of Health Care Journalists. In reporting stints around the South, she has covered courts, crime, real estate, and Gulf Coast communities in Louisiana, Mississippi, and Alabama. She lives in Los Angeles.